Thomas Wallace Knox

How to Travel. Hints, Advice, and Suggestions to Travelers by Land and Sea

All over the Globe

Thomas Wallace Knox

How to Travel. Hints, Advice, and Suggestions to Travelers by Land and Sea
All over the Globe

ISBN/EAN: 9783337209490

Printed in Europe, USA, Canada, Australia, Japan

Cover: Foto ©Andreas Hilbeck / pixelio.de

More available books at **www.hansebooks.com**

FISK & HATCH,

❖ BANKERS ❖

AND

DEALERS IN GOVERNMENT BONDS

And other desirable Investment Securities,

No. 5 Nassau St., N. Y.

Buy and sell all issues of Government Bonds, in large or small amounts, at current market prices, and will be pleased to furnish information in reference to all matters connected with investments in Government Bonds.

We are prepared to give information in regard to first-class Railway Securities and to execute orders for the same.

Buy and sell all marketable Stocks and Bonds on commission at the Stock Exchange or in the open market.

Receive accounts of Banks, Bankers, Merchants, and others, and allow interest on daily balances; and for those keeping accounts with us we collect U. S. coupons and registered interest, and other coupons, dividends, etc., and credit without charge.

☞ We give special attention to orders from Banks, Bankers, Institutions, and Investors out of the city, by Mail or Telegraph, to buy or sell Government Bonds, State and Railroad Bonds, Bank Stocks, Railroad Stocks, and other securities.

FISK & HATCH.

PASSENGER STEAMSHIPS.

FLEET.

SPAIN, EGYPT, ENGLAND, ERIN, HELVETIA, THE QUEEN, ITALY, FRANCE, HOLLAND, DENMARK, CANADA, GREECE.

THE STEAMSHIPS of this line are amongst the largest in the Atlantic service leaving the Port of New York. They have been constructed by the most celebrated builders in Great Britain, and are of great strength and power, and of beautiful model, enabling them to make regular passage in all kinds of weather. They are built entirely of Iron and Steel, except the merely decorative parts, and divided into watertight and fireproof compartments, with steam pumping, hoisting, and steering gear, and provided with fire-extinguishers, improved sounding apparatus, and generally found throughout in everything calculated to add to their Safety, and to the comfort and convenience of Passengers heretofore unattained at sea.

One of the Steamers will sail from New York every Saturday for Queenstown and Liverpool, and weekly from London direct, from Pier 39, North River.

RATES OF PASSAGE, in currency:—To Queenstown and Liverpool, $50 to $70. To London direct (Victoria Docks), $50 to $60; Excursion Tickets, $100 currency. Steerage passage, outward, $26 currency. Prepaid Tickets, $28, being $2 lower than most other lines.

For passage, Bank Drafts, Sovereigns, etc., apply to

F. W. J. HURST, MANAGER, Company's Offices,
Nos. 69, 71, and 73 Broadway, New York.

United States Mail Steamers
SAIL WEEKLY TO AND FROM
New York and Glasgow,
AND
New York and London.

THE ANCHOR LINE STEAMERS are first-class in every respect, built especially for Passenger Traffic; are safe, comfortable, reliable, splendidly equipped, and in their appointments and accommodations are not excelled by any other Line.

RATES OF PASSAGE FROM NEW YORK

To Glasgow, Liverpool, Londonderry, or Belfast.

Aft Outside Berth, $80		Excursion	$140
Aft Inside Berth, $75	FIRST CABIN.	Tickets, available	130
Forward Berth, $60		for One Year,	110

TO LONDON DIRECT.—First Cabin, $55 and $65; Excursion, $100 and $120, according to location of Stateroom.

For Books of Information for Passengers, Rates of Passage, Cabin Plans, etc., apply to

COMPANY'S OFFICES.

7 BOWLING GREEN, NEW YORK.
96 WASHINGTON STREET, CHICAGO.
7 and 9 STATE STREET, BOSTON.

HENDERSON BROTHERS, AGENTS.

AMERICAN EXCHANGE IN EUROPE,

(LIMITED.)

CAPITAL, ONE MILLION DOLLARS,

(In One Hundred Thousand Shares of Ten Dollars each, with power to increase.)

FULLY PAID-UP SHARES, $500,000.00.

PRESIDENT,	GEN'L MANAGER,
JOSEPH R. HAWELY.	HENRY F. GILLIG.

Financial Offices and Reading Rooms,
Passenger and Railroad Offices, . . } **449 STRAND, W. C.**
Exchange and News Department, .

Commission and Shipping Departments, } **3 ADELAIDE ST.,**
Emigration and Land Branches, .
Express and Storage Divisions, . . } **CHARING CROSS,**

LONDON, ENGLAND.

NEW YORK BRANCH OFFICE, 102 BROADWAY.

General Agent, ... W. C. BOONE.
Fiscal Agents, . . DONNELL, LAWSON & SIMPSON.

Branch Office of Commission and Shipping Departments,
50 BROADWAY, NEW YORK.

THE GENERAL OBJECT OF THIS COMPANY IS TO ADVANCE AND PROTECT AMERICAN INTERESTS IN EUROPE:

1st.—By establishing direct Business and Financial Relations between every important business centre of the United States and the great commercial and money centres of Europe.
2d.—By opening up and extending new markets in Europe for American Manufactures and other Products, and Railroad, Mining, Landed, and other Properties.
3d.—By promoting Emigration from England and other European countries to the United States.
4th.—By aiding and protecting American Travel in Europe through the extension of Financial Facilities to Travelers, and rendering other necessary services.
5th.—By promoting European Travel to the United States, and through the United States to Japan, China, Australia, etc.

TRAVELERS' CIRCULAR NOTES, available throughout the world, issued without charge, for actual value in cash.
N. B. The Circular Notes issued by this corporation are secured by deposit of United States Government Bonds.
LETTERS OF CREDIT issued either against deposit of cash, or satisfactory guarantee of payment.
MONEY TRANSMITTED BY TELEGRAPH to all points.
DRAFTS issued at current rates on all principal cities of the world.

HENRY F. GILLIG, *General Manager.*

PARTIES GOING ABROAD SHOULD LEAVE
THEIR PROPERTY SAFELY INSURED.

Condition January 1, 1881, of

CONTINENTAL
Insurance Company,
100 Broadway, New York.

Reserve for re-insurance of outstanding risks, $1,346,195.69
Reserve ample for all other claims, . . 286,387.95
Capital paid in in cash, ... 1,000,000.00
Unallotted Surplus [reserved for contingencies], 306,135.77
Net Surplus, ... 1,000,000.00

$3,938,719.41

Deduct for future decline [if any,] in market
values, ... 50,000.00

Total cash assets, January 1, 1881, . . $3,888,719.41

This Company conducts its business under the restrictions of the New York Safety Fund Law. The two Safety Funds together equal $1,000,000.

H. H. LAMPORT,   GEORGE T. HOPE,
    Vice-President.   President.

B. C. TOWNSEND, Sec'y Agency Dep't.   CYRUS PECK, Sec'y.
C. H. DUTCHER, Sec'y Brooklyn Dep't.   A. M. KIRBY, Sec'y Local Dep't.
J. K. OAKLEY, Gen'l Agent.   F. C MOORE, Agency Manager.

MALLORY LINES.

BRAZIL, TEXAS, FLORIDA, NASSAU, N. P., AND MATANZAS, CUBA.

The ONLY Direct Lines of Passenger Steamships from New York to TEXAS and FLORIDA, and the only Steamship Lines to BRAZIL, NASSAU, N. P., and MATANZAS, CUBA.

Brazil Steamers Sail 5th of Every Month

For St Thomas, Para, Pernambuco, Bahia, and Rio de Janeiro, connecting at St. Thomas with Steamers for Porto Rico, Jamaica, and the Spanish Main. Through rates and Bills of Lading given to Paranagua, Santa Catherina, Rio Grande do Sul, Pelotas, and Porto Alegre.

THROUGH TICKETS ISSUED TO ALL POINTS
reached by the Royal Mail Packet Company's Intercolonial Steamers, and to Monte Video, and Buenos Ayres.

Texas Steamers Sail Every Saturday

For GALVESTON, giving through Freight and Passage Rates to all points in Texas.

Florida Steamers Sail Every Friday

For JACKSONVILLE and FERNANDINA, FLA.

Pamphlets and Schedules mailed, and all information given upon application to

C. H. MALLORY & CO., AGENTS,

Pier 20 East River, near Fulton Ferry, New York.

BEFORE LEAVING HOME

PROVIDE YOURSELF WITH A SUPPLY OF

PARKER'S GINGER TONIC.

The occasional use of this delicious medicine will prevent any dangerous consequences from changing diet or water, and travelers will find it an unequalled appetizer and an invigorant to the highest degree, without intoxicating properties. It strengthens the Stomach, Bowels, and Digestive Organs, builds up the system, is a sure remedy for Sea Sickness, Dyspepsia, Dysentery, etc., and is the

BEST MEDICINE YOU CAN USE FOR

RESTORING HEALTH AND STRENGTH.

A bottle of this Tonic by keeping you in good health and spirits will greatly increase the pleasure of any journey.

Sold by all Druggists at 50 Cents, and $1.00.

LARGE SAVING IN BUYING THE DOLLAR SIZE.

HISCOX & CO., PROPRIETORS,

163 WILLIAM STREET, N. Y.

FLORESTON COLOGNE,

Is the most lasting, delicate, and fragrant of perfumes. As it relieves Headache, Prostration, and Nervousness, often induced by the fatigue of travel, it will be found an exceedingly refreshing and delightful toilet companion.

Price, 25 Cents; Large Bottles, 75 Cents.

Manufactured only by **HISCOX & CO.**, Chemists, New York

PARKER'S HAIR BALSAM,

THE BEST, CLEANEST, AND MOST ECONOMICAL HAIR DRESSING.

Elegantly perfumed and made from materials that are beneficial to the hair and scalp. Parker's Hair Balsam is far more satisfactory than any other hair preparation. It

Never Fails to Restore Gray Hair

to the youthful color, and beauty and is warranted to prevent baldness, falling of the hair, and dandruff.

50 Cent and $1.00 Sizes at all Druggists.

HISCOX & CO., NEW YORK.

HAND SAPOLIO.

Is far preferable to the best brands of Soap.

It is a perfect emollient, keeping the skin smooth and soft under all climatic changes and exposure.

It is delightfully Scented, and wears away slowly.

Its frequent use will remove tan, stains of all kinds, ink, and other blemishes from the skin.

It will also completely remove grease and stains from garments, and rust from metal.

EVERY TRAVELER SHOULD CARRY IT.

Each cake is wrapped in tinfoil, and a year's supply occupies but small space.

Sold by all Grocers and Fancy Goods Dealers throughout America.

MANUFACTURED ONLY BY

Enoch Morgan's Sons Co.,

22 PARK PLACE, NEW YORK.

FOR TRAVEL,
Nothing is so Refreshing and Invigorating
AS

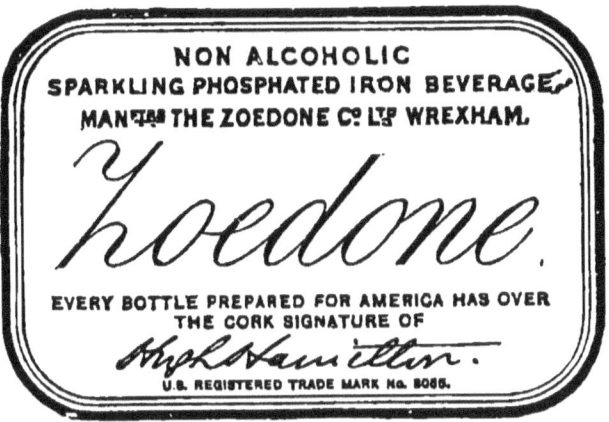

NO NEW UNTRIED BEVERAGE, BUT HAVING AN ESTABLISHED PRESTIGE
CONFERRED BY THE
ROYAL FAMILY, NOBILITY, GENTRY,
AND PEOPLE OF GREAT BRITAIN,
Consuming Annually Over Ten Million Bottles,
AND THE
INDORSEMENT OF HIGH MEDICAL AUTHORITY.

"The use of Zoedone is followed by all the refreshing and stimulating effects of champagne without fear of intoxication or after injurious reactionary effects. On the contrary the iron and phosphorus in Zoedone combine to convert what would otherwise be an agreeable but ephemeral stimulant into a valuable tonic."

PACKED WITHOUT STRAW.

$15 per case, Six Dozen Pints; $8 Three Dozen Pints.
SUPPLIED BY WINE MERCHANTS, GROCERS, DRUGGISTS.

ZOEDONE BUREAU, 27 PARK PLACE.

THE MOST RELIABLE
TRUNKS, BAGS, VALISES, &C.,
ARE MADE BY
CROUCH & FITZGERALD,
NEW YORK.

TRUNKS

FOR AMERICAN STEAMER AND EUROPEAN TRAVEL.

EXTRA FINE QUALITY OF TRAVELING BAGS, &C., &C.

STORES:
1 CORTLAND STREET.   (New Store,)
556 BROADWAY.   **723** SIXTH AVENUE,
                              Below Forty-Second Street.

☞ SEND FOR ILLUSTRATED CATALOGUE.

BOOKS
FOR TRAVELERS.

American Publishing Co.,
HARTFORD, CONN.

Publishers of MARK TWAIN'S Works:

"INNOCENTS ABROAD," "TRAMP ABROAD," AND OTHERS.

JOSIAH ALLEN'S WIFE'S Books:

"BETSEY BOBBETT," "MY WAYWARD PARDNER," ETC.

BOOKS OF TRAVEL IN VARIOUS COUNTRIES, MAKING VALUABLE GUIDE BOOKS,

By THOS. W. KNOX, BRET HARTE, and other Popular Authors.

═══ Send for Catalogue. ═══

Books sent to any part of the World on receipt of price.

Address,

AMERICAN PUBLISHING COMPANY,

Agents Wanted.   HARTFORD, CONN.

MILLIONS OF DOLLARS SAVED
TO THE WASTEFUL PEOPLE IN THIS COUNTRY
BY THE USE OF THIS SAFE GUIDE.

THE NEW YORK TRIBUNE says: "For comprehensiveness and precision, this book may be said to be unique."
THE BOSTON TRAVELLER says: "In her New Cook-Book, Miss Parloa has rendered a good service to humanity."
THE NEW YORK TIMES says: "It has no nonsense in it, and can be recommended for general use."
THE NEW HAVEN JOURNAL says: "It is in many respects the best book of its kind ever printed."

1 vol., 12mo, cloth, 430 pages, and 89 illustrations, $1.50.

Published by ESTES & LAURIAT, Boston.

For sale by all Booksellers.   Sent postpaid on receipt of price.

TRAVELING COMPANIONS.

BEFORE STARTING ON A JOURNEY, STOW AWAY SOME PLEASANT NOVEL IN YOUR SATCHEL.

We invite attention to the following choice selection of Novels:

THE NO NAME SERIES.

Mercy Philbrick's Choice; Afterglow; Deirdrè; Hetty's Strange History; Is that All? Will Denbigh, Nobleman; Kismet; The Wolf at the Door; The Great Match; Marmorne; Mirage; A Modern Mephistopheles; Gemini; A Masque of Poets. 16mo, Cloth, Black and Gold, price $1.00 each.

THE NO NAME (SECOND) SERIES.

Signor Monaldini's Niece; The Colonel's Opera Cloak; His Majesty, Myself; Mrs. Beauchamp Brown; Salvage; Don John. Manuela Parédes (in preparation). 16mo, Cloth, Green and Gold, price $1.00 each.

BY THE TIBER; a novel, by the author of "Signor Monaldini's Niece."
THE HEAD OF MEDUSA; a novel, by the author of "Kismet" and "Mirage."
BLESSED SAINT CERTAINTY; by the author of "His Majesty, Myself."

Uniform volumes, 16mo, Cloth, Black and Gold, price $1.50 each.

MY MARRIAGE; a novel, 16mo, cloth, price $1.00.
IRENE THE MISSIONARY; a novel, 16mo, cloth, price $1.25.
MOONDYNE; a story of the Under-World, by John Boyle O'Reilly; 16mo, cloth, price $1.50.
SARAH DE BERENGER; a novel, by Jean Ingelow; uniform with "Off the Skelligs" and "Fated to be Free"; 16mo, cloth, price $1.50.

These books can be procured of any Bookseller, or the Publishers will mail them, post-paid, on receipt of price.

ROBERTS BROTHERS, BOSTON.

BOOKS FOR EUROPEAN TOURISTS.

A SATCHEL GUIDE FOR THE VACATION TOURIST IN EUROPE. A compact itinerary of the British Isles, Belgium and Holland, Germany and the Rhine, Switzerland, France, Austria, and Italy. With Maps, Appendix, and Memoranda pages. Revised every year. 16mo, roan, flexible, $2.00.

"The book is indeed a model of perspicacity and brevity; all the advice it gives will be found of immediate service. The 'Satchel Guide' tells the reader *how to travel cheaply without a sacrifice of comfort*, and this feature of the book will recommend it to many Tourists."—PALL MALL GAZETTE.

SAUNTERINGS. By CHARLES DUDLEY WARNER. $1.25.

"The book contains a little about England and France, more about Switzerland and Holland, and a great deal concerning South Germany and Italy. There is not a dull page in it."—SPRINGFIELD REPUBLICAN.

CASTILIAN DAYS. A very attractive book by JOHN HAY, treating the history, country, cities, people, and politics of Spain. $2.00.

THE LANDS OF SCOTT. By JAMES F. HUNNEWELL. $2.50.

"It is a delightful epitome of the great author's life and works; the reader being introduced to a detailed acquaintance with these, while he is led through the localities which the genius of Scott has celebrated."—BUFFALO COURIER.

OLD ENGLAND: ITS SCENERY, ART, AND PEOPLE. By Prof. JAMES M. HOPPIN, of Yale College. 16mo, $1.75. Includes descriptions of Derbyshire, Devonshire, the Lake Country, Cornwall, the Old Cathedral Towns, and those Historic Scenes which most interest Tourists.

*** For sale by Booksellers. Sent postpaid on receipt of price by the Publishers,

HOUGHTON, MIFFLIN & CO., BOSTON, MASS.

PEOPLE WHO KNOW "HOW TO TRAVEL,"
GO TO EUROPE BY

THE STATE LINE,

Composed of new and powerful first-class Passenger Steamers sailing WEEKLY between

NEW YORK, GLASGOW, AND LIVERPOOL.

EVERY THURSDAY FROM NEW YORK. SAFETY AND SPEED COMBINED.

By taking this route, excursionists will economize in expenditures and yet enjoy all the comforts and luxuries of an ocean voyage, and a trip through Scotland via rail to Liverpool FREE OF COST.

No live stock carried on these steamers.

Passage and State-Rooms can be secured in advance by communicating by letter or telegraph with Agents, or to

AUSTIN, BALDWIN & CO.,

164 Randolph St., GEN'L AGENTS, 53 Broadway,
CHICAGO.   NEW YORK.

EXCURSIONISTS WHO MAKE PURCHASES ABROAD CAN SAVE TROUBLE AND EXPENSE BY PLACING THEM IN CHARGE OF

THE AMERICAN-EUROPEAN EXPRESS,

(Established 1848.)

BALDWIN BROS. & CO., PROPRIETORS,

53 BROADWAY, NEW YORK.

Parcels, packages, statuary, paintings, and valuables taken charge of and forwarded to America with care and at very moderate charges. Custom-house business attended to and goods delivered to any address in Europe or America.

PRINCIPAL AGENCIES.—H. Starr & Co., 19 Australian Avenue, Jewin Crescent, London; J. & R. McCracken, 38 Queen Street, London; Lherbette, Kane & Co., 19 Rue Scribe, Paris; Staveley & Co., 1 The Temple, Dale Street, Liverpool; Lherbette, Kane & Co., 9 Rue de la Bourse, Havre; Matthias Rohde & Co., Hamburg; J. H. Bachmann, Bremen; A. Warmuth, Berlin; Maquay, Hooker & Co., Rome; Maquay, Hooker & Co., Florence; W. J. Turner & Co., Naples; Guiseppe Scala, Naples; Carlo Ponti, Venice; E. Ramirez, 16 Mercaderes, Havana; John Wallis, Cork; John Wallis, 33 Bachelors' Walk, Dublin.

MAIL STEAMERS
BETWEEN
New York, Queenstown, and Liverpool.

| BRITANNIC, | GERMANIC, | ADRIATIC, |
| CELTIC, | BALTIC, | REPUBLIC. |

Sail from New York every alternate THURSDAY and SATURDAY.

They are all of them, without exception, among the largest and finest of ocean steamers, and were constructed with special reference to the conveyance of passengers.

The saloon and staterooms are located in the midship section, where but little motion is felt.

No Cattle, Sheep, or Pigs carried.

Rates of Passage as low as by any first-class line.

For inspection of plans, rates of passage, etc., apply at the COMPANY'S OFFICES, 37 BROADWAY, NEW YORK.

R. J. CORTIS, AGENT.

C. L. BARTLETT & CO., Agents for BOSTON.

BARRITT & CATTELL, Agents for PHILADELPHIA.

A. LAGERGREN, General Western Agent, CHICAGO.

Fine Art in Jewelry.

THREE centuries ago the Jewelers of Europe were Artists in every sense of the word, and Artists of such taste and skill that their works which have come down to us now command prices as utterly disproportionate to the intrinsic value of the precious substances of which they are made as the prices paid for the best works of the Sculptor in bronze and marble are to the intrinsic value of the materials out of which those works are hewn or moulded. Many such Artists bequeathed legacies, since enormously increased in value, to the Goldsmiths' Company for the purpose of keeping alive their art, and the enlightened public of London are now beginning to insist that these endowments shall be put to their legitimate use. We have no Goldsmiths' Company in New York, but an hour spent in such an establishment as that of MR. THEODORE B. STARR, 206 Fifth Avenue, in this city, will throw a great deal of light, for those who have eyes to see, on the possible importance, hitherto almost unappreciated among ourselves, of the æsthetic aspects of the beautiful industry by which that great corporation has been built up in the mother country. Mr. Starr has devoted himself steadily and successfully now for nearly twenty years to artistic work in Jewelry, and the display which he now makes of such work really deserves to rank among the the most interesting and instructive of our existing art collections. In the choice and conservation of the more brilliant gems—for there is an art in conserving as well as detecting the special perfection of special gems as respects alike their surfaces, their crystallization, and their color—Mr. Starr shows the taste and training of an Artist, not less than in the skill and judgment with which he combines and sets such gems.—NEW YORK WORLD.

HOW TO TRAVEL.

HINTS, ADVICE, AND SUGGESTIONS

TO TRAVELERS

BY

LAND AND SEA

ALL OVER THE GLOBE.

BY

THOMAS W. KNOX,

Author of "Camp-Fire and Cotton-Field," "Overland Through Asia," "Underground," "Backsheesh," "John," "The Boy Travelers in the Far East," Etc.

NEW YORK:
CHARLES T. DILLINGHAM.
BOSTON:
LEE AND SHEPARD.
LONDON AND GENEVA
THE AMERICAN EXCHANGE IN EUROPE.
1881.

Entered according to Act of Congress in the year 1880, by
THOMAS W. KNOX,
In the office of the Librarian of Congress, at Washington.

All rights of translation and foreign publication are reserved.

To all Travelers on Land and Sea,

This Volume

is sympathetically inscribed.

PREFACE.

IN preparing this volume for the press the author of "How to Travel" has endeavored to supply a want whose existence has long been apparent to him. Having journeyed somewhat over the earth he is frequently consulted by friends and acquaintances who are about to travel, and wish to know what to do before setting out on their undertakings, and how to meet the various perplexities that are sure to arise. In preparing this book he has answered a great many interrogatories that have been addressed to him in person, and if the manner of his response should be considered didactic, he begs the reader to remember that the author is endeavoring to meet the questions of the would-be traveler, and, therefore, addresses him in the second person. As nearly as possible he has embodied in "How to Travel" as much information as could be wrung from him by a vigorous and thorough interrogation of a couple of long winter evenings, conducted by an inquisitive couple who were about starting on a journey around the world and up and down its surface.

With the changes that are constantly going on, some of the information here given may be found slightly inaccurate, but it is hoped that instances of this sort will be rare. Prices of hotels, steamships, railroads, and the like are subject to alteration, and consequently no absolute rule can be laid down. But the author believes that in the instances where his figures may be found astray they are so near the mark that they will prove of material assistance to the traveler.

As the author is neither a lady nor a lawyer, he has found it desirable to invoke the aid of those important members of society in the preparation of the book. A reference to the table of contents will show the assistance they have given him, the one in a chapter of "Special Advice to Ladies" and the other in "Legal Rights of Travelers." All other parts of the book are of his own production and the results of his experience in travel, covering a period of more than 20 years and embracing many lands and seas.

With this explanatory preface, and trusting that the volume will be a sufficient apology for its existence, the author delivers it to the hands of the traveling public, and hopes for a verdict in its favor.

T. W. K.

NEW YORK, February, 1881.

CONTENTS.

CHAPTER.		PAGE.
I.	General Advice Applicable to all Kinds of Travel,	9
II.	Railway Travel in the United States and Canadas,	20
III.	American Steamboat Travel,	28
IV.	Sea and Ocean Travel,	37
V.	Sea Sickness and How to Avoid it,	48
VI.	Special Advice to Ladies, by a Lady,	55
VII.	Daily Life at Sea,	64
VIII.	Going on Shore — Hotels,	76
IX.	The System of Fees,	87
X.	English and Continental Money,	102
XI.	Languages and Couriers,	108
XII.	Railway Traveling on the Continent,	118
XIII.	Steamboat Traveling in Europe,	133
XIV.	Sea-going Steamers in European Waters,	139
XV.	Sea and Ocean Steamers in Various Parts of the World,	147
XVI.	Travel by Stage-Coach, Diligence, and Post,	155
XVII.	Traveling with Camels and Elephants,	167
XVIII.	Traveling with Reindeer and Dogs,	174
XIX.	Traveling with Man-power — Palankeens, Jinrikishas, and Sedan Chairs,	179
XX.	Pedestrian Traveling — Mountain Climbing,	186
XXI.	Traveling Without Money — Round the World for $50,	193
XXII.	Skeleton Tours for America and Europe,	201
XXIII. XXIV.	} General Directions for a Journey Round the World, with Routes, Distances, etc., etc.,	207
XXV.	Legal Rights of Travelers, by a Lawyer,	230
XXVI.	Wilderness and Frontier Travel,	242

CHAPTER I.

GENERAL ADVICE APPLICABLE TO ALL KINDS OF TRAVEL.

There is an old saying of unknown origin that a light heart and a thin pair of trowsers are the principal requisites for a journey. The proper texture of one's garments depends largely on his route of travel and the difficulties to be encountered; thin ones would be desirable in hot countries and for lounging on the deck of a ship in low latitudes, while they would be eminently out of place in the region of the north pole or in the rough traveling of the wilderness. But no one will deny that a light heart has much to do with the pleasure of travel, and the man who can be serene under all circumstances, who laughs at mishaps, and accepts every situation with a smile of content, or at least with a feeling of resignation, is the model voyager. For him the miles go by as on the wings of a bird, while to the grumbler and misanthrope they are weighted with lead. The former comes back from his wanderings refreshed and instructed while the latter is no better in mind and body than when setting out on his journey. For your own comfort and happiness, and your own mental and physical advantage, start on your journey with a determination to see the bright side of everything and to endure as cheerfully as possible the jolts and buffetings and petty disappointments that are sure to be your lot. And in the same proportion that a light heart makes you better for yourself it makes you better and more agreeable for those who may be traveling with you.

If you have been reared in the belief that your own country, or your own state, town, or hamlet, contains all that is good in the world, whether of moral excellence, mental development, or mechanical skill, you must prepare to eradicate that belief at an early date. That you and yours have the best and are the best we will not for a moment deny, but when you attempt to claim everything you claim too much. To an observant and thoughtful individual the invariable effect of travel is to teach respect for the opinions, the faith, or the ways of others, and to convince him that other civilizations than his own are worthy of consideration. At the same time he will find his love for his native land as strong as ever and his admiration for his own institutions as warm as on the day of his departure. An old traveler once said : " I have found good among every people, and even where there was much to condemn there was much to admire. I have never returned from a journey without an increased respect for the countries I have visited and a greater regard for my own land than ever before. The intelligent traveler will certainly be a true patriot."

So much for the mental conditions of travel. We will come now to the practical and tangible needs of locomotion.

Money is the first of these things. It is true that one can travel without money, and in a later chapter we will see how it may be accomplished; for the present we will look upon money as a requisite.

Never carry a large amount of cash about your person or in your baggage. A letter of credit, procurable at any banker's, is far better than ready money, as its loss causes nothing more than temporary inconvenience. It is best not to lose it at all; but, in case of its disappearance, payment may be stopped and the finder or thief can derive no benefit from its possession. The usual form of a letter of credit is about as follows :

"NEW YORK, 18 .
" *To our correspondents:*
" We have the pleasure of introducing to you * * * * * the bearer of this letter, whose signature you will find in the margin. We beg you to honor his drafts to the amount of * * * * * pounds sterling upon our London house. All deductions and commissions to be at the expense of the bearer.
" We have the honor to remain, gentlemen,
" Very truly yours,
"* * * * * *."

Some banking-houses have their letters printed in French instead of English, but the substance is the same. The amount is usually expressed in pounds sterling, and drafts are made payable in London; but if the traveler is going directly to the continent of Europe, some of the bankers will give him, if he desires it, a letter on Paris and state the amount in francs. Sterling credits are generally the best to carry, no matter what country you may be visiting, as London is the money centre of the world, and there is never any difficulty in ascertaining the rate of exchange upon that great city. The traveling letter of credit is printed on the front of a four-page sheet, letter size; the second page is left blank for the endorsement of the amounts drawn, and the third and fourth pages contain a list of bankers in all the principal cities that the voyager is likely to visit. Any respectable banker, even if not named on the printed list, will generally cash a letter of credit; but it is advisable to adhere as much as possible to the correspondents of the establishment that issued the document.

The traveler should only draw at one time sufficient money to last him for a few days, or till he reaches a convenient place for making another draft. A week's supply of cash is usually sufficient for a single draft; but, of course, no absolute rule can be laid down.

Another form of traveling credit is in the shape of circular notes, which are issued by some bankers, though not by all. They are for various amounts—five, ten, twenty, fifty, or a hundred pounds—and are accompanied by a letter of identification which bears the signature of the holder. The notes are useless without the letter, and the letter without the notes, and the traveler is advised to carry them apart from each other. The advantage of this kind of credit is that you can have the notes cashed at a hotel or at any large shop where you may be making purchases, and you may have remittances follow you from time to time in circular notes, the same letter of identification answering for all. The disadvantage is that they are bulky, and consequently inconvenient to carry, and the possession of two parcels in place of one, in different parts of your baggage, doubles the chances of loss. For a long journey where a considerable amount is to be carried, or where remittances are to follow, I would recommend that part of the funds should be in a letter of credit, and part in circular notes with an identification.

For domestic traveling, bankers' drafts and credits can always be procured; but American bankers are much more stringent about identifications than are those of Europe, and the traveler must be sure that he can be properly identified wherever he is going, or he may experience difficulty in obtaining his cash. An obliging banker has been known to pay a draft to an individual who had no other identification than his name written on his under-clothing or his initials tattooed on his arm. But such instances are rare, and the money-changer is very likely to be obdurate, though polite. It is said that a Boston banker once cashed a check payable to the order of Peter Bean, under the following circumstances :—The bearer said he knew nobody in the city, but he proved his identity by ripping open the lining of his coat-collar and revealing a pea and a bean, securely stowed away. "That's my name," said he, " P. Bean; and that's the way I mark my coats." But all names cannot be written with the products of the garden, and Mr. Bean is not likely to have many imitators.

Your letters can be sent to the care of any banker on whom your credits are drawn, and they will be forwarded by him as you may direct. This is the usual custom with European travelers, and there is rarely any cause for complaint.

When traveling, always be careful to have plenty of small change in your pockets, and be prepared to pay all obligations, especially the smallest, in their exact amount. The vast horde of cabmen, porters, guides, waiters, and all classes of people who render you services, or pretend to have done so, are proverbially without change, and if you cannot tender the exact sum due them you are pretty certain to overpay them. Even where they admit that they are possessed of small coin, they generally manage so as to mulct you in something by having their change give out before the proper return is reached. The New York hackman to whom you hand a five-dollar bill for him to deduct his fare of two dollars will usually discover that he has only two dollars, or perhaps two and a half, in his possession; and the London cabman will play the same trick when you ask him to take half a crown from a five-shilling piece. All over the world you will find it the same. There may be an occasional exception, but it only proves the rule. And when you enter the great field of gratuities, you will find that the absence of small change will cost you heavily. Many a man has given a shilling where a sixpence was quite sufficient, and all that was expected; but he did not have the sixpence in his pocket, and the shilling had to go.

Have as little baggage as the circumstances will justify. Don't carry anything on the principle of Mrs. Toodles, that it may come handy some time, but take only what you know to be absolutely necessary. No rule can be laid down, and each person must judge for himself. For a man, a suit of clothes in addition to the one he wears is sufficient for outward adornment, unless he is "in society," and expects to dine, attend parties, or make fashionable visits. In the latter case a dress-suit is indispensable, and in European travel it is generally well to have a dress-suit along, since there are many public ceremonies where the wearer of ordinary clothing is not admitted. For ladies, a traveling-dress, a walking-dress, and a black silk dress may be considered the minimum. The black silk garment corresponds to the masculine dress-suit, but it comes in use on many occasions where the latter is not demanded. The quantity of under-clothing will depend largely on personal habits. It should never be less than to cause no inconvenience in a week's absence of the laundress, and if a long voyage is to be made by steamship the supply should be proportionally increased. It is a good rule never to omit an opportunity of giving your soiled garments to be washed, even if only a day or two has elapsed since your last employment of the laundress. In all civilized parts of the world where there is an appreciable volume of travel, washing is done in from twenty-four to forty-eight hours, but away from the routes you must count on a week, or four or five days at least.

A single trunk of moderate size will contain all that is needed for the actual traveling wants of a reasonable being, of either sex, except on a long journey. To this add a hand-satchel to hold your toilet articles, and any little odds and ends of reading matter, or other personal comforts. Some travelers are content with such toilet materials as they find in hotels, and do not object to a public comb or hair-brush; but the majority of individuals are more fastidious. In most hotels in America, soap is supplied in private rooms; but in Europe the traveler must provide his own.

Endeavor as much as possible to avoid being in a hurry. Go to your train, boat, ship, diligence, or other conveyance, in ample season, so that all needed arrangements can be made without pressure for want of time. You will save money and temper by adopting this rule.

Respect the rights of other travelers, and by so doing you will lead them to respect yours. Keep your disposition as unruffled as possible at all times, and even when angry inside don't let the anger come to the surface. If you find yourself imposed upon by any official or employé of railway or steamer, state your views quietly but firmly, and, if he declines to redress the wrong, ask him to be kind enough to call his superior. If the latter is inaccessible, ask, in the same polite tone, for his address, and the chances are ten to one that your cause of complaint will be removed without more discussion.

Expenses may be roughly set down at five dollars a day, not including railway or other fares, and not including luxuries of any kind. Ordinary hotel expenses will be not be far from three dollars a day, leaving two dollars for incidentals. Most persons would be likely to exceed rather than fall below this figure, and in the United States they will find that money melts away more rapidly than in Europe. England is at least twenty-five per cent. dearer than the continental countries, and only a trifle cheaper than America. The traveler who is not economical on the one hand and not wasteful on the other can get along very well on six dollars a day in England or America, and five dollars on the continent, with the exception of Spain and Russia, which are dearer than Germany, France, Italy, or Switzerland. The usual allowance to commercial travelers for their expenses, exclusive of railway fares, is one pound sterling daily in England, and twenty francs on the continent; and it is probable that the most of them manage to keep within their allowances.

A party of two or more will travel somewhat cheaper than the same number of individuals alone, for the reason that many items are no more for two than for one. Including all the expenses of travel—railways, steamships, hotels, carriages, fees, and the like—an extended journey may be made for ten dollars a day in England and Europe, and twelve dollars for the United States. This allows for first-class places on all conveyances, and good rooms at good hotels—requires no rigid economy, and permits no extravagance. For a journey around the world, to occupy ten or twelve months, and visiting Japan, China, Siam, Java, India, Egypt, Italy, France, and England, together with the run across the American continent, the cost will be about four or five thousand dollars. But, as before stated, there can be no fixed rule, and the amount of expenditure depends largely upon the tastes and habits of the traveler and the amount of money at his disposal. More will be said on this topic in subsequent pages.

Whenever you go out of your own country carry a passport. It may not be needed, as passports are now demanded in very few countries, but it is a good thing to have along, since it serves as an identification in case of trouble with the authorities, and is useful in civil actions or where the assistance of your consul may be required. In many countries the post-office employés refuse to deliver registered letters to a stranger except on presentation of his passport, and the document will occasionally be found useful at the banker's. An old frontiersman once said of the revolver which he habitually carried, " You don't need it often; perhaps may never need it at all, but when you do want it you want it awful bad, I tell you." The same may be said of the passport.

Passports may be procured through a lawyer or notary public, and a single passport is sufficient for a family. They may also be obtained at any United States legation abroad on presentation of proofs of citizenship. The government fee for a passport is five dollars.

At the custom-house, whatever its nationality, be as civil as possible and anticipate the desires of the officials. They have a duty to perform, and if you facilitate their labors the chances are they will appreciate the politeness and let you off as easily as they can consistently. Unlock your trunk or valise, or offer to do so, before they ask you, and open the various compartments immediately. Declare anything that may be liable to duty and call attention to it, and conduct yourself generally as though it was one of the delights of your life to pass a custom-house examination. If you are inclined to defraud the revenue, do it gracefully and conceal your contraband articles so that it will not be easy to find them yourself after you are out of reach of the officials. Honesty is, however, the best policy in this business, and the smuggler is just as much a violator of the law as a burglar.

The ways of the custom-house may sometimes be smoothed by a numismatic application to the hand of the inspector, but it is not altogether a safe operation. In

Turkey, Egypt, Syria, and other Moslem countries bribery is considered a legitimate and honorable transaction, and the customs officer looks at the outside of your trunk and extends his open hand for your money with as little attempt at concealment as does the cabman when he asks for your fare. At the Italian Dogana fees are taken on the sly, but you may sometimes make a mistake and hit the wrong man, and the same is the case in Spain and Russia. In the other continental countries generally, and in England and the United States, fee-taking at the custom-house is a pretty rare exception, and the traveler will do far better to avoid crooked ways than to attempt them. Instances have been known of American inspectors who went straight to the point and suggested that a five-dollar bill would make things easy, and when it was not forthcoming they gave all the trouble in their power. Happily such occurrences are rare, and if customs officials are occasionally dishonest it should be remembered that they are no worse than those who encourage them to be so. A bribe, like a bargain, requires two persons for its consummation, and of this twain the officer is but one.

Before starting on any journey buy a copy of "How to Travel," and if you find the book useful be kind enough to recommend it to your friends and acquaintances. Find the best guide-books for the region you are to visit and study them carefully; if you make a mistake and get hold of a poor one, remember that even a poor guide-book is better than none at all, and you will generally obtain the worth of your money from it.

For the United States Osgood's and Appleton's guides are to be recommended, though there are others that contain a great deal of information. The name of guide-books for the trans-continental journey is legion; all have their merits and their faults, and as they are to be found at all the news-stands on the great railway lines the tourist can choose for himself.

For Europe the principal guide-books are those of Murray and Baedeker. Baedeker's books are the most convenient, and contain more practical information than their English rival; and there are probably ten copies of Baedeker sold to one of Murray. Where a traveler wishes to learn about the hotels, railways, cabs, roads, and other things of every-day life, Baedeker is his friend, but where he desires a long historical sketch, or perhaps a dissertation on art, he will choose Murray. It is well to have both these guides, as the one supplies oftentimes what the other lacks. Harper's and Appleton's guide books to Europe and the East, each in three volumes, are popular with many Americans, on account of their compactness.

Syria, Palestine, and Egypt are also covered by both Baedeker and Murray, and the latter has a guide to India, but it has not been revised for a long time. There are no complete guide-books to China, Japan, and the Far East generally, and the tourist must rely on general works of history and travel. In this connection the writer respectfully calls attention to his volumes, named on the title-page of this work.

CHAPTER II.

RAILWAY TRAVEL IN THE UNITED STATES AND CANADAS.

Travel in the United States and Canada virtually comprises but two kinds of conveyance, the railway and the steamboat. Once the stage-coach was an American feature, and it still remains in some parts of the country, but the rapid advance of the railway has almost swept it out of existence, and where it still lingers it is but the shadow of its former self. Long ago we had the canal-boat, a slow but remarkably safe mode of locomotion; it could not leave the track or be overturned, nor could it explode; The water beneath it was so shallow that it could not sink, and in case it took fire you had only to step ashore and be out of danger. But the canal-boat is a thing of the past, with here and there an exception still more rare than that of the stage-coach. We are a progressive people, and when the quicker mode of travel was developed the old was forgotten and sent into obscurity.

Until within the last fifteen or twenty years we had but a single class of passenger cars in America, as the emigrant trains on a few of the trunk lines were hardly to be considered by travelers, but the invention of the palace and sleeping-coaches (generally coupled with the name of Pullman, their inventor), has given us two classes which are virtually as distinct as are the first and second of a continental railway. Hardly a train runs on any road of consequence without a Pullman car attached, and a seat may be had in this vehicle on payment of an extra fee. There is the parlor car for day use only, but the "sleeper" is intended for both day and night. By the magic wand of a colored porter the seats are converted into comfortable beds, and the traveler may be whirled along at the rate of thirty miles an hour, and all the while he sleeps as calmly as at home. Toilet-rooms are at the ends of every carriage, one for gentlemen and the other for ladies, where you may perform your ablutions and put your hair in shape, so as to present as creditable an appearance as when starting on your journey. That "necessity is the mother of invention" is well exemplified in the history of the Pullman car. The great distances to be traveled in America called for something which should soften the asperities of sitting in an ordinary seat by night as well as by day. Step by step the work went on, till finally we have the perfection of railway travel.

The expense of a place in a parlor or sleeping-car on American railways varies from two to three dollars for twenty-four hours, with the addition of a fee to the porter of 25 cents a day. For this he looks after your personal needs, polishes your boots, and opens or closes your bed when you desire it. There has been considerable mystery relative to the sleeping hours of a porter in a palace car on long routes, as he appears to be on duty all the time from one day's beginning to another. It is suspected that he belongs to a race apart from the rest of humanity, and is so constituted that he never sleeps. The tickets for the palace car are not usually sold at the same place as the regular passenger tickets, but at a separate window or in an office by itself. It is well to secure your place in advance, as the cars are often crowded and you may arrive at a station to start on a long journey and find that every bed has been sold. Places may be secured hours and days ahead, and the earlier you take them the better choice do you have. The tickets for the car are collected by a conductor, and if any places are unsecured he can sell them to those who apply for them.

Never buy your tickets, either for passage or for a place in a palace car, of strangers in the street or of chance "runners." Such tickets may be good, but the probabilities are not in their favor, while there can be no doubt about the tickets at the regular offices. Where there are rival routes it is often difficult to get the exact facts concerning them, as the runners are apt to be inexact about the merits of their own lines or the demerits of others. They have been known to state that the track of a rival railway had been torn up and sold for old iron in order that a dividend might be declared to the stockholders, and the steamboat agent who told a timid old lady that his company had removed all the boilers from their boats, so as to destroy the possibility of an explosion, is not without imitators.

Beware of playing cards with strangers who wish to start a friendly game of euchre which is subsequently changed to draw-poker or some other seductive and costly amusement. This advice is superfluous in case you are in the gambling line yourself, and confident that you can "get away" with any adversary you may be pitted against. Be cautious, however, about "waking up the wrong passenger," as not unfrequently happens to skilled performers with cards.

On most of the railways each passenger has an allowance of 100 pounds of baggage, but it is never weighed unless the amount is greatly in excess. West of the Missouri river they are more particular, and all trunks must pass the scales. On the Pacific railways all extra baggage above the allowance is charged for at a certain rate per pound, but on the eastern roads the extra charge is generally for the trunk or box without much regard to its weight. On most of the eastern roads a passenger can take a single trunk without extra payment, even though it may rival a square piano in size. Sometimes a question about extra trunks may be settled by a fee to the man in charge of the baggage-room of the station or the baggage-car of the train. The passenger's ticket must be shown at the baggage-room, where a metal check will be given to the place of destination. The check secured, the traveler may proceed to the palace or other car of the train and give his trunk no farther consideration till he nears the place to which it is checked.

Baggage expresses exist in most of the large cities. They undertake to deliver your impedimenta on payment of a fee of from 25 to 50 cents for each parcel, at any hotel or private residence in the place, on the surrender of your check. If you are in a hurry and must have your trunk within a few hours after your arrival, it will be unsafe to trust to the baggage express; the agent who passes through the train to collect the checks will assure you that your baggage will be delivered within an hour of arrival, but if you ask a written guarantee to that effect he will be pretty sure to refuse it, and admit that he does not know when the delivery will take place. The writer speaks knowingly and feelingly of his experience with baggage expresses in New York; in only one instance in a period covering more than twenty years has a baggage express delivered his trunk or valise in the time promised by the agent, and he has been compelled to wait all the way from two to ten hours beyond the time stipulated. On one occasion a trunk that was promised for 7 A. M. was delivered at 8.30 P. M., and on another a valise promised for 2 P. M. did not reach its destination till 11 P. M. and the driver of the wagon demanded extra payment for night delivery.

Carriages from railway stations are always to be had, and in some of the cities, notably in Boston, the rates are reasonable and honestly stated, and the service is good and prompt. In New York very little can be said in praise of the carriage system, as the drivers are inclined to make as much as possible out of the stranger within the gates, and are more likely to overcharge him than to state the proper and legal fare. Most of the large hotels have their own coaches at the stations on arrival of the principal trains, not only in New York but in other cities, and by taking one of these coaches the traveler will greatly lessen the probabilities of being defrauded. If he intends to take a carriage from the station, and has only ordinary baggage, he will not give his checks to the express agent, but will hand them over to the driver whom he engages.

In the western cities there is an omnibus system of a very satisfactory character. As you approach a city, an agent of the omnibus company (generally called a Transfer Company) passes through the train, and interrogates each passenger. You state your destination—whether hotel, private house, or another railway station—surrender your baggage check, and with it your transfer ticket, if you have one; or if not, you pay a fee of from twenty-five to fifty cents. The agent tells you the number or letter of the omnibus you are to enter, and when you arrive at the station you find the vehicles drawn up in a row against the platform. Selecting the one that is to carry you, you enter it, and in a little while it moves off, followed by the wagon that holds your trunk. You are taken with reasonable directness to your destination, the omnibus sometimes making slight detours to drop passengers along its route. The same vehicles take passengers to the stations, and, by leaving notice at the company's office, you can be called for in any part of the city, at any hour you name.

Most of the American cities are well provided with street railways, or tramways, and with cheap omnibuses that ply along the principal streets. To make use of these to advantage, a knowledge of the city is necessary; but strangers will have little difficulty in securing the proper directions by applying to a policeman. Professional guides are unknown in American cities, but the services of a bootblack or other small and somewhat ragged boy can generally be secured to put the traveler on the right track.

On all the lines of railway there are eating-stations, where passengers may save themselves from starvation, and generally do a good deal more. The time allowed varies greatly, but the usual limit is twenty minutes; on some lines it is half an hour, while on others a quarter of an hour is deemed sufficient. The price of a "square meal" varies from fifty cents to a dollar, and there are a few places where it is a dollar and a quarter. The square meal is not, as might be supposed, a dinner, supper, or breakfast in the form of a cube; it includes the right of eating as much as one pleases from any or all the dishes on the bill of fare, and if the traveler chooses to repeat, again and again, any favorite article of food, the proprietor offers no objection. The service is generally good, and the supply of food palatable and bountiful. The majority of travelers are apt to eat with considerable velocity at these stopping-places, and there are few spots in the world where one can witness greater dexterity with knife and fork than where a railway train halts " fifteen minutes for refreshments." The performances of the East Indian juggler are thrown in the shade, and the famous swordsman of Runjeet Singh, who could wield his weapon with such rapidity that it was altogether invisible while removing the head of an antagonist, might learn something if he would make a visit to the eating-house of an American railway.

Those who do not wish a full meal will generally find a counter at the eating-stations where coffee, tea, sandwiches, and cold meats may be bought cheaply, and on some roads there are stations where the trains stop for five or ten minutes only, to enable passengers to take a slight lunch, of a solid or liquid character. On many of the roads the sale of intoxicating liquors is forbidden; but these are not held to include beer, cider, and light wines.

It is a good rule for a traveler never to miss the opportunity of taking a meal. Sometimes the hours are a trifle inconvenient, and he may not feel hungry when an eating-station is reached; but if he allows it to pass he will find himself faint with hunger before he comes to the next. On long journeys it is well to carry a lunch-basket of such things as may strike the owner's fancy and palate, but care should be taken to avoid articles that give out disagreeable odors. Limburger cheese is not to be recommended—nor, in fact, cheese of any sort; cold tongue is another objectionable article, as it will not keep many hours, and has a way of smelling badly, or even worse. Crackers, English biscuit, and fruit, with a bottle of claret or some similar drink, are the best things for a railway lunch-basket, and sometimes they tend greatly to preserve the temper unruffled, by filling an aching void when the train is delayed and the square meal unattainable.

On several of the great lines running westward, dining and hotel cars have been established. The latter are both eating and sleeping-coaches in one, but they are not generally in favor, as it is found in actual practice that the smell of cookery is disagreeable to the slumberer, while that of the sleeping-room is not acceptable to the nostrils when one sits down to breakfast or dinner. The dining-car is kitchen and dining-room, and nothing more. It is attached to the train at a convenient time for a meal, and runs with it for a couple of hours or so, when it is turned to a side track and waits to serve the next banquet for a train going the other way. The dining-car is a most admirable institution, as it enables the traveler to take his meals leisurely while proceeding on his way. It is generally well-managed and liberally supplied, and one may be fed as bountifully, and on as well-cooked food, as in the majority of hotels. On some of these cars meals are served *a la carte;* but the most of them have the fixed-price system, at the same rates as the stations along the lines where they run.

In the parlor cars, your seat is designated on a ticket specially marked and numbered, and no one has any right to occupy it during your absence. On the ordinary cars, the seats are common property, and cannot be retained; though it is almost universally recognized that the deposit of an overcoat, shawl, bag, or some other article of the traveler's equipment in a seat is *prima facie* evidence that it has been taken. Impudent persons will sometimes remove the property of one who is temporarily absent, and appropriate the seat to themselves; but they generally vacate it on being reasoned with. If they are obstinate, the conductor may be called, and sometimes the muscular persuasion of a strong brakeman or two is necessary to convince the intruder of his mistake.

CHAPTER III.

AMERICAN STEAMBOAT TRAVEL.

The railway system of the United States had its beginning about fifty years ago, and is consequently a third of a century behind the adoption of the steamboat. According to the best authorities, the first American steamboat that carried passengers and made regular trips was built by John Fitch, at Philadelphia, and was the successor of two experimental boats by the same inventor. She ran on the Delaware river during the summer of 1790, and made altogether more than two thousand miles, at a maximum speed of seven and a half miles an hour. Fulton built the *Clermont* in 1806, and her regular trips began in 1807, seventeen years later than the achievement of Fitch. From this beginning, river-navigation by steam was spread through the United States till it reached every stream where boats could ply, and some where they were of no use. Of late years the steamboat interest has declined in some parts of the country, owing to the extension of the railway system; but it is still of great magnitude, and will doubtless so continue for many years to come.

American steamboats are undisputedly the finest in the world, and every foreigner who visits the United States looks with wonder at our floating palaces. Whether on eastern or western waters, the result is the same. The most ordinary boat surpasses the finest that English or European rivers or lakes can show.

(28)

The largest and most elaborate of the eastern boats are on the Hudson river and Long Island sound; the finest of the western boats are on the Mississippi. Some of those that connect New York and Albany and New York and Boston are capable of carrying six hundred first cabin passengers with comfort, and they have been known to transport as many as a thousand. On the night-boats there is a general sleeping-room below deck, and a bed in this locality is included in the ticket. Separate rooms on the upper deck must be paid for extra; but they are worth their cost in the privacy, better ventilation, and superior accommodations that they afford, besides being easier to escape from in case of accidents. The saloons are large, and elaborately furnished; and, if the boat is crowded to repletion, the sofas are used as sleeping-places by those who were not lucky enough to obtain rooms or beds below. Sometimes extra beds are put up in the saloon and lower cabin, so that the place looks not unlike a hospital, or the dormitory of a charity school.

A crowded steamboat at night is the paradise of the pickpocket, who frequently manages to reap a rich harvest from the unprotected slumberers. Even the private rooms are not safe from thieves, as their occupants are frequently robbed. On one occasion, some thirty or more rooms on a sound steamer were entered in a single night. The scoundrels had obtained access to the rooms in the day-time, and arranged the locks on the doors so that they could not be properly fastened. The night traveler on the steamboats plying in eastern waters should be very particular to fasten his door securely, and if he finds the lock has been tampered with he should report the circumstance to an officer or to one of the stewards. The windows should be looked after as well as the doors, and the rules that apply on railways to social games of cards with polite strangers should be remembered on steamboats.

Where steamboats are in competition with railways their fares are generally much cheaper, owing to the longer time consumed on the route. Where time is not an object the steamboat is the preferable conveyance, as the traveler is not inconvenienced by dust, the ventilation is better, means of circulation are far superior, and on river routes there is a better opportunity to study the scenery. Tickets may be bought and rooms secured at the offices at the terminal points in advance, and they may also be had on board the boats at the time of departure. It is needless to add that the earlier they are taken the better is the choice of rooms.

Meals are not included in the price of the ticket. They are served on nearly all boats, sometimes at a fixed price, as at the railway stations, and sometimes *a la carte*. The latter system appears to be gaining in popularity, as it is now adopted on many lines that formerly adhered to the old method.

On the great lakes there are propellors on the general model of the ocean steamer, and in summer they ply to all the principal ports. Interesting excursions may be made on these steamers, provided the traveler is not disturbed by a little roughness of the water now and then; of late years the voyage around the lakes has become highly popular, and is very pleasurable in Summer. Paddle steamers also abound on the lakes, but they do not equal those of the Hudson and Long Island sound, either in size or in the splendor of their accommodations.

On the Western rivers the model of the boat differs materially from the Eastern one. The main saloon is quite above the engine-room, which is on the lower deck, where the freight is piled and the steerage passengers are congregated. The Eastern and lake boats are propelled by low-pressure engines, while the craft of the Mississippi and its tributaries are generally high-pressure, and sometimes work a hundred and thirty pounds to the square inch. Explosions are less frequent now than formerly, but there are still enough of them to make traveling a trifle hazardous. Not infrequently fifty or a hundred lives will be lost by a steamboat explosion, and on one occasion the number of deaths by the blowing up of a steamboat and her consequent destruction by fire exceeded fifteen hundred.

Steamboat racing was once one of the amusements of the Mississippi and is not altogether unknown at present, though it has greatly declined. In the annals of the West there are many famous races recorded, where large sums of money were risked on the result, and where the passengers were as much excited over the event as the owners of the boats. In 1853 there was a race from New Orleans to Louisville, between the steamers *Eclipse* and *Shotwell*, on which seventy thousand dollars were staked by the owners of the rival craft, and probably the private bets were fully equal to that amount. The two boats were literally "stripped for the race;" they were loaded to the depth that would give them the greatest speed, and their arrangements for taking fuel were as complete as possible. Barges were filled with wood at stated points on the river and dropped out to mid-stream as the boats approached; they were taken alongside and their cargoes of wood transferred without any stoppage of the steamer's engines. At the end of the first twenty-four hours the *Eclipse* and *Shotwell* were side by side, 360 miles from New Orleans. They continued in almost this way to Louisville, and, though the race was supposed to have been won by the *Eclipse*, there was so much dispute about it that the wager was never paid.

Passenger travel on the Western rivers has been greatly

reduced in the last twenty years, owing to the creation of lines of railway parallel to the rivers, and the majority of the boats now running are far behind those of the palmy days between 1850 and 1860. Fares are lower than on the railways, and they include rooms and meals as of old, but the table is less bountifully supplied than formerly, and the number of servants is not so large. There is less competition, and the schedule of fares is generally adhered to. In the old days there was comparatively little regularity, and the clerk or captain of each boat could do pretty much as he liked about terms to passengers. On the Red river the clerks were accustomed to graduate the fare according to the locality where the passenger came on board. The more fertile and wealthy the region, the higher was the price of passage. Travelers from the cotton districts paid more than those from where tobacco was the staple product, and those from the sugar country paid more than any other class. With few exceptions there was no ticket system, every man paying his fare when it best suited him to do so. At present *on a changé tout cela.*

The departure of a steamboat from one of the great landings is a matter of some uncertainty. If she is advertised to leave at a certain time, those familiar with the business will understand that she will not leave before that hour, and her departure after it will be guided by circumstances. She will go when her freight and passenger-list are sufficiently full to make the trip a profitable one, unless she belongs to a line performing a regular service, in which case she is held to her schedule. The writer once took passage on a Mississippi steamer that remained at the wharf twenty-nine hours after her advertised time, and all the while she had steam up and her whistle was blown every half hour or so to indicate that she was "just going." And a friend of his once took passage on a steamboat from St. Louis to Cincinnati before the days of the railway. He lived on board for nearly a week with the boat tied up to the landing. At the end of that time the trip was abandoned, as the boat could not obtain a cargo for Cincinnati, and the passage-money was refunded in full.

When you go on board a Western steamboat proceed at once to the office and pay your fare. The clerk will hand you the key to your room or assign you to a berth in one that already contains a passenger, and then you can make yourself at home. You will find the manners of the Western waters more free than those of the East, and it is quite possible that your room-mate, if you have one, will commence the cultivation of your acquaintance with an invitation to drink; the custom of shooting a man who declines this politeness does not prevail at present, and the records of its having ever occurred are shrouded in obscurity. Western and Southwestern passengers are often rude and uncouth, but the rudeness is almost always unintentional, and the coarse exterior is very apt to cover a warm heart. The stranger will find much to amuse and interest him, and there are few places where human nature can be studied to better advantage than in the saloon of a Western steamboat.

The gambler once flourished on the Mississippi. He is less abundant than of yore, but the supply is still quite equal to the demand. He is generally not so polished as his confrere of the eastern boats and railway trains, but his ways are no less winning, so far as the taking of money is concerned, and he goes much further in the science of cheating. The unsophisticated stranger who takes a fourth hand with a trio of the light-fingered fraternity, "just to make up a game," might as well hand over his pocket-book at the start, unless he prefers going through the form of losing his cash.

Never be in a hurry on a western boat, as the time of arrival at your destination is a matter of more or less uncertainty. Delays at the landings, to take or discharge freight, are sometimes vexatious, and the journey may require double the time that was expected at the start. In the season of low water the boat is liable to get aground, and may lie there for hours, days, or even for weeks, before she is again afloat.

The dangers of the western waters are greater than those of the east. The boats are more liable to take fire, owing to their form of construction, and, as their engines are on the high-pressure principle, the chance of explosion of the boilers is much greater. The navigation of the rivers is hazardous, as the sand-banks are constantly shifting, and the course to be followed by the pilots is rarely the same for three months at a time. Snags and sawyers present dangers quite unknown to eastern waters, and in the Missouri river especially they are very numerous. A snag is a log or tree-trunk imbedded in the bottom of a river, with one end at or near the surface. The current causes it to incline down stream, and it is more dangerous to an ascending boat than to a descending one. The flat bottom of the boat is pierced by it, and sometimes the craft is impaled as one might impale a fly with a pin. On one occasion, on the Missouri river, some twenty years ago, a snag pierced the hull of a steamer, passed through the deck and cabin, and actually killed the pilot in the wheel-house. The sawyer is a tree that is loosely held by the roots at the bottom of the river, while its branches are on the surface; the current causes it to assume a sort of sawing motion, and hence its name. It is nearly if not quite as dangerous as the snag, and some of the pilots hold it in greater dread, for the reason that sawyers frequently change their position, while the snags, being more firmly imbedded, are less likely to drift away.

The current of the lower Mississippi is very strong, and it is a common remark that when a man falls into that stream his chances of escape are small. Many good swimmers have been drowned in it, and the great majority of those who dwell on its banks have a wholesome dread of attempting to bathe in its waters.

When we go westward beyond the valley of the Mississippi we find very few inland lakes and streams that are navigable. Great Salt Lake maintains a steamer or two for excursion purposes, and the waters of California had at one time a fair-sized fleet of boats that navigated San Francisco bay and the streams flowing into it. Their importance has diminished since the construction of the railway, and at present the steamboats of the Golden State are of no great consequence. Those that exist are managed more on the eastern than on the Mississippi system, but the rates are generally higher than on the Atlantic coast.

The Columbia river and its navigable tributaries have some thirty odd boats, most of them of small size, and intended to run where there is little water. The models in use are a modification of those of the Hudson and Long Island sound, and the rooms on the boats intended for night travel are generally large and comfortable. In going up the river from Portland, Oregon, the regular boats leave at five o'clock in the morning, and travelers making that journey will find it to their advantage to sleep on board instead of spending the night at the hotel and rising at an unseasonable hour in the morning.

On all the river steamers of America it is advisable to get a forward room rather than one near the stern. There is less jarring of the machinery, less heat from the engines, and, when the water is rough, there is less "pitching." On the other hand, there is more danger from collisions, and, on the Mississippi boats, a greater chance of being blown up. You pay your money, and you take your choice. But don't trouble yourself about accidents; don't put on your life-preserver before you go to sleep, as timid persons have been known to do; and if anything should happen try to face the danger coolly, and do the best you can. If you have occasion to don a life-preserver, be sure to fasten it well up under the arms, and not around the waist. In the proper position it will support the head above water, while, if fastened around the waist, it is apt to sustain the lower part of the body and submerge the head. If compelled to take to the water, divest yourself of the greater part of your clothing, and have your feet bare, or, at best, only stockinged. Ladies should reject their corsets under such circumstances, as they are serious hindrances to breathing in the water, and it is hardly necessary to say that long skirts are great impediments to swimming, or even to floating. Some persons have recommended their retention, on account of their buoyancy; but this only lasts for a few moments. As soon as they become soaked with water they become heavy, and have a tendency to drag the wearer down, rather than to support her.

CHAPTER IV.

SEA AND OCEAN TRAVEL.

The landsman who has never been on a sea-voyage looks with more or less hesitation at the prospect of making one. His thoughts are occupied with what he has heard or read of the perils of the great deep, and he regards with a feeling akin to veneration the bronzed sailor who has plowed every ocean on the globe, and tasted the delights of every climate. He questions his friends who have been to sea before him, and from their varied experience lays up a store of knowledge more or less useful. He wonders how he will enjoy sailing over the blue waters, how the spectacle will impress him, and more than all else he wonders whether or no he will be sea-sick. He busies himself with procuring a suitable outfit for his nautical journeys, and in nine cases out of ten selects a quantity of articles he never uses, and which it is not always easy to give away.

Before the days of steamships a sea voyage was an affair of considerable moment, as it implied an uncertain period on the waters, and the passenger was obliged to take along a good many articles of necessity or comfort, or go without them altogether. Nowadays the principal preparation is to secure your place and pay for your ticket, and, unless you are very eccentric in your wishes and desires, you will find everything you want to eat or drink on board the ship that is to carry you. In selecting your place, if you are inexperienced in sea travel, try and get as near the middle of the ship as you possibly can, and if you are forward of "amidships" you are better off than if the same distance "aft." In the middle of the ship there is less motion than elsewhere in a pitching sea, and the further you can get from the screw the less do you feel the jarring of the machinery. The rolling is the same all over the craft, and there is no position that will rid you of it. Several devices in the shape of swinging-berths have been tried, for the benefit of persons with tender heads and stomachs, and some of them have been quite successful in smoothing the rough ways of the ocean, but the steamship companies have been slow to adopt them, and the old salts do not regard them with a friendly eye.

Close all your business and have everything ready the day before your departure. It is better to sit around and be idle for a few hours than to have the worry of a lot of things that have been deferred till the last.

If you are going on a long voyage by sailing ship and expect to pass through the torrid and both temperate zones, you should provide yourself with thick and thin clothing suitable to all latitudes. If you are a society man of course you will carry your dress suit and a goodly stock of fine linen to match, but if you are "roughing it," and have no letters of introduction nor social designs, the dress suit will be superfluous. Take three or four suits of linen for wearing on shore in hot countries, a medium suit of woolen for temperate lands and a thick suit of the same material for high latitudes north or south. The roughest clothing procurable is what you need for wearing on shipboard, thin for the torrid zone and thicker for the temperate. Woolen or "hickory" shirts are the proper things for sea wear, and the only occasion when you need a white shirt is when you go on shore. Your own judgment must be your guide as to the proper supply of collars, handkerchiefs, and the like; don't forget to be well provided with underclothing, and remember that wool is a much safer article to wear against the skin than cotton or linen. Take plenty of woolen undershirts of the lightest texture for hot climates, and of course you will have thick ones for the cold regions. An umbrella and a cane are desirable for protection against sun and rain, or dogs and beggars, when going on shore. A sun hat, or *sola topee*, as it is called in India, is desirable in the tropics, but there is no need of taking it along at the start. It can be bought in the first tropical port you visit, and will be found there at a lower price than where it is not in regular use.

If you are going to China or India from an American port you need take only enough shore clothing to last you till you arrive there, as the tailors in those countries can outfit you very expeditiously, and at lower prices than you have at home. Of course you should have something to wear during the day or two it will require them to make up the goods after taking your measure. They will not give you a very snug fit, and quite possibly your garments may look as if they had been made on another man's measure, but if they are comfortable and succeed in touching you here and there they are about all you can expect. The Chinese tailor generally suggests "no fittee no takee" when he measures you, but his ideas of a fit are different from those of the fashionable clothiers of New York and London.

If you carry gloves through the tropics be sure to wrap them well in oiled silk before starting. It is well to observe this rule with gloves on all sea voyages, as the marine atmosphere is very injurious to them.

If you are a smoker carry your own cigars and tobacco. Fine cigars should be put up in tin or glass, as they are apt to suffer from the sea air; it is the opinion of many travelers that it is not worth the trouble to carry good cigars on an ocean voyage, as they are quickly spoiled, and soon taste no better than common ones. A fine cigar may be desirable after each meal, but for other times and for " smoking between smokes " an ordinary one is just as well. The author has tried all kinds of cigars at sea, and gives his verdict in favor of the manilla cigar of the quality called "seconds (understand that the manilla cheroot is not intended, but only the cigar). Seconds are preferable to firsts, as they are lighter in size and quality; the firsts make a very fair after-dinner cigar, and in the Far East many persons prefer them to choice Havanas. If you smoke a pipe be sure and have a supply of pipes with perforated covers for use on deck when the wind is blowing.

For the trans-Atlantic voyage, between America and Europe, there is very little need of preparation, beyond getting your ticket and putting affairs in shape for your absence. Take plenty of thick underclothing, your roughest suit of clothes for wearing on the voyage, the roughest and heaviest overcoat that you possess for wet weather, and an equally rough rug or other wrap for keeping you warm on deck when the north wind blows merrily. If you are of a sedentary habit buy a steamer chair, and when you buy it make up your mind that you will occupy it when you want to. A great number of people who say they "don't want the bother of a chair," or "didn't think to get one," are in the habit of helping themselves to the chairs of others without the least compunction of conscience and without caring a straw as to the desires of the owners for their property. Women are worse offenders than men in this matter, and the young and pretty are worse than the older and plainer. If you have a stony heart you will turn an intruder out of your chair without ceremony, whatever the age or sex, but if you cannot muster the courage to do so your best plan is to send the deck steward to bring the chair, and while he is getting it you can remain quietly out of sight. When you buy the chair have it marked with your name or initials, so that it can be easily distinguished from others of the same shape and color.

You are expected to come to the dinner-table in a black coat on most of the steamship lines. The rule is not imperative, however, but it is well to comply with it, as you will encounter many people whose notions about dressing for dinner are rigid, and, besides, the half hour spent in arranging the toilet before the bell calls you to the table is a variation of the monotony of the voyage.

Everything needed for the voyage may be contained in a valise or "steamer trunk," with a toilet satchel, and all heavy luggage should be sent below at the dock. A steamer trunk is designed to be stowed under the berth out of the way; its proper dimensions are 30 inches long, 15 or 16 wide, and 12 high. Its length or width may be greater, but its height should not exceed 12 or at most 13 inches, or it will be often found too large for the space where it is intended to go.

An old valise or sack should be taken along for containing the rough sea-clothing which may be left with the steamer-chair at the company's office in Liverpool or whatever port the passenger may land at. There they remain till his return, in a storeroom specially provided for them. They should be properly marked, so that the storekeeper will have no difficulty in selecting them when wanted.

The servants who wait upon you will expect a reward for their attentions, and you will be flying in the face of a long-established custom if you fail to give it. On the English steamers half a sovereign (ten shillings English) is the proper fee for the room-steward on the voyage either way, and the same to the table-steward. You will not diminish the attention upon you if you say to these men at starting that you will remember each of them with a ten-shilling piece, provided you are satisfied with them; they know what to expect and will act accordingly. On the French and German steamers a ten-franc piece is the usual fee to each of the servants above mentioned. The "boots" expects a five-shilling or a five-franc piece, according as the steamer is English or French, provided he polishes your boots during the voyage, and the man in charge of the bath comes along for a similar amount if you make regular use of his services. If you frequent the smoking-room the steward in charge of it expects to be remembered with a half crown, and a similar coin will not be refused by the deck-steward who looks after your chair. None of these fees should be paid until the last day of the voyage and the service of the men has ended. It often happens that the room-steward is very attentive through the voyage and in every way satisfactory; he answers your bell promptly and you consider him a model servant, but if you give him his fee before he has carried your impedimenta on deck it is quite possible that you will carry them yourself or hire another man to do it. His interest in you has ceased and he is looking after somebody who hasn't yet rewarded him. The same thing may happen with the table-steward, and he cannot hear your summons after he has been paid off, though before that event he was the very beau ideal of all you could wish.

It is always well to provide yourself with the money of the country you are going to, or with that of the nationality of the steamer. On an English ship, take ten pounds or so of English money, to cover all your fees and extras, and to have a supply on landing until a visit can be made to the banker. On the French steamers, take a proportionate amount in francs, and on the German steamers, a supply of marks will be quite in order. You can get this cash at a money-changer's without as much trouble as you will have in case you find no one on the steamer to make change for you, and the discount will be less.

The perils of the transatlantic voyage are now practically reduced to the dangers resulting from fog on and near the banks of Newfoundland. The ships performing the service of the best of the lines are built so strong that no wind to which the North Atlantic is accustomed can injure them, and the captains are men of experience and ability. But the fog is an evil which will not disappear at our bidding; the most intelligent commander is helpless in the fog, and he cannot be sure at any moment that he is not rushing to destruction upon a pitiless iceberg, or dashing forward to collide with another ship, in which one or both of the unlucky vessels may be lost. The ice is probably the greater of the dangers, as the steamers give warning of their presence to each other by the sound of whistles or fog-horns, and of late years there has been an attempt to establish steam lanes across the Atlantic, so that steamers going eastward should be several miles from the track of those that are westward-bound. The iceberg hangs out no lights and blows no whistle, and the first warning the captain can have of its presence is when its white outline looms through the fog less than a ship's length ahead. Many a steamer has had a narrow escape from destruction, and not a few have been lost by encounters with the ice. Of those that have never been heard from it is conjectured that the majority were lost by collisions with the ice, as in most instances it was abundant at the time of their disappearance.

The ingenuity of man has been taxed to avert the dangers from the ice and fog, but thus far comparatively little has been accomplished. At times the density of the fog is so great that the eye cannot penetrate it more than twenty yards; experiments have been made with the electric light, but the result has not been favorable to its general adoption. A careful observation of the thermometer will sometimes show the proximity of a berg, as the melting ice causes a fall in the temperature of the water, frequently amounting to ten or twelve degrees, and sometimes there will be a chilly blast of air, that says very plainly there is ice in the vicinity. The early summer months are the most dangerous on the score of ice, but the bergs abound till late in autumn; they come from the west coast of Greenland, where they are broken off from the immense glaciers that flow down from the interior and push out into the sea. The great polar current carries them southward, past Labrador and Newfoundland, till they are thrown into the warm waters of the Gulf-stream and there melted away. They rarely go further south than to the fortieth parallel, but are sometimes drifted as far east as the Azores.

By taking a course that will carry them to the south of the Grand Banks the steamers might avoid the fog and its consequent dangers; some of them do so, and others advertise that they will. After they get at sea the mind of the captain sometimes undergoes a change, and the ship is headed so that she passes near Cape Race. The more to the south a ship is kept the longer will be her course, and in these days of keen competition to make the shortest passages the temptation is great to run away to the northward as far as possible. The author was once a passenger on a steamer that laid her course within fifty miles of Cape Race, although he had been assured at the office of the company that she would "take an extreme southerly course," and the promise to do so had been inserted in the advertisements. A passenger ventured to say as much to one of the officers and to ask if the managers of the company had not ordered the southerly route. "The captain commands here," was the reply, "and the managers have nothing to do with his course; he can run wherever he pleases, and trust to Providence for the result."

It is to be hoped that the great companies will some day make an agreement, and keep it, that they will all take the southerly course and make an end of a competition that is dangerous in a certain degree. They would be greatly aided to such an arrangement if the American government would withdraw its offer to give the carrying of the mails to the company making the shortest average of passages across the Atlantic. Public opinion might also do something in this way, but, unfortunately, public opinion happens to be in favor of the most rapid transit, and looks upon safety as a minor consideration. Whenever the majority of travelers shall think more of the pleasure of staying longer on the earth than of going over its surface at the greatest speed there will be a move in the right direction.

But do not disturb yourself with unpleasant thoughts of what may happen in the fog. Remember, rather, that of the thousands of voyages that have been made across the Atlantic only a few dozens have been unfortunate, and of all the steamers that have plowed these waters only the *President, City of Glasgow, Pacific, Tempest, United King-*

dom, *City of Boston*, and *Ismailia*—seven in all—are unheard from. The chances are thousands to one in your favor, and if this does not satisfy you, try and recall the philosophy of the man who said it was none of his business whether the ship was in danger, as he had paid his fare to the company and they were under obligations to carry him safely to the other side. If the wind rises to a gale, don't worry in the least, and if you have any doubt about the matter ask your room-steward what the appearances of things are to a sea-faring man like himself. Quite possibly his answer may be in the substance, if not in the words, of the mariner's song:—

"A strong nor'-wester's blowing, Bill;
Hark! don't ye hear it roar now!
Lord help 'em, how I pities them
Unhappy folks on shore now!"

When a steamer is in a rough sea, especially if she is lightly laden, the screw is frequently out of water for several seconds at a time. Relieved from the resistance of the water, the screw whirls with the rapidity of lightning and gives the stern of the ship a very lively shaking. This is called "racing," and it is anything but pleasant, but there is a comforting assurance when you hear it that everything is all right and the machinery in order. Whenever you hear the racing of the screw in rough weather you will hear a welcome sound. If a wave seems to hit the ship a staggering blow, and send her half over, do not listen for a commotion and spring from your berth, but bend your ears to catch the sound of the engine, and when you hear its "choog! choog!" you may make yourself easy. In rough weather or in smooth, the first thing to listen for on awaking is the engine, and when you hear its steady breathing and feel its great heart pulsating, as if it were the vital force of an animate being, you may turn and sleep again, satisfied that the ship which carries you "walks the water like a thing of life" and is bearing you safely onward to your destination.

Inventors have busied themselves to devise something that should put a stop to the racing of the screw, with its liability to derange the machinery and its certainty of disturbing the nerves of excitable passengers. Several plans have been tried, but, up to the date of writing this volume, none of them have proved successful. Somebody will doubtless accomplish the desired result before the end of another decade, and when this is done he should give attention to the jar caused by the machinery. It is hardly reasonable to expect that a fast steamer will ever go over the water with the steadiness of a sailing-ship, and with no perceptible jarring, but so much has been done in the last twenty-five years in smoothing the ways of the ocean, and the vessels that plow it, that the scheme here suggested is by no means impossible.

While sitting on deck some afternoon you may be at a loss for a subject to think about. Busy yourself with imagining what will be the style, model, speed, and propelling force of the transatlantic ship of twenty, fifty, a hundred, and five hundred years hence! Here is enough to occupy you for many hours, and perhaps you may devise something that will benefit the human race, and, also, not the least consideration, put money in your pocket.

CHAPTER V.

SEA-SICKNESS AND HOW TO AVOID IT.

We come now to the momentous question of *mal de mer*. It is a question that has puzzled the scientific men of all ages since the departure of the Argonauts in search of the Golden Fleece on the first ship that ever sailed the sea, and, from present appearances, it will continue to be a puzzle as long as the waves of the ocean continue to roll. By some it is claimed to be a nervous disturbance, others contend that it is purely a stomachic affair and the nerves have nothing to do with it, and there are others who argue that the brain is the seat of the disorder and disturbs the stomach by sympathetic action. There are wise men who charge sea-sickness to the spleen, the liver, or other internal organs, and it is not impossible that we may yet hear of a savant who attributes it to corns on the toes. Sea-sickness is a mystery, and the more we study it the more are we at sea as to its exact operation.

Some people, who are bundles of nerves, are not affected by the motion of a ship, while others, who are nerveless as a paper-weight, are disturbed with the least movement. Weak stomachs escape while strong ones are upset, and there seems to be no rule that can be laid down with exactness or anything that approaches it. But on one point there can be no two opinions, that sea-sickness is a most disagreeable malady, even in its mildest form, and that any means of relieving it, or even of mitigating it in a small degree, will be hailed with delight by all who suffer from it. It will also be a boon to those who are never sea-sick, as it will relieve them from a companionship that is not always the most agreeable in the world.

For some persons there is no escape, and they will be prostrate in their berths during the whole voyage of the ship, or just able to get around. But, in the majority of cases, sea-sickness may be wholly prevented by a free use of cathartics or anti-bilious remedies a day or two before departure on a voyage. In America, the pills of Ayer, Brandreth, or Wright will serve the purpose; in England, the famous "Cockle's pills," and in France the *Pilules Duhaut*. The relaxation of the system should be sustained during the voyage by the same means or by the use of Seidlitz powders, or similar effervescent substances; this simple precaution will save most persons from being disturbed by sea-sickness, no matter how wildly the ship may toss, provided they combine with it an abundance of air and exercise. As before stated, there is no relief known at present for the other fourth of humanity, except to stay at home.

Dr. Fordyce Barker, an eminent physician who has made a careful study of sea-sickness, opposes the previous use of cathartics, and advises that a hearty meal be eaten a short time before going on board. Those who are subject to sea-sickness he enjoins to undress and go to bed before the vessel moves from her dock or anchorage. He says they should eat regularly and heartily without raising the head for at least one or two days, and in this way they will accustom the digestive organs to the performance of their functions. He advises the use of laxative pills the first night out and, if necessary, during the entire voyage. The following is his prescription:—

LAXATIVE PILLS.

℞. Pulv. Rhei. (Turk.), ʒss.
Ext. Hyoscyami, Эj.
Pulv. Aloes Soc.,
Sapo Cast., āā gr. xv.
Ext. Nux Vomicæ Alchoh., gr. x.
Podophyllin p., gr. v.
Ipecac., gr. ij.
M. ft. pil, (argent) No. 20.
S. Dose—one, two, or three.

Where there is a tendency to diarrhœa, which sometimes happens at sea, he recommends the following, and he also advises the traveler to carry it in his journeys over the Continent to counteract the effects that occasionally come from drinking bad water. The dose is, for an adult,

℞. Tinct. Camphoræ, ʒvj.
Tinct. Capsici, ʒij.
Spts. Lavendul. Comp.,
Tinct. Opii, āā ℥ss.
Syr. Simp., ℥ij.

M. S. A small teaspoonful in a wineglass of water after each movement.

Dr. Barker says that in cases where the victim has suffered several days from sea-sickness, with constant nausea, nervous depression, and sleeplessness, he has found great benefit in the use of bromide of potassium. The powders are to be taken in a half-tumbler of plain soda-water, and, if this cannot be obtained, in cold water sweetened with sugar. It is to be sipped slowly, so that the stomach may be persuaded to retain and absorb it. The powders should be kept in a wide-mouthed vial, or in a tin box, so as to protect them from the effects of the sea-air. The following is the prescription:

℞. Potass. Bromide, ℥j.
Div. in Chart No. 20.
S. One, two, or three times a day.

He also recommends a person about making a sea-voyage to take a supply of "mustard leaves," which can be had at the druggist's. They are useful in allaying the nausea and vomiting by getting up a counter irritation, and should be applied over the pit of the stomach.

Many individuals, especially those inclined to corpulency, find relief in wearing a tight belt around the waist. This is so well understood that some of the makers of surgical appliances advertise " belts for sea-sickness " as part of their stock in trade. Some persons recommend a tight-fitting undergarment of strong silk, but, in order to be of use, it must be altogether too close for comfort, and the wearer is quite likely to say that he considers it the greater of the evils.

A recumbent position is better than the erect one when a traveler is suffering from the nautical disturbance, and, in most cases, he is too weak to take any other. It is better to lie flat on the back than in any other way, and there are many persons who are well when thus lying down, but become ill the minute they attempt to rise. A friend of the writer belongs to this category. His mode of taking his meals when at sea is to lie flat on his sofa, while the steward cuts his meat into small pieces and gets everything ready. At a given signal the sufferer rises to a sitting posture, and swallows a few mouthfuls as rapidly as possible. Then he drops back, rests a few minutes, and repeats the feeding operation. In half a dozen performances of this sort he will take in a creditable dinner; as long as he remains on his back his digestion goes on all right, but he cannot be five minutes on his feet without a return of nausea.

A round of heavy dinners and champagne suppers before starting is not a good preparation for a sea-voyage, neither is a "send-off" on board, with farewell glasses of inspiriting liquids. Many a man has suffered at sea from too much conviviality before his departure.

The sufferer on the water is not charmed with the mention of the table, and even the greatest delicacies fail to arouse his appetite. Give him anything he wants, it wont make much difference, though it is well, perhaps, to deter him from ham and eggs, chicken or lobster salads, and anything, in fact, that contains grease or oil. Tea and toast are the great articles of diet for the sea-sick, and they may be safely trusted with baked apples, and with nearly all kinds of fruit. A cracker or an Albert biscuit will sometimes have charms when nothing else can be swallowed, and when the victim is convalescent he feels as though a pickle would do him good. Lemonade is admissible and soda-water is a safe beverage; brandy and soda may be ordered by those who do not shine as members of a temperance society, but it should be taken with caution and the doses must not be repeated too frequently. All drinks that contain carbonic-acid gas are beneficial, and many persons find relief in occasional small allowances of champagne. Those who intend to put any reliance on this wine during sea-sickness should equip themselves with a "champagne tap" before starting; they can then draw what they desire from a bottle and keep the rest without fear that it will become stale through loss of gas.

Hartshorn, cologne, and other substances intended for inhalation are all good at this time, partly because of their effects on their lungs and partly by the distraction of taking them. A volatile article used with great success in sea-sickness is the nitrite of amyl; it is prepared in the form of a pearl with a thin shell of glass around it so as to prevent its evaporation. Any reputable druggist can procure it, and with the pearls it is desirable to have a tube for crushing them and liberating the liquid. In the absence of the tube they may be crushed in the handkerchief, but when taken in this way a large part of the effect is lost.

Always go on deck when you are able to do so, even if you are carried up by your friends or the stewards and deposited in your chair like an armful of wet clothing. Wrap yourself well against the cold, and on the first instant of chillness get more covering or go below. Whenever you feel the impulse to feed the fishes in the early stages of a fit of sea-sickness always go to the lee side of the ship (the one the wind blows from) and never to windward. By so doing you will save a considerable amount of damage to your clothing, and also to that of any who may be near you.

Many persons will tell you that it is an excellent thing to be sea-sick, as you are so much better for it afterwards. If you are a sufferer you will do well to accept their statements as entirely correct, since you are thereby consoled and soothed, and the malady doesn't care what you think about it, one way or the other.

And now comes a bit of advice which might have been given at the opening of this dissertation on the discomforts of the heaving deep, but has been reserved to the end in the hope that it will leave a lasting impression. When the ship casts loose from the dock, or lifts her anchor and gets under way, you should think of anything and everything except sea-sickness, and if any one starts the topic in your hearing leave him and walk away, or ask him to change the subject. If you cannot be thus abrupt, change it for him by starting a political discussion or other agreeable wrangle; do anything rather than allow a continuation of his remarks. Many a man and many a woman has been talked into being sea-sick, or has meditated and wondered on the possibility of it till the malady has put in an appearance. We all know how much the mind dominates the body, how bad news takes away the appetite and good news increases it, and we have all heard how a well man was driven to his bed by the concentrated efforts of a dozen practical jokers who separately informed him that he looked very pale and something must be the matter with him. Don't talk or think of sea-sickness; you will know it fast enough when it comes, and till that time it is the wisest course to assume that you are to be the healthiest passenger on the ship.

Prof. A. G. Wilkinson, of Washington, D. C., says:

"During Atlantic crossings for four years past I found but one instance in which from twenty to thirty grains of bromide of soda in ice-water three times daily for four days, commencing two days before sailing, failed to prevent loss of a single meal. Get dry powders put up in foil and enclosed in ground-stoppered bottles, to prevent deliquescence. I learned this from experimenting for several years with chloral and the various bromides. Soda alone was never distasteful. Dr. G. M. Beard, of New York, was independently experimenting at the same time, and first published his conclusions. *After vomiting commences* he recommends,

Bromide of soda, ʒi. Tinct. belladonna, xxx guttæ. Aqua, ℥vi.

Teaspoonful every ten minutes until relieved.

A lady friend had never been able to take a single meal at sea; the second day out, while she was sick, I gave her the above, and she took every meal for the rest of the voyage."

CHAPTER VI.

SPECIAL ADVICE TO LADIES.

For the following the author is indebted to a lady who has made several trans-Atlantic voyages, and is consequently familiar with the necessities and comforts of ocean travel:

"It is simply preposterous," says a fashionable friend of mine, "Here you are, going to sail for Europe in three days, to be gone three months, and you have nothing ready but that same old trunk, plastered all over with baggage labels, every color of the rainbow." *J'ai repondu,* "*C'est assez, mon ami.*" If you wish to examine its contents I will show it you with great pleasure, and any one else who may desire to see how I "stow away" my traps can look on at the same time. But as the steamer-clothing, etc., will be the first to be used, I'll show you the contents of this little fifteen-inch square box first. This I call my "steamer-trunk." It is not a steamer-trunk proper, but I find it much more convenient than a long flat one such as is used to go under the berth. This will stand on one side of the wash-stand in the state-room, where a camp-stool is generally found, and by placing a folded shawl on top it makes a permanent, comfortable, and firm seat, saves trouble of stooping and dragging it out, as is the case with an ordinary steamer-trunk, when you want to open it. The lid has a flat leather loop in the center for a handle and can be easily lifted when closed. There is a small tray inside which I use as a "catch-all," and there is plenty of room under the tray for all the clean linen I shall require on the voyage. This and my dressing-bag, with one shawl-strap, is all the baggage I put into my state-room.

Some ladies strew things, "conveniences" they call them, from the top to the bottom of the state-room; quite regardless are they to the convenience and comfort of a possible fellow passenger. Do whatever you please if you can afford a state-room to yourself. But if not, pray keep your own side of the house. Other folks put a lot of eatables in their berths and then complain of rats. Don't take anything in the eating line except a basket of lemons, and if you must take something to drink let it be Chartreuse. Take a box of cathartic pills, and if you need a dose make it a little larger than you would under the same circumstances on shore. Coarse blue flannel or serge is the best for deck wear. Have the skirt of the dress as short as possible without looking odd. Attach the skirt to the waist of the dress and make the front without side forms so that it will look well without a corset. A blouse waist, if well made, will be suitable for almost any figure, and is the most comfortable, but it must fit perfectly round the neck and shoulders.

One flannel skirt, one thin skirt of some bright clean gingham, warm flannels next the body, one pair of overall flannel drawers, bright turkey red, to be worn over the ordinary underclothing and slipped off on going below, two pair stout boots with good square heels, and buttons or laces to support the ankles properly, warm stockings of silk or very fine wool. Don't weigh yourself down with a lot of skirts. Have the limbs well covered and free for walking. No matter what season of the year, take along a good stout cloth ulster, reaching to the bottom of your dress and securely buttoned from the throat to the bottom; no hood nor cape for the wind to make a sail of, only one good broad collar for turning up to keep your ears and neck warm while promenading the deck or sitting in your steamer chair; two or three good outside pockets are indispensable. Never venture on deck without this coat, and a big shawl to cover your feet while sitting down.

Wear an ordinary night-dress in your berth, and have a flannel dressing-gown made without any lining to wear over it when going to or from the bath-rooms, some of which are very luxurious if you enjoy bathing in seawater. Don't fail to have gauntlets sewed on to your gloves to keep your wrists warm. You must make your own selection for head-wear; soft felt hats are very comfortable, but not always becoming. One of the prettiest and most comfortable head-coverings for ladies over 30 is a sort of Normandy cap or bonnet made of silk with soft crown and the breast of a grebe on one side; it will not spoil or get out of shape easily. The best way to dress the hair is to make a smooth coil at the back of the neck and keep the front tidy by brushing each time you go to the state-room; frizzing and curling are impossible and ludicrous. A pretty opera-hood will do good service for a change.

If the weather is very warm on the day you are to sail, carry your steamer-clothes in your shawl-strap and wear a dress that will do you service for a change on the journey. On your arrival in Europe put the same dress on to go ashore and put your steamer-clothes into the little trunk, taking out the underclothing, which will now be soiled, and put it into your shawl-strap. Leave your steamer-trunk, chair, shawls, etc., with the steamship company, subject to your order or return. Put your name in full, and make all into one package, if possible.

The large trunk is a Saratoga, 36 inches long, 23 high, and 20 inches in width. There is only one tray, one end of which has a separated compartment for bonnets or hats, and it is quite large enough to contain three without injury if properly packed round with tissue paper to prevent their falling from side to side. The other two-thirds of the tray is open and flat. Here are collars, cuffs, gloves, ribbons, pocket-handkerchiefs, a few bright bows, ready looped or tied, for hair, neck, and corsage, eight pairs of stockings, such as I wear ordinarily, four pairs extra thick for cold weather, or for mountain climbing, one small box in one corner for cuff-buttons and some inexpensive jewelry which can be worn without constant fear of losing. One little plump pincushion with plenty of short shawl-pins, three or four long hat-pins and plenty of black and white, small ones, some safety-pins, and a few needles on the under side. Make a loop at one corner to hang it up by.

Into the convex portion of the lid (which has a separate cover with hook to fasten), are three pairs of boots, one for dress, one for walking, and one extra stout pair for bad weather. Into the remaining space I have put a shawl and wrap, which will not spoil by being put into so small a space; also my bathing-suit of blue flannel, which is always kept in a rubber water-proof bag, with drawing strings, thereby making it portable whether wet or dry, which is a great convenience, both at home and abroad, for the reason that when you take it off you can immediately put it into the bag, draw the strings together and carry it back by them to your hotel to be dried by the chambermaid. Never leave a nice bathing-suit at the bath-house to be dried. If you do, the probability is that when you need it you will find it wet from some one else having worn it, and the buttons off at the places where they are most needed. There is yet space enough left in this little convexity for a few books, and also for a small bundle of things for a friend whom I wish to remember.

When all these things are taken out for use on arrival, the space is very convenient for soiled clothing, it being quite separate and distinct from any other compartment. Do your own packing if you do not keep a maid. Have a place for everything, so that when you want anything in a hurry, or you feel tired, you will not have that interminable bug-bear of "having to unpack everything to find it." Many a good manager or housekeeper seems perfectly lost when she contemplates the possibility of "living in a trunk," as it is vulgarly called. But if she will bring some of her good common sense to bear upon these smaller details, she will find it not only adds greatly to her own comfort, but it will save her friends from the depression of listening to her uninteresting complainings.

Now we lift out the tray, which has two strong loops for that purpose. You can do it yourself, for it is not heavy, having no heavy articles placed in it. Into the body of the trunk put all undergarments first. Don't roll anything up; lay all as smooth and even as possible. About twelve of each article will last you twenty days. Whatever the season of the year, don't fail to take a couple of flannel skirts and some warm underflannels for extra cold or damp days, and before dressing each morning take a peep at the sky and ask the weather which kind of undergarment you shall put on, thick or thin? One of the greatest comforts for breakfast wear is a wrapper of very dark, soft summer silk costing about 50 or 60 cents per yard; line it throughout with unbleached muslin; twelve yards of silk will make it if cut sparingly, *a la princesse* robe, loose in front with demi train. Trim the front from the throat to the bottom of the skirt with some cheap cream color or black lace, with a few bright bows of your favorite colored ribbon, about one inch wide, tack some of the lace in pleats round the neck and fasten securely down the front with buttons concealed under the lace, put a patch pocket on each side with one bow on each, one bow and a little of the lace on each sleeve, and you have a dress that will not spoil if you wish to lie down. It is always tidy with or without a corset. You can go through the halls of the hotels in it, and if indisposed you can receive your intimate friends without making a change. It will do more service than a dozen dressing-sacques, and it saves washing, which is quite an item to the economical.

One black grenadine walking dress, made fashionably, looks pretty for evening wear, but it must be lined throughout. No transparent sleeves and neck for rheumatism and consumption. One black silk made to wear with or without extra wraps for the street. One black or very dark green, or smoke-color cashmere for rougher wear, trimmed with satin bands, will not catch the dust and looks handsome. One India silk and one alpaca ulster with plenty of pockets, and if you have a couple of dresses which you wish to finish wearing out, see that the skirt braid is in good order and take them along to wear under the ulsters, for railroad traveling, staging, etc. See that the ulsters fit properly. Don't imagine that because the material is thin it will accommodate itself to your shape. Have the silk one washed as often as required, and it will look like new every time. A blue gauze veil worn with either of these ulsters looks stylish, and a soft felt hat, if suitable to your face, will be the most comfortable for your head. Put a wing or bow of ribbon on the left side, but no ostrich feathers. I would remark that a due regard should be given to the color of the bonnet or hat, also to bows of ribbon or lace, selected to be worn with the dresses. The reason is obvious, viz., when traveling from place to place you have very little time for dressing and arranging becoming toilets, therefore—do n't mix things. Put on each article which is intended to be worn with its particular dress, and instead of the fatigue of "changing your dress" every time you go somewhere, you will have only to put on bonnet, gloves, and wrap, and there you are, smiling and ready in three minutes. Husbands, brothers, and fellow-travelers will appreciate this when they find that it is not necessary to ask you, "How long will it take you to get ready?"

Get a yard and a half of unbleached glazed linen and bind it all round with wide red worsted braid. Put this into the trunk with a good long shawl-strap, also your umbrella and parasol. One black parasol with white lining will do for every dress, and look as if it were made for each one in particular. You will not *need* any of these things on the voyage, so you can put "*Hold*" in large letters on the trunk, and that will insure you against the temptation of opening it on the steamer. When you arrive at the end of your ocean journey, you will appreciate the comfort of having everything to your hand directly you open your trunk.

Rest for one night (at least) at the place of landing, whether Queenstown, Liverpool, Havre, or elsewhere, and have your soiled linen washed. If at an English port, you will probably go on to London for your first sightseeing; if at Havre, your destination will probably be Paris. In either case you will find it pleasant to stop over night at one or other of the most attractive towns on the way, and for your greater comfort you will take out one complete change of clothes, viz., a fresh dress and some under-linen, and your lace-trimmed wrapper. Spread the afore-mentioned "linen wrap" out smooth, lay your dress lengthwise in the center first, then put the other things on top (lengthwise also), and lastly your umbrella and parasol. Fold each side of the linen cover over so as to nearly meet in the center, and then roll up from end to end, and put your shawl-strap around it. This, and your dressing-bag, is your baggage when you expect to be away from your trunk for a few nights. Send the trunk on by *petite vitesse*, or ordinary freight, to your ultimate destination. It will make an appreciable difference in your expenses, and like a thoughtful friend it will be waiting for you on arrival, and will have secured a room at the hotel to which it has been addressed. By following this plan you will always have a complete change with you, and will be relieved from the bother of looking after a trunk while on your journey. The hotel manager can always tell you about forwarding your trunk, and the porter of the hotel will attend to the matter. And now let me tell you about my hand-bag and what it contains.

The best satchels, and the most convenient, are those which open very wide and display their contents without obliging one to hunt for each little article needed.

Fold a nice clean night-dress in a piece of paper and place it in the bottom. It is a great comfort to have such a necessity so handy in cases of late arrival at hotels, great fatigue, and possible accident. Don't forget a clean towel. A good-sized sponge, in a water-proof bag long enough to contain a tooth or nail-brush (some of these bags have a separate pocket for the brushes), have a piece of soap in a tight metallic soap-box; one good-sized bottle of cologne-water or bay rum, well corked; one powder-box, with cover screwed on firmly; one medium-sized hand-mirror; a small bag (with drawing string), into which you have put plenty of buttons, spools of silk, thread, needles, and thimbles.

One thin blotter containing writing-materials, and which is small enough to lay flat against one side of the hand-bag, and can be slipped in and out without disarranging the other things, small bottle of ink, with screw or spring top, a couple of pens, and plenty of pencils. Comb and brush in a bag made for the purpose out of a dark silk handkerchief or a piece of chintz. Silk is the best because it will not so easily catch the dust. There is always a little pocket on one side of bag for a paper of pins, a button-hook, and hair-pins, also a pair of scissors.

Put everything back after using, and make your handbag your catch-all in the state-room, and when the weather is rough you have only to close it and so keep everything secure and in its right place. When going a journey by rail put in your guide-book and a magazine. Also, a common fan on top to be easily reached.

For a becoming head-covering to wear in railroad carriages, and to keep the dust from your hair when you wish to rest your head, which often gets tired from wearing a hat for several hours, take a gentleman's small-sized silk pocket handkerchief, of becoming color, and trim the edges with some cheap black Spanish lace, gathering it round the corners so it will lie flat and round. Fold it crosswise, and lay it with two corners on the top of the head, and tie the other two together either under the chin or back-hair. Then make two little pleats on each side of the head near the temples, making it fit the arch of the head nicely, and you will find that it is very comfortable, and takes up little room in your bag.

CHAPTER VII.

DAILY LIFE AT SEA.

On shipboard you may rise as early or sleep as late as you choose, provided you do not extend your slumbers beyond the breakfast-hour; you are not by any means compelled to get up when the bell rings, but it is best to do so unless prevented by illness. You will find the fresh air of the deck invigorating, and a better appetizer than all the cordials or other stimulants in the possession of the bar-keeper, and besides, the room-steward desires to put your cabin in order sometime during the forenoon. Time is kept on shipboard by "bells," and those who wish to show their familiarity with the sea are in the habit of dropping the ordinary nomenclature of the hours and reckoning by the sound of the bell. The nautical day begins at noon, and all calculations regarding the movements of the ship are made with 12 M. as the starting-point. A little practice and observation will accustom the landsman to "ship's time," and afford him a slight distraction when inclined to think the voyage a monotonous one.

The bell strikes every half-hour from noon to noon again, the even strokes representing complete hours, and the odd numbers the half-hours. The marine day is divided into "watches" of four hours each, with the exception of the period from 4 P. M. to 8 P. M., which forms two divisions of two hours each, known as "dog-watches." The object of this arrangement is to prevent the same men being on duty at the same time day after day, as they would be if the whole twenty-four hours were divided into unbroken watches of four hours each. The crew is divided into "watches" that relieve each other every four hours, with the exception of the "dog-watch" just described. These divisions of the men are known as starboard and larboard, or starboard and port, and each watch has an officer in charge of it. The captain does not "stand his watch" like the other officers, and when the weather is fine and everything lovely he has little to do. But when a gale arises, or the ship is enveloped in fog, it is a time of great anxiety for him, and sometimes there are days together when he hardly leaves the bridge for more than a few minutes at a time. The prudent passenger will avoid speaking to him during this anxious period, and it is a good rule never to address the captain until he has first spoken to you. For the most part, the transatlantic captains are genial and inclined to be sociable, but you will now and then encounter one who evidently descended from a bear or some other ill-mannered animal, if the theories of Charles Darwin are correct.

To know the hour at sea by the bell remember the following: At half an hour past noon there is a single stroke of the bell, and at one o'clock there are two strokes. At half-past one we have three strokes, and at two o'clock four strokes. Thus it goes on, adding a single stroke every half-hour till four o'clock, when "eight bells" are struck. As before explained, the time from four to eight is divided into two short watches, and at eight o'clock a full watch begins, in which the hours are sounded the same as from noon to 4 P. M. This watch ends at midnight and is followed by another till 4 A. M.; from 4 to 8 A. M. is another, and from 8 A. M. till noon is another. If you happen to wake in the night and hear five bells you may know that it is half-past two, unless you have gone to bed very early, and slept briefly, in which case it may be half-past ten. But as the lights are not put out till 11 P. M., and on some ships at 11.30, you are not very liable to mistake the time of one watch for another.

And while we are talking about watches we will consider the one you have in your pocket. The change of longitude in a transatlantic voyage implies a corresponding change of time. There is a difference of four hours and fifty-six minutes between New York and London, *i. e.*, when it is noon in New York it is fifty-six minutes past four in the afternoon at London. This variation of time is spread over the transatlantic voyage and amounts to not far from half an hour daily with the majority of steamers. When going to the east a ship's day is actually only twenty-three and a half hours long, while it is twenty-four and a half when she is on her westward course. This may account for the fact that steamers make their best daily runs when their prows are pointed towards the setting sun.

If you have a costly watch it is not well to change it daily to correspond with the ship's time. Let it run without alteration till you are at the end of the journey, and depend on the bells or the cabin clock for the actual hours. The writer has found that a cheap watch—such as can be bought for five or ten dollars—is an excellent adjunct to a valuable gold one when traveling. It can be altered daily to correspond with the change of longitude, and if it is left around carelessly there is little danger that any intelligent thief will care to steal it. In a journey around the world he changed the hour of his pocket-chronometer only five times—at San Francisco, Tokio, Calcutta, Naples, and Paris—and depended upon his "brass" watch for daily service.

So much for keeping time on shipboard; let us see how

we can spend it. Carry enough books to give you ten or twelve hours reading every day, and if you get through a quarter of them you will be lucky. You will find an unaccountable disinclination to read, especially if you have been very active just previous to departure, and will develop a decided tendency for sleep. What with sleeping, and eating, and associating with other passengers, you find no great amount of time for literature, and unless you devote yourself to a blood-curdling novel, in which you are constantly on the strain to know how the plot ended, and whether she married him or the other man, you can only get through a few pages at a time. If you are going abroad for the first time it is advisable to confine the reading to descriptions of the countries you are about to visit, rather than to light literature, but, if you are determined to stick to fiction, you will find sea-stories more interesting than land ones, for the reason that you are on the great deep, and the pictures of the novel will be more vivid than if the book were read on shore.

A ship is a world, and the ocean is the measureless azure in which it floats. Sea and sky are your boundaries, and the horizon-line is ever the same. The weaknesses of human nature, as well as its noble qualities, are developed here, and sometimes they are limned in sharper outlines than on land. Persons whom you have known for years will develop on shipboard qualities that you never suspected them of possessing. You had always thought your neighbor on the right was a selfish mortal, but you now find that he is self-sacrificing to the extreme; on the other hand, the man whom you believed a model of politeness turns out to be quite the reverse. Never in your life have you heard as much gossip in a month as you now hear in a single week; the occupation, character, peculiarities, hopes, desires, and frailties of everybody are canvassed by a goodly proportion of busy tongues, and the ship will very likely impress you as a school for scandal which Sheridan might envy.

Don't take a share in the gossip, and don't concern yourself about the private affairs of anyone else. Be polite to everybody, but don't be in a hurry to make acquaintances; by so doing you will stand higher in their estimation, and will have time to find out those whom you would like the best. A shipful of passengers is generally broken into several parties of persons congenial to each other; sometimes the groups and parties are on the best of terms, and at other times there is considerable hostility, generally caused by a few turbulent spirits, not always of the sterner sex. The weather has much to do with the formation of cliques on an ocean steamer. When the sea is smooth for a day or two at the start the passengers become generally acquainted and are agreeable all around. But if the steamer puts her prow into a rough sea immediately on leaving port those of tender stomachs disappear before they have had time to exchange a word with a stranger. The unruffled ones get together, the men in the smoking-room, and the ladies in the cabin, and companionship begins. By the time the sea is level again, and the sea-sick ones appear, the circles have been formed, and some of them closed completely; then the new-comers form rings of their own, and out of these primary and secondary formations jealousies often grow.

Join in all the innocent sports that while away the time. By day, in fine weather, there are quoits, shuffle-board, and other games, for which the ship furnishes the material, and in the evening there are impromptu entertainments of a mixed character in the cabin. Contribute whatever you can to the general fund of amusement, and if you can neither sing, recite, tell stories, play on an instrument, or do anything else to please your fellow passengers, try and be a good integral part of the audience. You can look on and listen at any rate, and with a little practice you can do it well. Perhaps you can find diversion by investing in the daily pool on the run of the ship, and, when coming westward, there is the inevitable speculation as to the number of the boat from which you take the pilot. But this pool business is sometimes expensive, and if your purse is thinly lined you will do well to stay out of it. The smoking-room affords opportunities for dropping your spare cash to gentlemen of a playful turn of mind, and there are usually adepts at cards who will accommodate you with any game you like. The Atlantic is crossed every year by men who boast that they are always able to cover their expenses, and very often the boast is far below the reality. The fashionable steamers are sometimes the scenes of very high play, and gambling at sea seems to be on the increase in the last few years. They can never be made the field of operations similar to those of the river and railway gamblers of America, for the reason that there is no station or landing-place where a performer on the cards can disappear when he has fleeced his victim, but, at present, there is good reason to believe that the business of occasional passengers is less while ashore than when afloat.

If you have any complaints to make address them to the purser; it is his business to look after the welfare of the passengers, and he nearly always does it. Where you desire to make a first-class row you can appeal from the purser to the captain, and if they are not on the best of terms, and you lay your schemes carefully, a great deal of bad blood will be engendered. As a last resort, you can carry the affair up to the general management of the company, where complaints are investigated with more or less care, and satisfaction is given or refused. The great competition between the various lines causes them to be particularly attentive to the wants of passengers, and it is very rarely that one hears of a well-founded complaint against the captain or purser of a transatlantic steamer. If they err at all it is in paying too much attention to passengers who are often quite willing to be let alone after they have been comfortably settled on board.

Never attempt to go on the "bridge" which is exclusively reserved for the officers of the ship, and do not be anxious to penetrate the mysteries of the engine-room or handle the steering apparatus. On some of the ships notices are posted requesting passengers not to speak to the officers when on duty; it is well to heed these, and also well not to get too near the ropes when sails are being hoisted or taken in. When the ship is pitching violently in a head sea, avoid going forward on deck, as you may get a drenching unexpectedly, and possibly may be washed overboard. Be cautious about leaning over the taffrail or stern at any time, and especially in rough weather, as the ship may "jump from under you" without the least warning, and drop you in the sea. Old sailors as well as landsmen have been lost in this way.

The hours for meals vary on the different lines, but whatever the arrangement, there is no danger of starvation. Most of the English lines give you breakfast, lunch, dinner, and supper, four meals altogether, and all of them pretty "square" ones.' The breakfast consists of fish, ham and eggs, steaks, chops, Irish stew, hot rolls, and a half dozen, or perhaps a dozen, other things, with all the tea or coffee you choose to drink. Lunch consists of cold meats and biscuits, and is not a very heavy affair, but the dinner is of that solid character which is one of the boasts of British liberty. You can eat yourself into dyspepsia without making any apparent impression on the abundance set before you, and if you try to go through the bill of fare without missing anything, you will wish you had n't. Of soups, fish, roasts, boils, stews, and fries, there is apparently no end; the cooking is generally good, and leads the thoughtful passenger into a profound admiration of the culinary artists of the sea. And it also leads him to wonder why so much is prepared when comparatively little is eaten, especially in the first touch of rough weather, when half the passengers and more are confined to their rooms, and a goodly number of the other half display microscopic appetites. This matter has been discussed by the managers of the lines; it has been proposed to make the experiment of serving meals on the " European plan," and ultimately to abandon the old system, if the new one is found acceptable. Under this scheme the price of passage would be reduced, and include only the room and transportation; meals would be served as in a restaurant, and the traveler could spend much money or little, according to the dictates of his purse and appetite. The cost of feeding the passengers would be much less than at present, and all the waste would be borne by the public, instead of the company.

For supper you have toast and cold meats, with Welsh rarebits and other things, such as dreams are made of, and the strong-hearted Englishman generally washes it down with a bottle of ale to give him a good digestion. Some of the companies give an additional meal called tea, which runs closely into the supper; so close is the connection that you can go from the one to the other without leaving the table. In fact, the meals are so numerous that they are crowded against each other, and you are hardly through with one and settled into your chair on deck before you are summoned for the next. But if even these are not sufficient for the keen appetite and hearty digestion you have acquired at sea, you can get something to eat between times by application to the steward. Verily, there is little danger of starvation on a voyage by trans-Atlantic steamer.

On the French line the arrangement differs somewhat from the English. At seven in the morning, tea or coffee is given, with bread and butter and a bowl of soup. From half past nine to eleven breakfast is served, and consists of preliminary appetizers, such as radishes, anchovies, cold ham, and other trifles, followed by steaks, chops, eggs in every form, fish, chicken, and similar solids. Then comes a selection of cheeses and fresh and dry fruits, and the meal ends with a cup of black coffee. Dinner is at half past four, and resembles the continental table d'hote; it is served in courses, and is sufficiently comprehensive to cover the demands of any appetite not altogether unreasonable. Wine, either white or red, is included for both breakfast and dinner, and the passenger may drink as freely of it as he likes. Tea is served at eight in the evening, and there is a light lunch of cold meats at one o'clock. The writer has fared admirably on one of the ships of the French line, and on a subsequent voyage by the same steamer, he fared badly; on the whole, he believes the system a good one, and acceptable to the majority of the passengers.

The gastronomic service of the German steamers combines certain features of the French and English lines, and the hours for meals correspond very nearly to those of the latter. The cooking is Teutonic, and the bill of fare includes a liberal allowance of the toothsome sausage and the savory sour-kraut. There is less waste on the French and German steamers than on the English ones; and it has been remarked that the sea gulls understand the matter very clearly, and will always follow an English ship in preference to one of the others, for the reason that the chance of picking up a delicate morsel that has been tossed overboard is much greater.

Seats at table are assigned by the chief steward or taken by the passengers when they go on board. A card with the name of the individual is placed at the desired seat; the novice might suppose that this would be sufficient to retain the place, but it is not so by any means. Other passengers, who desire the same places, will remove the cards and substitute their own, and sometimes they display great "cheek" in the transaction. It is best to have the chief steward approve your selection at the time you make it, and then you will have an appeal in case of the removal of your card. The captain's table is the post of honor, and the location of the greatest dignity, but if you are not specially invited by the commander to a place there, and have no acquaintance with him, it is best not to seek it. Sometimes the purser's table is a pleasant one, and sometimes the reverse; and the same may be said of the doctor's table. Purser and doctor are proverbially good fellows, with very few exceptions, and wherever you may be seated, your fortune in eating depends more on the table steward than on any one of the officers. When you have once occupied a seat at dinner you retain it through the voyage unless you change with the approval of the steward. A seat in the middle of the saloon is preferred by some to one near the side, but there is really very little difference in the places, so far as the motion of the ship is concerned. Most of the best steamers have adopted the revolving seat, so that you may come to or leave your place without disturbing any one, which is not the case with the old-fashioned bench. Where the benches remain, the passenger should make an effort to secure an end seat, especially if he is liable to sea-sickness and may suddenly discover some day that he does n't want any more dinner.

If the chief steward assists you to secure a desirable seat, he will expect a pecuniary compliment for the service; on most ships it is well to be on the right side of him, but on some it makes no difference. The first time you go forward beyond a certain line one of the sailors will chalk your boot, or draw a chalk-mark around you. This is a time-honored custom of extracting a shilling from the novice, and the money so obtained is invested in liquid refreshments for the crew. There is only a single chalking for each passenger on the voyage; after he has paid the penalty once he may go forward as much as he pleases without danger of molestation.

The days will run on with more or less monotony, according to circumstances. You will be interested in trivial matters; a sail that is a mere speck on the horizon will awaken a lively discussion, and the appearance of a shark, or a school of porpoises, is sure to draw at least half the passengers to the side of the ship to watch the movements of the inhabitants of the sea. The birds will be a source of amusement, and when a wearied land bird, driven far out to sea by the wind, and with strength nearly exhausted, lights on the rigging, the excitement rises to almost fever heat. What he is, and whence he came, are momentous questions, and if he can be caught and tamed, as sometimes happens, he becomes a popular pet throughout the ship. Some years ago, while a steamer was on her way to New York, a crow came on board a hundred miles or so from the Irish coast. He was caught by the sailors, and soon became perfectly tame and fearless. He liked his new home so well that he did not try to leave it when the ship returned to Ireland; he continued to cross and re-cross for several months, till he was accidentally killed on the dock in New York, where the ship was lying.

Land is in sight, and we will prepare for shore. The old clothing is packed away for deposit in the store-room of the company till our return, and the steamer chair is folded, tied, and tagged. We don our good garments and may cause a sensation to those who have seen us only in the habiliments of the sea, but as every one else will do likewise, the sensation is doubtful. We are ready for the tender that takes us to terra firma, where the formalities of the custom-house await us.

As we leave the ship that has brought us safely over the ocean, it will be no discredit to our manhood if we say good-bye to her, and wish her many prosperous voyages. A feeling akin to affection is not unfrequently developed by the traveler for the ship that has carried him, and ever after he will take a personal interest in her fortunes. A passenger on one of the transatlantic steamers once gave vent to his sentiments in some doggerel verses, of which the following was the concluding one:—

"Old steamer, good-bye, there's some brine in my eye;
 I can't say where'll be our next meeting,
But wherever it is I shall welcome your phiz.,
 And give you a right hearty greeting."

CHAPTER VIII.

GOING ON SHORE.—HOTELS.

The English and French custom-houses are not as difficult to pass as the American, and the examination is generally quite brief. The traveler should get all his pieces together, so as to facilitate the labors of the officials, and if he has anything liable to duty it is best to declare it before any questions are asked. Spirits and tobacco are the things mainly looked for, and, if any are found that have not been declared, they are liable to confiscation. Where the passenger has only a small quantity of luggage it is generally passed without being opened; and if there are several trunks they investigate every second or third one, making the selection themselves. It is well not to have any of your trunks nicely corded and made up for a long journey, as the officers have learned from long experience that such packages are more liable to contain contraband goods than any other, and consequently they are the ones generally chosen to be opened.

Landing in America has more formality than landing in England or France. The officers come on board at quarantine, and while the ship is making her way up the harbor the declarations of the passengers are taken. The number and character of each one's packages is marked on a blank, to which is appended an oath to the effect that the passenger has told the truth. He receives a card bearing the number of his declaration, and when he reaches the dock and has his baggage ready for examination, he presents his ticket to the officer in charge; the latter assigns his subordinate who is to conduct the examination, and hands him the declaration that the passenger has made. If the number and character of the packages is found to be correct, and no dutiable goods are discovered that have not been declared, the inspection is over in a few minutes, the officer puts a cabalistic mark on each article, and the passenger may then breathe freely. Sometimes the officials conduct the search with a great deal of rigor, and at others they are not at all particular. There appears to be no regular system about the business, and the officials are lax or vigilant, according to the temper of their chief. A change in the office of collector of customs at New York is followed by a great deal of energy, but nobody can tell how long it will last. On some occasions the inspectors have actually turned the contents of trunks on the dock in order to facilitate their examinations, and a great deal of needless rudeness has been displayed by them.

For the information of travelers, the following caution is published :—

" All articles such as wearing apparel, not having been worn, must be declared at the custom-house. Travelers not conforming to this regulation will incur not only the confiscation of the articles not declared, but also the payment of a fine. Silks, laces, and other foreign goods, packed with articles of apparel, or otherwise concealed, are, as well as the articles in which they may be placed, liable to seizure; and travelers are warned that the seizure is strictly enforced, unless the examining officer is informed of the articles being in the package, and the goods duly declared before it is opened."

Clothing in actual use is admitted free of duty, and those who return home with a supply of new garments should be particular to wear each article at least once, in order to be within the regulations. Ladies are informed that a dress that has simply been "tried on" is considered liable to duty, but if it has actually been worn once or twice, it is admissible. Gloves are exempt from this condition, but the traveler should not expect to import a large quantity. The strict allowance is one dozen pairs, but in most cases three or four dozen may be carried without question. The regulations say that each passenger may bring, free of duty, a fair amount of clothing, according to his condition in life, a statement that has given rise to a great deal of dispute. Half a dozen costly silk dresses of the latest fashion would be manifestly out of place in the baggage of Bridget Maloney in the steerage, and fresh from the bogs of Ireland, while they would be regarded as a moderate allowance for Miss Flora M'Flimsey, whose father is a millionaire.

In the continental ports, generally, there is often considerable delay in examining baggage, and the following regulations have been made to facilitate the movements of travelers :—

"Passengers, on landing, are not permitted to take more than one small bag with them on shore. The custom-house porters, who are responsible for its safety, convey it direct from the vessel to the custom-house, where the owner, to save personal attendance, had better send the hotel commissionaire afterwards with the keys. The landlord of the inn is responsible for his honesty."

Leaving the custom-house behind you, the way is clear to seek a hotel. Generally there are plenty of runners at the landing-place, and if you have chosen the establishment where you are to stop, you have only to name it, and the runner for that house will step forward to take charge of yourself and your belongings. Sometimes the baggage is taken on the cab or carriage which carries you, and at others it is intrusted to licensed porters, who are responsible for its safe delivery, and can be trusted without much hesitation. As far as possible, it is best to keep your baggage always with you when traveling, but there are many instances where it is not convenient to do so. Before you leave the custom-house there are some fees to be paid to the porters who have handled your luggage, but none to the officers who examined it. You will find, too, that the man who puts it on the carriage desires to be remembered, and you discover very early in your travels that you are in the land of fees. If you are in charge of the hotel runner you can let him settle these matters, or, if you prefer to attend to them yourself, you can do so, but you run the risk of giving too much. The runner is not always to be trusted, as he sometimes has a secret arrangement with the porters to compel strangers to bleed freely with the understanding that he is to receive the surplus. For putting the ordinary baggage of a traveler through the custom-house and on the top of a cab, a shilling is sufficient, and if it is handled by two persons they should be satisfied with a sixpence each.

It is best to ask the hotel proprietor to settle for your cab rather than attempt it yourself. It is next to impossible to ascertain from a driver how much he is legally entitled to; he either lies about it, or will not give a direct answer. He will "leave it to the gentleman," and the more you persist in knowing, the more he will "leave it to your honor." And finally when you make a venture, and through fear of giving too little give too much, the chances are, five to one, he will declare himself under-paid, and demand more. He promises beforehand to leave it to you, but rarely does, and therein is the aggravating part of the business. The only way to do under such circumstances is to walk off and leave him to shower imprecations on you; if you prefer peace and quietness you will pay what he demands. This payment will be followed by a request for an additional something for drinking your health, and possibly by a hint that the horse is hungry, and a trifle to buy oats would be appreciated by the beast. Don't expect a driver in the United Kingdom to change a coin for you; his pockets may be bulging with shillings and sixpences, but he declares with the most solemn face that he has no change, and possibly insists that you are the first patron he has had for two days.

Our copy-books at school generally inform us that the horse is a noble animal. No one will be likely to dispute the statement, as we all have a respect for the horse, and many of us are familiar with incidents that show his excellent character. But, admitting his nobility, it is a little singular that he should be associated with so much that is the reverse of noble, or rather that the great majority of those who associate with him are inclined to rascality. The whole race of hackmen and cabmen, from one end of the world to the other, are distinguished for their swindling tendencies; horse-trading and horse-jockeying are synonyms of cheating, and the race-track is the resort of scoundrels of all grades and kinds. If the traveler is not prepared to accept this proposition before landing in the old world, he will have excellent opportunities to verify it before he has been a month on the eastern side of the Atlantic.

In the English hotels the traveler will find many things to remind him that he is not in the United States. Instead of an office with a marble counter, a heavy register, and a clerk gorgeous as to hair and sparkling as to breast-pin, he finds a little window opening into a room only a few feet square, and behind the window a woman. She takes his application for lodging, and as he peers into the nook where she sits he wonders how the New York hotel clerk would get along in such narrow limits. Perhaps he may see a door opening beyond the office into an equally small apartment, where the book-keeper is stationed, and, in many instances, he finds that the accounts are kept by one of the gentler sex.

In many hotels not a man is visible about the office, with the possible exception of the porter, and the entire management is in feminine hands. The proprietor is rarely seen, and even the manager, where there is a masculine one, is a personage who is reached with more or less difficulty. At a famous hotel in Ireland, which bears the name of its proprietor, the story goes that a gentleman asked one day if that individual was in.

"He's in his private office, sir," was the reply.

"Say that I wish to see him a moment," said the gentleman, who was a London merchant of considerable prominence, and well known as a frequent patron of the hotel.

The clerk disappeared, and shortly returned with the following message:—

"Mr. ——— is engaged at present over some papers, and will send his secretary out in a few minutes to see what you want."

The American will miss the wide corridors of the hotels of his native land, and he finds the space usually given up to the public in the United States is here reserved for the strict use of the house. There are no broad reading-rooms and parlors, with a plentiful supply of papers from all parts of the country, as in the great hostelries at home; the bar is a dingy nook, scarcely larger than the office, and the most conspicuous ornaments in it are the handles of the beer-pumps. The bartender is absent, and in his place the bar-maid presides; those who are bibulously inclined will find comparatively little to tempt them, as the array of "mixed drinks," so common in an

American bar, is practically unknown in England. A few drinking establishments in London have sought to attract the patronage of strangers from the United States by advertising " American drinks," but those who have tried them say that the British concoctions are base counterfeits of the great originals.

In some hotels there is no public bar whatever, and drinks are served to order in the dining and smoking-rooms, or in the private apartments. Smoking is usually forbidden in the corridors, and sometimes the stranger who ventures to light a cigar in his private room will be told that he is violating the rules, and must go to the smoking-room.

In the last few years the English appear to have taken a hint from their transatlantic cousins in the way of hotel-keeping, and several establishments containing many of the American features have sprung into existence. The most of them have been successful, and it is probable that the crop will increase.

Bedrooms in the English hotels are usually larger than in American houses, and furnished on a more liberal scale. The beds are spacious, and frequently you find an old-fashioned four-poster of considerable antiquity, together with others that were fashioned in the present time. A hotel in Liverpool boasts of a bed in which Oliver Cromwell once slept, and certainly he could have occupied it without being cramped for space. Those who are liable to colds and rheumatic pains should be particular to have the sheets well aired and dried before retiring; the moist climate of the British Islands is apt to leave a disagreeable dampness on bed-linen, and make it very detrimental to the general health. Many a man has taken a severe cold by sleeping in damp sheets on his arrival in England, and discovered to his sorrow that his recovery was a thing of several weeks, if not longer. The prevailing moisture of the United Kingdom is an excellent thing for the ruddy cheeks of the women, and beneficial to the potato crop, but the stranger is not usually enamored of it, especially if he comes from a region where dry atmosphere is the fashion.

There are only a very few hotels where the traveler is received on the American system, and pays a lump sum per day for everything. The engagement is nearly always for the room alone, and all meals are charged extra, and may be taken wherever the customer chooses. There is an extra item for "attendance," and custom has fixed this at one shilling and sixpence at the majority of the English hotels. Some hotels compel you to breakfast in the house, or at all events they charge you for that meal, whether you take it or not, but the dinner is quite optional with you. The dining-room is generally known as the "coffee-room," but in some hotels there is a larger hall in addition to the coffee-room, where the table-d'hote dinner is served. One can breakfast very comfortably in the coffee-room, as he will find the morning papers there, and frequently a stock of guide-books and writing materials, with which he may amuse himself while his chop or steak is being prepared. Chops, steaks, ham and eggs, and cold meats are the principal items of an English breakfast, and there is hardly any variation from day to day.

If the dinner is served in the continental style, the traveler has no choice, but takes the courses in the order in which they are brought. A dinner "off the joint" is another thing, and a peculiarly British institution. Soup is served, and then fish, and then comes the joint, which is the *piece de resistance* of the day. A huge round of beef, smoking hot from the fire, or perhaps an equally huge piece of mutton, is mounted on a small table whose legs terminate in casters; by means of this table the joint is wheeled before each customer, who indicates to the carver the exact morsel he desires. There can be no deception, and no opportunity to serve up slices that have been warmed over from a previously cooked joint. The form of service is quite a novelty to the newly-arrived American, and various opinions have been passed upon its advantages. Some are loud in its praise while others declare that the sight of the steaming joints destroys their appetite.

The dinner costs from two shillings, sixpence, to five shillings, and there is an extra charge of threepence or sixpence for attendance, if the customer is not stopping in the hotel, and sometimes when he is. This attendance business is a nuisance, and many a stranger has spoken his mind freely in denouncing it as a well-regulated swindle. The theory is that it pays for the service, but it does nothing of the kind, and every waiter who has done the least thing for you, as well as others who have not lifted a finger in your aid, expects to receive a fee before your departure. Some of the hotels have the impertinence to print on their bill-heads "the service is all included, and nothing more is expected," a falsehood as glaring as any that has ever been told in the history of the world. The stranger who takes them at their word, and leaves the house without distributing sixpences and shillings to the servants, would be looked upon as little less than a downright swindler, and be received with coldness and negligence if he had the temerity to venture there again.

The prices of bedrooms vary according to their location and character; they are rarely less than two shillings—with the inevitable attendance—and often as high as five shillings. The following may be taken as a fair average of charges in an English hotel of medium pretensions:

Bedroom, - - 3 shillings.
Breakfast, - - - 3 "
Dinner, - - - 4 "
Supper, - - - 2 " 6 pence.
Attendance, - - 1 " 6 "

If tea is added to this it will cost not less than one shilling, and generally more. The fees to the servants are not likely to be less than a shilling a day for each person of the party, and it requires careful management to bring them down to that figure. The fees should never be given till the moment of departure, for the reason already mentioned in our talk about steamships.

At all hotels in the United Kingdom and on the Continent be sure to have the price of everything distinctly understood at the time the room is taken. Perhaps it is from a consciousness of the dishonesty of the charge for attendance, the manager or other person who assigns your room never mentions that item, and a direct question is needed to bring it out. The following inquiries will cover the ordinary circumstances of arrival at a hotel :—

" What is the price of a bedroom ? "
" What is the charge for attendance ? "
" How much for dinner ? "
" How much for breakfast ? "
" What time must a room be given up ? "

The last interrogatory is necessary in consequence of the varying rules of the hotels. Most of them have their day, like the nautical one, begin at noon, and a person who remains till one or two P. M. must pay for an extra day of room and attendance. Some hotels begin their day at 11 A. M., and some as early as 10; it is a noticeable fact that in several of these latter instances important trains leave a couple of hours after the termination of the diurnal reckoning. The traveler who holds his room till it is time to go to the train finds to his astonishment that the last hour of his occupation has cost him the same as an entire day. But the hotel keepers have a living to make, and must keep an eye to the main chance.

Guides for the city or neighborhood can be had at all hotels, and are preferable to those picked up the street. Carriages and cabs can also be ordered at the hotel, but if the traveler can trust himself to make a bargain it is better to secure them outside, since the house not infrequently adds a commission for its services. Besides it is well to learn as much as possible of the people you are among, and there are no more sharply-defined characters in the world than the professional drivers of Irish, Scotch, or English cities.

CHAPTER IX.

THE SYSTEM OF FEES.

Allusion has been made in preceding paragraphs to the system of gratuities that prevails in Great Britain and on the Continent. It is the greatest of all the annoyances of European travel, not so much for the money it consumes as for the perplexities it makes, and the perpetual irritation of being asked at every step to give an indefinite sum for real or fancied services. It would be a good deal mitigated if the expectants would name the exact amount they are entitled to; a regular tariff for gratuities would be a vast relief to the traveling public, but this boon is emphatically refused. The amount is always left to the stranger, partly for the reason that custom has so ordained, and partly because an avenue is thus left open for an increased demand.

The waiter is much less likely than his friend the cabman to tell you he is under-paid, but he vouchsafes that information far more frequently than is agreeable to the traveler. He rarely speaks when conveying this reproof, but his manner is unmistakable. Occasionally he puts the money back in your hand, and declines to accept it; his manner is as lofty as the summit of Mount Blanc, and quite as cold, and to judge by his appearance his most tender susceptibilities have been sorely wounded. The novice generally soothes him by an addition to the amount of the offer, but the experienced voyager does nothing of the kind. He drops the returned cash into his pocket and turns away; the movement brings the offended dignity to his senses, and for a moment he undergoes a mental struggle over the situation. Shall he preserve his haughty manner and refuse to pursue the subject, or shall he accept what he has just declined? These are the questions that flit through his brain, and he carefully balances the pros and cons. The usual result is in favor of the last-named course, and he pockets his fee in silence and thankfulness, not unaccompanied with a sullen air.

Occurrences of this kind are more rare in England than on the Continent, and the Continent again is freer from them than the countries farther East. Perhaps the worst of all is Egypt, where "backsheesh!" ("a present") is dinned into the traveler's ears from morn till night; it is the word he first hears on his arrival, and the last at his departure, and in after years it haunts his dreams, and is by no means banished from his waking hours. Whatever he does or does not do, he is expected to pay for; services are impudently forced upon him, and then the demand for compensation is as insolent as it is exorbitant. The manner of the Egyptian Arab in this matter of backsheesh is most insulting, and the wonder is he has been allowed to practice it so long. Give him what you consider a fair return for his services, either real or fancied, and he pushes the money back into your hands and lifts his nose into the air; you have been in his estimation a miser, and your coin is unfit for him to touch. But if you drop it into your pocket and turn away, his whole attitude changes; he is no longer the proud descendant of the Mamelukes and the kings of Egypt, but the most cringing suppliant you can imagine. He begs you to give again what he has just refused, and if you persist in keeping it he has resource to tears. Not unfrequently he rolls on the ground and screams like an angry child, and he will follow you for hours in the hope that you will relent. Sometimes, instead of thrusting the money into your hand, he throws it on the ground, knowing that you will be very unlikely to stoop to pick it up; by so doing he endeavors to make sure of the original offer, and takes his chances in shaming or bullying you into giving more.

The question naturally occurs to an American, 'How shall I ascertain what is proper to give when a service has been rendered to me?' No general rule can be laid down, and the traveler must depend often on his judgment. Where it is possible to do so, you can ask any person who is familiar with the subject, and he will tell you; when this cannot be done you have only yourself to rely upon. Remember that in England and on the Continent money has a greater purchasing power than in America, and gauge your fees accordingly. Where you have engaged cabmen, guides, or other individuals whose rate of service is previously arranged, or is regulated by a tariff, you will be about right if you add ten per cent. for a gratuity. Thus a guide whose tariff is five francs a day should be satisfied with half a franc, but, if he has been specially zealous and useful, you can give him a franc with safety. The Paris cabman expects four sous additional on the course or six sous an hour; his fee is obligatory in a certain sense, as his wages are too low for him to live upon without the *pour boire*. The German cabman expects his *trinkgeld* as a matter of course, and you will really under-pay him if you do not give it. The same is the case with his class in all parts of the Continent, as well as in Great Britain, and you will fully hit the mark if you augment the regular tariff by fifteen or twenty per cent.

In the restaurants the waiters generally receive nothing in the form of wages; they rely entirely on the donations of patrons for their compensation, and the system is well understood by the public. The money thus obtained is dropped into a box at the cashier's counter, and divided among all the waiters of the establishment at the end of the week. This has been found after long experience the best way to secure uniform attention to all customers,— better than to allow each waiter to pocket the money he receives. In the latter case, a patron know to be liberal would be carefully looked after, while the man who gave only the regulation fee would be neglected. Under the present arrangement a waiter can have no great inducement to neglect the niggardly man to an undue extent, and, on the other hand, he will not be over-serviceable to the generous one. The box for the money is in full view of all the waiters, so as to prevent any frauds on the revenue; it is usually of metal, and a foot or so in height. The shape and material cause the coin to jingle when it falls, and thus the waiters can be taught by the ear as well as by the eye that the donations are properly bestowed.

A French barber shop frequently amuses the stranger on account of the way the *pour boire* is received. You have whatever tonsorial operation you choose, and when the work is finished you pay according to the tariff. When change has been made you leave a few sous on the counter for the inevitable extra; the cashier drops them in the metal box which stands ready for their reception, and the sound of their fall is followed by a chorus of "Merci, monsieur," from all the barbers in the place, be they few or many. Half a dozen masculine voices pronouncing those words in measured cadence have a strange effect on the ears of a novice.

In many hotels and restaurants in England, and on the Continent, not only do the servants receive no wages, but they even pay something to the proprietor for their places.

In the restaurants of Vienna there is a man who is designated the "*zoll-kellner*," (pay-waiter) who carries a leather sack at his side to hold the coin for making change. Your accounts are settled with him, and not with the waiter who has served you, and it is to the zoll-kellner that you give your gratuities. Out of the gratuities he pays the wages of the waiters, and reimburses himself for his services, so that the attendance costs the establishment nothing. Some of the larger bier-halles in Vienna derive a revenue from the service, as they require the zoll-kellner to pay some hundreds of dollars annually for his privilege, besides giving his time and paying the waiters.

The usual fee in a restaurant on the Continent is a sou on each franc of the bill, or one sou in twenty. Thus, if you have ten francs to pay for your dinner, you give half a franc, or ten sous, to the waiter, and if you have expended only five francs you give him five sous. A sou on a franc is a good general rule; it is followed by the great majority of Frenchmen and other continental people, but you should not adhere to it by giving a single sou when you have only a franc to pay. Never give less than two sous, where you give anything at all, except to the professional beggar of whom you wish to rid yourself. The cashiers of the restaurants always arrange the change, so that you will have the material for the *pour boire*. Suppose your bill is exactly ten francs, and you put down a twenty-franc piece from which the amount is to be taken. The cashier sends back, not a ten-franc piece, but a five-franc piece, four francs, half a franc, and the rest in copper. Sometimes there is an attempt to cause the stranger to bleed freely by making change so that he will be compelled to give more than is necessary. Thus in the instance described above, the cashier would send back a five-franc piece and five pieces of one franc each, so as to compel a donation of a franc. Whenever this is done you can be entirely sure that it is an effort to extract more than is due; you can meet it by asking change—*la monnaie*—for one of the franc pieces, or better still, give the exact *pour boire* from the reserve you should always have in your pocket.

The regulation of the fees necessary for a hotel is more difficult than for a restaurant. The amount given should be proportioned to the time you have been in the house, the services of the waiters, the demands you have made upon them, and the size of your party. It is best to let one person of a party pay all the gratuities, and do it in a systematic way so that each servant receives his or her due. Suppose you are four in number, and have been a week in the house; you pay the concierge from five to eight francs, the chambermaid four to six, the waiter who has brought the coffee in the morning, and otherwise looked after you, five to eight, and the porter who has handled luggage and blacked your boots, five to six francs. These figures are for a fair amount of service, and are liberal enough for most cases. Every traveler must judge for himself whether he has made an undue demand upon the servants, and gauge his gratuities accordingly.

So much has been said about the fee system that some of the hotels have adopted the plan of certain English ones in announcing that the service is all included and nothing more is expected. But the pretence is a very thin one, as the departing traveler will surely ascertain. The servants come to his room while he is putting the finishing touch to his packing, they lie in wait in the halls and on the stairways, and they assemble at the door to see him off. There is often a preconcerted system of signals by which all the servants can be notified of the approaching departure of a patron of a hotel. Bells will be rung, or somebody will be called in a loud voice to bring something either real or imaginary. The writer had the following experience in a hotel in Paris :

He had been in the house nearly a week, and followed the usual custom of leaving his key with the concierge whenever he went out. If he came in in the afternoon he was usually informed that the chambermaid had the key upstairs, and on proceeding to his hall he summoned that damsel by touching a bell at the head of the stairway; the concierge never made any pretence of calling her, but simply indicated that the key was above. One afternoon he came in, asked for his key, and received the usual response that the chambermaid had it. As he turned to go upstairs he asked to have his bill made out, as he was going away immediately.

The half-asleep concierge seemed to have been struck with a shock from an electric battery. She protruded her head from the window of her office, and shouted so that she could have been heard to the uttermost parts of the house :—

"*Fifine! Fifine! apportez le clef pour numero trente deux ; monsieur va partir—il va partir.*" (" Bring the key for number 32; the gentlemen is going away; he's going away!")

The echoes of the last syllable of the last word of her call followed number 32 up the stairs to his door. When he had arranged his packing and descended, he found the servants waiting for him, with the exception of those he had already encountered on his way down. At least half of them he had never seen, but all had their hands open for any tokens of remembrance in the shape of the current coin of the country.

The custom of assembling all the servants on the departure of a traveler is descended from the Middle Ages when the retainers of a castle were summoned by the bell at the portcullis to welcome the coming and speed the parting guest. Like many another honorable usage of olden times it has suffered degradation; at present it is simply a form of extracting money from the traveler, and not one servant in a hundred is aware of its origin, or thinks of it in any other light than the practical one. The fee system to the hotel waiter had a similar origin, and is likewise a relic of feudalism. The guest at the castle of a baron of the Middle Ages was not expected to pay for his accommodation; he was in every sense a guest, and like many a guest of modern days, he often felt that he was causing a good deal of trouble and extra work on the part of the servants and retainers. Consequently he opened his purse at his departure and scattered his cash among those who had cared for him; the shell of the custom has been retained, but its sentiment is altogether gone. The patron of a hotel pays his bill, and is in no sense a "guest," as many keepers of hostelries like to call him, and the excuse for his distribution of money among the servants has the lightest possible foundation.

In high circles the habits of the olden time remain in all their purity, and princes and kings and nobles are obliged to pay heavily for their entertainment. After his sojourn in Paris in 1867, the Emperor of Russia gave 40,000 francs to be distributed among the servants of the palace where he was lodged, and the King of Italy gave 10,000 francs under similar circumstances at Vienna in 1873. American and other foreigners of distinction who visit Egypt are often honored with lodgings in one of the Khedive's palaces, or with one of his private steamers to go up the Nile. But it is bad economy to accept these courtesies, for the reason that the backsheesh to servants and officers amounts to a large figure, frequently to several hundreds of dollars. It was said of Ismail Pacha that he paid nothing to the attaches of his boats and palaces but reimbursed them by giving them an occasional distinguished visitor to pluck.

The fee system has grown into so many abuses in these latter days that several governments have passed laws restricting it, and forbidding its servants to accept fees. This is noticeable in the public galleries of France, Italy, and other countries, where no fees are demanded except a slight charge for taking care of a cane or umbrella, and sometimes an entrance fee, which is bought at a ticket-office, and must be paid by everybody who enters. At the ruins of Pompeii signs are posted in all the languages of Europe forbidding the guides to accept fees in any form under penalty of dismissal; the regulations are so stringent that no guide dares to accept a piece of money, no matter how willing you may be to give it. But there is a form of keeping the word of promise to the ear and breaking it to the hope; the guides are allowed to sell photographs of the various objects of interest, and sometimes they pester you with them to an extent far worse than any direct application for gratuities.

The traveler should be cautious about making a "half-bargain" with guides, valets, *et id omne genus*, who will be sure to make all kinds of claim against him. Never accept the services of one of these men without a positive agreement as to the amount he is to receive, and if you can have it include his *pour boire*, so much the better. He always desires to leave something open for a demand, while you should be equally certain to have no loop-hole in the contract. A Neapolitan guide will fix his services at five francs a day, "and something for myself if you are satisfied." Now this something breeds a great deal of trouble. The writer had one of these fellows to accompany him up

Vesuvius on his first visit to Naples. The 'something' was left undetermined; the guide received five francs at the end of the day with a franc extra, which was thought to be quite sufficient. He struck an attitude of astonishment and declared himself outrageously treated; "gentlemen always gives me five francs extra," he remarked, "and some of them gives ten." This was said with an air of withering contempt, but there was nothing in his neighborhood that withered immediately. When a guide proposes to hire himself for five francs and something if you are satisfied, endeavor to fix the amount of the "satisfaction." If he will not do it he is a good subject to drop, unless he is the only one of his kind attainable, and you happen to be in a hurry. Remember always that a half-bargain is a bad bargain, everywhere, and especially in the countries where the fee system is in vogue.

Sometimes even a careful bargain will not protect the traveler from trouble. Italian boatmen will agree for a certain sum, and while on the way they demand more. If you are going on board a steamer at Naples they are apt to be extortionate, as they know you are leaving port and are not likely to give them trouble with the police. A boatman agrees to carry you and your baggage for two francs; you enter his boat and off you go. Half way to the ship he stops rowing and demands four, or perhaps five, francs, and threatens to return to shore unless you comply. If you are strong, and carry a cane or good umbrella, a threat to break his head, accompanied with a gesture to that effect, will generally cause him to proceed. If you are weak and timid, the best way is to say nothing, and if you are tough in conscience and don't mind meeting downright rascality with a white lie, you can nod assent and let him go on. Before he gets to the ship he will increase his demand, and you may nod again. When you reach the vessel do not show your money till your baggage is safe on board, the heavy trunks in the hold, and the lighter things in your cabin. Then pay the sum you first agreed to give, and not a centime more, and, having discharged the obligation, descend to the saloon. The boatman is not allowed to follow you there, but he will give vent to a volley of imprecations that fall harmless on your devoted head if you happen to be ignorant of Italian. When these fellows get too noisy they are ordered away from the ship, and after their departure you may mount again to the deck and enjoy the wonderfully beautiful panorama of the bay of Naples.

The boatmen of Alexandria, Egypt, are worse than their Neapolitan brethren, as they sometimes resort to downright violence. A strong cane is the best argument for them, and if you are two or three men against an equal or inferior number, you have a moral force that stands in good stead. One man alone may face two or three of these rascals, but he is not altogether safe, as they would have little hesitation in robbing him and then throwing him overboard, if they could be sure of escaping undetected. They have been known to pull around the harbor for an hour or two to compel their victim to come to terms, and if brought before the police for their misconduct they generally manage to bribe themselves out of trouble, unless their prosecutor is able and willing to pay more for their punishment than they can for their liberty.

The inhabitants of Switzerland have been noted in all ages for their thrifty habits and their ability to make much of an opportunity. In former times their genius was displayed in watch-making and other industries; in these latter days, they have devoted themselves in great measure to fleecing the tourists that come among them, and some of their performances in this line border on the wonderful. Watch-making and wood-carving still exist, and quite probably there are yet many honest people in the land of the Alps. Down to a recent period the exploitation of the stranger was left to the hotel-keepers, guides, porters, and others with whom he came in contact, and if he felt aggrieved and brought complaint against his swindlers he could receive redress at the hands of the law. *On a changé tout cela,* the government has come to the assistance of the exploiting class, and what was before optional is now official. At every step the tourist encounters a "tariff," and if he objects to anything his attention is called to the fact that is "official." The hotel porter takes your trunk to the door of the establishment where you have been lodged, and hands it over to a licensed porter, who carries it to the boat, train, or diligence. He stops at the dock, or at the front of the station, where another licensed porter comes forward and bears the trunk to the baggage-man; each of the porters must be paid, and the baggage-man also expects something, and if you object you are shown the official tariff, from which there is no appeal.

The official tariff is made the scapegoat of a great many extortions and downright falsehoods; the writer will give a bit of his personal experience to illustrate this statement. He was in Martigny, on his way to Chamouny, in the summer of 1880, and wished to hire a carriage for the journey; he had been told that one could be had for thirty or forty francs, and asked the proprietor of the hotel Clerc where carriages were to be had and the price to be paid. The latter answered that the tariff for a carriage for two persons was fifty francs, and there was no other price.

"But," said the stranger, "I have been told that a carriage can be had for thirty or forty francs. Is it not so?"

"Not at all," was the proprietor's answer; "there is

only one price, fifty francs. They will tell you so at the office of the Association of Drivers." (*Societe des cochers de Martigny.*)

He indicated the office, which was close to the hotel, and the stranger went there. The agent assured him that no carriage could be had under fifty francs, and he pointed to the official tariff, by which all drivers were bound. Convinced of the truthfulness of the landlord's statement, the stranger engaged a carriage and paid twenty-five francs in advance, the balance being due on arrival at Chamouny. Then he strolled up the street and came upon an office bearing the announcement:—

" Carriages for Chamouny.—Two persons, thirty francs ; three persons, forty francs ; four persons, fifty francs."

Full of wrath at having been swindled, he returned to the hotel and interviewed the landlord. There was a good deal of frankness to the square foot of the conversation, and the landlord became very indignant when told that he had dealt sparingly with the truth. He defended his action on the ground that the official tariff was fifty francs, and he did not recognize the existence of the opposition. In whatever light the case was presented, he responded that the opposition was not " recognized," and he would not allow his patrons to travel by it if possible to prevent their doing so. He denied receiving any commission from the "official" drivers, and waxed wroth at the intimation of such a thing, but the writer ascertained afterwards to his full satisfaction that the drivers gave ten per cent. of their revenues to the hotel-keepers on condition that the latter would ignore the existence of the opposition, and give all patronage to the association.

Cases like the foregoing may be found all over Switzerland in one form or another. Great stress is laid upon the words "official" and "tariff," and matters are so arranged that the traveler can be bled as much as possible with the least possible chance of redress. The authorities connive at the frauds, and the chances are twenty to one that a tourist who has the temerity to bring his disputes before them will be required to pay the sum in question, with a heavy addition in the shape of a fine. As an instance of official connivance, the following may be cited:—

Tourists going from Zermatt to the railway station at Visp have a journey of about eight hours, partly by saddle and partly by wagon; it is customary to forward trunks and valises by the government post, which is due at Visp at 4 P. M., while the train for Lausanne and Geneva leaves at five o'clock. The traveler times his movements so as to get to Visp to claim his baggage and take it to the railway station in season for the train, but he finds on arrival that the postmaster is busy with the verification of the lists, copying them, sorting letters, and arranging parcels in general, so that there is no delivery till after the departure of the train. This neat arrangement compels the traveler who wishes to keep with his luggage to spend a night at Visp, to the profit of one of the two hotels that adorn this uninteresting place, and, furthermore, they have a habit of closing the office half an hour before the departure of the forenoon train, and the hotel-keepers manage to keep you at breakfast until this half-hour has been reached. In this case you must wait till afternoon, or go on without your property, either of which is unpleasant, and if you venture to complain you are told that such is the regulation of the office, and as the postmaster represents the government the futility of any opposition is at once apparent.

The Swiss excel even the Chinese in their genius for combinations and guilds; and the object of these enterprises is not, like those of the Chinese, altogether in the interest of legitimate labor, but to the end that the pocket of the stranger can be depleted to the advantage of the inhabitants of the land of William Tell. Items that were formerly regarded as gratuities, and therefore optional, are now obligatory, and they are frequently demanded with an insolence that rouses the traveler's ire. There are doubtless many honest people in Switzerland, but it is not easy for the ordinary traveler to find them, and the difficulty seems to be increasing every year.

CHAPTER X.

ENGLISH AND CONTINENTAL MONEY.

We have already considered the subject of letters of credit and the uses to be made of them. We will now look at the perplexities of the English and Continental currencies. The English stand at the head of the list in having one of the most troublesome monetary systems imaginable; it is a never-failing source of inconvenience to the stranger, especially if he has come from a land where the decimal system in one form or another is in vogue. We all know it from the school-books:—

> 4 farthings make one penny,
> 12 pence make one shilling,
> 20 shillings make one pound,
> 21 shillings make one guinea.

It is easy enough to commit the above to memory, but not at all easy to put it into practice. The farthing is imaginary, like the American mill, the smallest coin being two farthings, or half a penny, usually called a ha'penny, with the accent on the first syllable. This coin is about equal to the American cent, so that a penny is worth two cents, or very nearly. The shilling is nearly the equivalent of twenty-five cents. Four shillings may be reckoned as a dollar, and a pound as five dollars. The actual value is less than five dollars, but it is near enough for rough calculations. The guinea is obsolete, and does not exist in circulation, but the coins can be bought as curiosities, and may be seen occasionally dangling from the watch-chains of their possessors. English tradesmen are fond of stating prices in guineas when dealing with foreigners, as they can thereby add five per cent. to their revenues; the English customer is on the look-out for this trick and cannot be caught by it, but the American is very likely to confound pounds with guineas and not think of the difference. Some unscrupulous tailors and other tradesmen are in the habit of making their bills in guineas when only pounds have been mentioned, and not infrequently the bills are paid without the discovery of the swindle.

The smallest bank-notes in circulation in England are of five pounds each, though the banks in Ireland and Scotland, and some of the private banks in England, issue notes of one pound. The gold coins are twenty shillings and ten shillings each, and known as sovereigns and half-sovereigns. In common usage the larger is frequently called a "sov.," and a ten-shilling piece a "half-sov." Silver coins are for five shillings, two and a half shillings, two shillings, one shilling, sixpence, fourpence, and threepence. The copper coins of a penny and a halfpenny complete the list. The two-and-a-half-shilling piece is called half a crown, the five-shilling piece sometimes a crown and sometimes, in slang language, "five bob." A shilling is designated as a "bob" by the lower classes, and a sixpence as a "tanner." "Two bobs and a tanner," means "two shillings and sixpence."

The two-shilling piece is the newest of the English coins, and is heartily detested by the cabman, the waiter, and all others whose existence has any dependence on gratuities. Where half a crown was formerly given, the two-shilling piece comes in use; the giver saves a sixpence, and the receiver is "out" just that amount. If a vote of the fee-taking classes could be had on the subject it would be unanimous for the abolition of this hated coin. Travelers economically inclined would do well to consider the advantages of this piece of money, and govern themselves accordingly.

On the Continent the currency in nearly all countries is far simpler than in England, for the reason that it is on a decimal basis. The franc is the acknowledged unit of France, Belgium, Switzerland, and Italy, and it is divided into a hundred parts, known as *centimes* in the three countries first named, and as *centissimi* in the last of the list. Reckonings are in francs and centimes; the approximate value of the franc is twenty cents of American money—though in reality it is a trifle over eighteen cents. The centime is consequently one-fifth of a cent, but no coins of that value are stamped except in Italy; five centimes make a sou in all the countries except Italy, where the coin is known as a soldi, and it is the smallest of the coins in general use. The sou is practically the equivalent of the American cent, and is about as large as the old-fashioned "copper" of twenty years ago. There is a two-sous piece of copper in all the countries named, and quite recently some of them have adopted nickel coins of the value of five, ten, and twenty centimes. There are silver coins of twenty and fifty centimes (the last being a half-franc), and then come the pieces of one franc, two francs, and five francs, the last being about the size of the American dollar. The gold coins are of ten and twenty francs, and occasionally we encounter pieces of forty francs, and also some slender ones of five francs. Bank-notes are of 10, 20, 50, 100, 500, and 1000 francs, and rarely smaller except in Italy, where there is a depreciated paper currency with forced circulation. Gold and silver are as scarce in Italy as they were in the United States in the decade following our civil war; the rate of discount for paper varies according to the condition of the national treasury, and for other countries, and can always be ascertained at any banker's, or in the hotels. Where it is not expressly stipulated to the contrary, all hotel and other bills in Italy are payable in paper at par whatever may be the rate of discount; if a hotel-keeper attempts to compel the payment of his bill in gold, without previous notification, he can be brought to terms by referring him to the police. The franc is commonly called a *lira* in Italy, especially among the lower classes, who have a tendency to stick to their national terms.

The unit of Austria is the florin (about fifty American cents), which is divided into a hundred kreutzers. The currency is in paper, at a varying discount, with coins of one, five, ten, and twenty kreutzers, based on the paper values. There is a ten-florin piece of gold which is intended to be equal to the twenty-franc piece, but is just a trifle short of it, and is consequently refused by bankers and others, except at a discount. The unit of Russia is the rouble (about seventy-five cents American), and it is divided into one hundred kopecks; the circulation is in paper, and it fluctuates in value with the varying conditions of the public treasury, and the alternating events of war or peace.

The German States had until within a few a years a bewildering array of currencies that would require whole pages of this book for their enumeration. Since the unification of the Empire the old currencies have mostly disappeared, and a uniform system has been adopted. The unit is the mark (twenty-five cents American, or one shilling English), and the mark is divided into one hundred pfennings. The silver coins are five marks, two marks, and one mark, and fifty and twenty pfennings, the nickle of ten and five pfennings, the copper of two pfennings and one pfenning; the gold coins are twenty, ten, and five marks, and the largest of the three is intended to be equal to the English sovereign.

English sovereigns can be exchanged in any country of Europe for the local currency, and so can the French, Italian, or other pieces of twenty francs. The latter are generally called napoleons, but since the establishment of the French Republic there has been a revival of the old name *louis*, or *louis d'or*. Some intense Republicans denominate the coin in question " *une piece de vingt francs*," and do not seem to mind the loss of time requisite for pronouncing four words instead of one. The traveler who has a stock of sovereigns or napoleons, either or both, can always settle his bill at the hotels with those coins, but he must be careful to have a supply of the money of the country for paying railway fares. In most countries of Europe the railways are more or less under government control, and the ticket-sellers are forbidden to accept foreign money. Sometimes a ticket-seller will change the traveler's money for him, but he naturally expects to be paid for his trouble.

At the frontier railway stations there are money-changers who do a very good business on small capital. Travelers can exchange the money of the country they are leaving for that of the one they are entering, and the changer can turn his capital as many times as there are trains each way daily, and make a small percentage on each operation. He has a fine profit and no risk, except that he may take an occasional counterfeit, but in the latter case he will have little difficulty in passing it on the first verdant customer. Counterfeit coins abound in Spain, Switzerland, England, and some other countries, but not in great number. The traveler is sure to be caught by them once in a while, and also by coins which have been called in and are declared uncurrent. The latter can be disposed of as gratuities to waiters and guides, and the former may be kept as curiosities, or dropped into the hats of importunate beggars.

For a rough calculation you can turn your dollars into pounds by dividing their amount by five, and into francs by using the same number as a multiplier. Multiply your dollars by four for German marks, and by two for Austrian florins; and if you get as far as Turkey and wish to reckon in piastres, you must multiply by twenty. To reach the amount in dollars of any values in the above currencies, you have only to reverse the operation, and after a little practice you will do it very rapidly.

CHAPTER XI.

LANGUAGES AND COURIERS.

As long as the American is in the United Kingdom he finds no trouble in making himself understood, but when he crosses the channel and lands on the Continent, the situation changes. Strange languages assail his ears, and the farther he goes the more languages he finds. If he has never studied any tongue save his mother one, he will often find himself helpless, and he execrates the memory of the man who first proposed the erection of the tower of Babel, and thereby brought trouble on the whole human race. He wishes he had studied some of the foreign lingo before he left home, and vows that before he comes again he will be able to make himself understood in French and German. An excellent resolution this is, and, like most good resolves, it is rarely kept.

An American who is entirely ignorant of any language beyond the vernacular of his own land may travel from one end of Europe to the other without any very serious trouble. But he will pay dear for his lack of lingual accomplishments, as he will be regarded as a fair subject for exploitation by the inn-keepers, guides, and others with whom he is brought in contact, and he cannot go out of the beaten track of tourists. In the principal hotels throughout Europe there are English-speaking clerks and servants, and it is usually easy to find guides and valets who are able to get on in the language of the British Isles. Those with deep and well-lined purses may employ a courier who will look after everything—engage rooms at hotels, buy railway tickets, attend to the luggage, and in various ways relieve the traveler from a great deal of perplexity. But he is a luxury that only the affluent can afford, as he not only has his wages and traveling expenses, but he obtains a commission, or "squeeze," on nearly every disbursement in your behalf. He takes you to the best hotels and secures the best rooms in them, and he leads you to the shops where the prices are highest, with correspondingly large commissions. He is generally honest so far as actual plunder of your money is concerned, and he takes care that no one but himself fleeces you, unless he can have a share of the spoil. His operations are conducted upon well understood principles, and he regards the taking of a commission as entirely compatible with rigid integrity. Now and then a courier can be found who disdains commissions, and faithfully watches the interest of his employer, and when such a man is obtained he may be regarded as a treasure.

Be very particular in employing a courier, as your happiness or misery will depend in great measure upon his goodness or badness. Your banker in London or Paris can generally recommend a trustworthy man, and there is a couriers' association in London that is well spoken of. The association is responsible for the honesty of each member, and also for his sobriety and general good conduct, but in any event the credentials of the man you are considering should be carefully examined. Especially should this be done with a courier who seeks you and offers his services, and if he cannot produce good references he should be rejected at once. The genuineness of the testimonials should also be investigated, as there have been instances where these documents were mostly imaginary, and written to order.

A courier should be familiar with English, French, German, and Italian, and if you are going to Spain, Russia, or the Scandinavian countries, you should seek for one who knows the languages along your intended route of travel. You can hire a good courier for fifty or sixty dollars a month, though he will frequently ask more, and you must pay extra for one who speaks Russian, Scandinavian, or Spanish. Whenever there are second-class carriages on the train he will travel in them, but it often happens that the express trains have none but first-class coaches, and in that event you must provide him with a first-class ticket. He should be called by his surname, without any preliminary "mister," and, if he understands his business, you can be perfectly free with him without fear that he will overstep the proper bounds. Don't invite him to sit with you at table or to ride with you in a carriage, as he does not expect anything of the sort; if you do, you will encourage him to undue familiarity, which may result in his assuming the air of a gentleman who is per-permitting you to travel with him for companionship.

In your financial relations with him, do exactly as you would with a clerk or cashier in business affairs. Have the contract carefully drawn in writing so as to avoid misunderstandings, and examine his accounts frequently and thoroughly, going over every item, whether small or large. It is well to arrange beforehand that he shall bring the accounts to you every second or third morning, and if he neglects to do so, and shows a persistence in the neglect, you will have reason to believe he is not honest. When you start on a journey give him money enough to pay the various items of expenditure to your first stopping-place. It is not good policy to be "close" with him, and, on the other hand, it is very impolitic to be careless of his accounts.

The courier is supposed to pay his own hotel bill, or to be boarded free of charge by the establishment. The real fact is that your own bill is sufficiently augmented to cover the courier's expenses, and in some instances he has been known to receive a commission in money in addition to his free living. Make it a part of your contract that he is to act as local guide in the cities you visit; otherwise you will be compelled to employ a guide in each place in addition to your courier. Some of the grand ones refuse to do so, and it is for you to determine whether to engage a man of high notions, or another who is not so exacting.

If not disposed to incur the expense of a courier you can hire a traveling servant for about half the price you will pay for the more distinguished attaché. These servants are not generally satisfactory, for the reason that they do not claim to understand all about the cities, routes, etc., and cannot speak the continental languages. Very often they are quite as helpless as the traveler himself, if not more so, and some of them are continually getting lost and giving no end of trouble to their employers to find them.

If you undertake to get along without any assistance, it is advisable to learn something of the language of the country you are to travel in. Ever so little is better than none at all, and you will be surprised to find how much you can accomplish with a very limited capital of words. Learn to count in French; you can do so in a few hours if you give your mind to it, and you will never regret the time you have devoted to the accomplishment of enumeration. Commit to memory a few phrases, such as "where is?" "how much?" and the like, and make yourself able to understand the bills of fare in restaurants and hotels. When you have done this you can look proudly down on the unfortunate wretch who knows nothing, and cannot help himself. After being thus perfected in French, you can attack German in the same way, and afterwards Italian; if you are to be ten days or more in a country it is worth your while to learn to count in its language, and when you have acquired the numerals you will want to know something more.

Don't practice your lingual acquirements on your friends if you can find anybody else to try them on. But don't be afraid to talk when on shopping excursions, or in other places where your French can be used; the continental people are polite, and will help you out of difficulty when you lose your footing, and they never smile at your most awkward blunders.

Books of the sentences and phrases in most frequent use are abundant and cheap. They are given in English, French, German, and Italian, in parallel columns, and are generally divided according to the subjects of conversation. They are excellent in theory, but it is generally discovered in practice that you can rarely find the sentence you wish to use, and may turn the leaves over and over again to no purpose.

If you find that you are not understood in your native language, and know no other, remember that it will not help the listener's understanding if you shout into his ear, or repeat a question over and over again with an increased emphasis each time.

Many laughable mistakes will occur in your efforts to get on in a country where you do not know the language, but they are part of the experiences of travel, and a good deal of instruction can be obtained from them. Sometimes a slight change in the pronunciation of a single word or syllable, or the incorrect use of an article, causes an awkward misunderstanding, but all such accidents should be taken good-humoredly and made the subject of merriment rather than of vexation. An American one day, in a Paris restaurant, wished to call for bread, and was astonished when the waiter after some delay brought him stewed rabbit. He pondered over the subject, and finally remembered that instead of saying "*du pain,*" he had made it "*le pain,*" which was naturally supposed to be "*lapin,*" the French word for rabbit or hare. He ate the stew in silence, and never allowed the waiter to understand that a mistake had been made.

A story is told of a party of Americans taking a ride in the Bois du Boulogne, and they wished to induce the driver to go faster, but the more they urged, the more angry he became, and their attempts at the French for "go faster, driver," seemed to set him wild. At last he stopped and wanted to fight, and when they refused to indulge in a trial of muscular capacity, he called a policeman. Some one happened along at this juncture who could act as interpreter, and it was discovered that they had been addressing the jehu as "*cochon*" (pig) instead of "*cocher*" (driver). An explanation was made, the driver received a franc as a salve to his wounded dignity, and the drive was continued at a more satisfactory speed.

Many things may be said in pantomime where you are ignorant of the words that are needed. If you wish to employ a carriage by the hour, and cannot grapple with "*a l'heure,*" you can show the face of your watch to the driver and point to the time; he will understand your meaning at once, and will indicate his comprehension of it by a nod. If you wish the carriage for only a single course you do not show your watch at all, but simply give or show the address to which you want to go. A desire for food or drink may be manifested by the conveyance of imaginary viands or liquids to the mouth, and following the said conveyance with equally imaginary mastication or deglutition. Mistakes will occur in pantomime as well as in spoken words, and the traveler should be prepared for them. An Englishman at a German inn endeavored to show that he wished to go to bed, and did it by commencing the removal of his clothing, and making a motion with his arms, as if he would spread himself over the invisible couch. The inn-keeper nodded, and disappeared; and he soon returned, followed by the servants, bringing a large tub and some water, under the impression that the stranger wished to take a bath. The latter made himself understood by resting his head on his hand and closing his eyes, whereupon there was a laugh all around, and he was shown to his sleeping-room.

Not infrequently you will throw yourself into a condition of exhaustion by mustering all your French for an effort; after it is made, and you are at your wit's end, you are answered in English, and find that your mental struggle has been thrown away. During the last Paris exposition one of the hotels imported a lot of waiters from London for the benefit of their English patrons. A Briton arrived at this house one morning, unaware of the importation, and after making himself presentable he proceeded to the breakfast-room. Beckoning to a waiter, he gave his order.

"*Donnez moi du biftek, du pomme de terre, et du cafe au lait.*" (Give me a beefsteak, potatoes, and coffee with milk.)

He was at the end of his French, and drew a long breath as he finished the sentence. The waiter listened attentively, with a blank expression on his face, and replied:—

"If it's all the same, sir, couldn't you just as well do it in English? I've only been here three days."

Whether you can speak the continental languages or not, you must put yourself into the hands of a dragoman when you go to the Orient and endeavor to make a journey into the interior. The dragoman differs from the courier in being a contractor who undertakes to manage your journey for a fixed sum per day, or for the entire trip, and he makes a margin sufficiently large to include the compensation for his own services. He combines the services of courier, butler, and maitre d'hotel all in one, and a good dragoman is able to relieve the traveler of all trouble by attending to every kind of petty detail, and managing the journey so that the tourist has nothing to think of beyond enjoying himself.

Dragomen are of all kinds, from the worst to the best; most of them bring recommendations from former employers, and, while these should have due weight, it is best not to rely on them implicitly. There are some of the profession who enjoy a high reputation, and their prices are fixed accordingly; a cheap dragoman is almost sure to be a poor one, but not all high-priced ones are necessarily good. If possible, when starting for a journey in Syria and Egypt, get a friend who has been there before you to recommend a dragoman, and make a careful note of the name and address, so that there can be no mistake. Good ones may also be heard of around the consulate of your country, and in whatever bargain you make you should have the consular approval. The dragomen who hang about the hotels are not to be relied on, as they are often in league with the establishments to make something out of the stranger, or have agreed to pay a commission to whoever can get them an engagement.

George William Curtis, in his Nile Notes, says, "The dragoman is of four species; the Maltese, or able knave; the Greek, or the cunning knave; the Syrian, or the active knave; and the Egyptian, or the stupid knave." The description is by no means inaccurate, but it gives the impression that all are knaves, whatever their race or nationality.

There is little to choose between them, and whatever kind you employ it is quite possible you may wish you had taken another. There are honest and efficient ones among all the different races, and also a liberal allowance of those who are worthless, or even worse.

Detailed directions for engaging dragomen, and the forms of contracts to be made with them, can be found in the guide-books of Murray and Baedeker, to which the reader is referred. Never trust yourself to draw a contract that will be "iron-clad," but go to your consulate and have the matter attended to there, at a cost of five dollars. Then, in case of trouble, the consul can be called to arbitrate the matter, and his decision will be final. As you are required to pay half, or more, of the engagement-money at the time of making the contract, you thus place yourself at the mercy of the man you are engaging, and it is worth while to be cautious.

If a particular dragoman has been recommended to you by some friend at home, you will very likely be told on enquiring for him that he died a few months ago. Of course, it is just possible that he is no longer alive, as drago—like other men—are but mortal, but his death at that time is by no means a certainty. His rivals have a convenient way of ridding themselves of his competition by killing him metaphorically, and they are particular to state time, place, and circumstances with great minuteness. Bayard Taylor became much attached to his dragoman in his journey up the Nile in 1852, and recommended him, a few years afterwards, to some friends. They brought back the information of the man's death, but on visiting Cairo in 1874 Taylor found his old companion alive and well, and very much chagrined at the announcement of his demise. "He is dead," or "He has just left with a party," is the stereotyped answer of the dragomen you encounter around the hotels when you ask for one whose name has been given to you by a friend at home, although it is well known by them that the man in question is within a dozen blocks of them, and waiting for a job.

It is the custom at the end of a journey in the Holy Land, or on the Nile, to make a present to the servants in addition to the contract-price agreed upon with the dragoman or manager of the party. The dragoman is always ready to attend to the distribution of this gratuity, and shows great activity in looking after it. Verdant travelers are apt to place the affair and the money in his hands with the expectation that he will carry out their wishes; the only distribution he makes, in nine cases out of ten, is to distribute the cash around the pockets of his own garments, and leave the other servants without a penny. Unless you give the money to the waiters with your own hands the chances are ten to one they will get nothing, and the whole amount will go to enrich the dragoman; it will not even answer to allow that worthy to distribute it to them in your presence, as he will manage by certain dexterous turns of the wrist to retain the larger portion for himself. Complaints of his misconduct are unlikely to reach your ears, as the servants are his subordinates, and liable to lose their places if they incur his displeasure. The writer was once a member of a party on a Nile steamboat that made up a purse for the servants; while the money was being raised two or three of the cabin-waiters intimated privately that if the money was put in the hands of the dragoman they would get nothing, since he always kept the whole of it. "Whatever you give us," said they, "please put in our own hands," and we acted on the hint to the great disgust of the dragoman.

CHAPTER XII.

RAILWAY TRAVELING ON THE CONTINENT.

The American traveler who makes his first tour abroad will come upon something new as soon as he visits a railway station. The cars are quite unlike those to which he has been accustomed at home; they have no passage-way running the whole length of the vehicle, and most of them present a Lilliputian appearance when compared with the American passenger car. They are divided into compartments which generally contain seats for eight persons, and are entered by doors at either end. The occupants of a compartment face each other, so that when the place is full half the passengers are riding backwards and the other half forwards. Some persons are made ill unless they have their faces in the direction they are traveling; a tourist who belongs to this category should make sure of his place by the aid of a porter, and there is generally no trouble about the matter. Those who are not disturbed by the aforesaid nausea prefer to sit with their backs toward the locomotive, as they escape a good deal of the dust and smoke that fall to the lot of those in the "front-face" position. There is a large window in the upper half of the door, and there are smaller windows at the ends of the rows of seats; if you have your back towards the engine, and are in an end seat, the open window in the door will give you all the air you need, while in the opposite seat you might find the breeze too strong. A seat on the windward side of the train is preferable to a leeward one, though much will depend upon the position of the sun and the scenery along the route.

On the Swiss railways many of the carriages are on the American system, with doors at the ends and a passageway in the center, but they still cling to the compartment idea, and have partitions with doors that permit free circulation. In Italy, and some other countries, you occasionally find a carriage with a saloon in the center, capable of seating twelve or sixteen persons, but such cars are not common, and are considered a luxury to be specially ordered. Some of the first-class carriages have the compartments arranged for six passengers—three on a side— but the majority are intended for eight. On every train you will usually find one or more carriages with a coupé at the end; it can be made to hold four persons, but there is no advantage in securing it for more than two. It is considered as a *place de luxe*, and can only be occupied by payment of an extra charge, which is usually about one-sixth of the price of the passage ticket. Two persons in a coupé are tolerably certain not to be disturbed by the entrance of other passengers, but a single passenger is not so safe. The coupé may be engaged beforehand on application to the station-master, but the companies will never guarantee that a particular train will contain coupé carriages.

The Pullman palace and sleeping-cars have not been introduced in Europe to any extent, nothwithstanding persistent efforts by the Pullman Company for a decade or more. The Midland Railway Company, of England, has adopted them, and they are used on two or three smaller lines in the United Kingdom, but not in any great number. On the Continent they have found their principal footing in Italy, under the auspices of the *Strada Ferrata del' Alta Italia* (Railway of Upper Italy), which has adopted them for the comfort of passengers on the Indian mail route between London and Brindisi. On several of the continental lines the Mann Boudoir sleeping-car has been introduced; it is the enterprise of an American, and is a very serviceable vehicle, though less comfortable than the famous Pullman. The Mann car is the ordinary European railway carriage equipped with sleeping accommodations, lavatories and the like; the traveler must have a first-class ticket to be admitted, and he pays in addition about $2.50 per night. There are offices in Paris, Berlin, Vienna, and other large cities, where places may be secured in the Mann sleeping-cars just as they are secured in the Pullman cars in America.

Some of the companies have cars fitted up with the "fauteuil-lit," or bed-chair; it is the ordinary seat so arranged that it may be coverted into a bed, or a poor substitute for one, and the extra cost is nearly, if not quite, equal to a third of the price of the ticket. Three fauteuils-lits fill a compartment, and the occupants of those away from the door must climb over the one nearest to it in getting in or out after the beds have been opened. Very few of the roads have any kind of sleeping-carriage whatever, and the night traveler on long journeys will miss the luxuries that he finds in the United States. " Bless the name of Pullman," he will often exclaim, as he crawls, dusty and disjointed, from where he has sat bolt or limply upright for hours, and contrasts his present feelings with those he would have at the end of a journey from New York to Chicago. There are no toilet facilities on the European trains, with the exception of those on the few sleeping-cars in use, and retiring-closets are by no means universal. Most of the coupés contain them, and they can generally be found in the baggage-wagon or under the brake-van. The keys of these "cabinets" are in charge of the conductor, who will readily open them on application, but they can only be reached or left while the train is halted at a station.

The carriages are of three and sometimes four classes, and their character is indicated in different ways in different countries. In England they are labelled " first-class," " second-class," or " third-class," as the case may be; in France they are marked " premiere," "seconde," "troisieme," or with the abbreviation of those words into figures and letters, and in Germany and some other countries by " I," " II," " III." Sometimes you find only the figures " 1," " 2," and " 3 " on the doors of the carriages to indicate the class, and sometimes the designation is by a number of stars, corresponding to the class. When you leave a carriage temporarily at a station, be careful to observe and remember its number, or you may have difficulty in finding it when you return. If you have the number and class well in mind, you will not be likely to make a mistake.

Nearly every train will have one or more compartments exclusively for ladies; they are labelled " Dames Seules " in France, " Damen Coupé," or " Fur Damen," in Germany, and " Per Signore " in Italy. The sterner sex is not allowed in these carriages under any pretext whatever; even the offer of a piece of money, so potent in other matters, will not secure the violation of the rule. Smoking is forbidden except in compartments specially designated for that amusement; in France smoking-carriages are labelled " Pour Fumeurs," and in Italy " Per Fumare." The Germans get at the subject in the opposite way by allowing smoking in all carriages save those wherein it is forbidden; these are labelled " Nicht Rauken," but if an entire party in one of them chooses to suspend the rules, it may do so. It is customary in case of doubt to ask permission to smoke, and if any person objects, the rule must be obeyed.

In Germany the second-class carriages are quite comfortable, but they are apt to be crowded, and the traveler who desires plenty of room will do well to buy a first-class ticket. The first-class vehicles are upholstered with velvet, and the second with cloth; the former are often the more uncomfortable in hot weather, as the velvet retains more heat than the cloth. The third-class carriages have seats of plain boards, and the fourth-class no seats at all; if you travel fourth-class in Germany, you must stand and cling to an iron rod, or, if there are not many passengers, you may sit or lie on the floor. Fourth-class is rarely found in any other country than Germany, and only where there is a considerable amount of travel among those who cannot afford to pay for the higher grades. Second-class in Germany is nearly if not quite as comfortable as first-class in France or Italy, and this is so well understood that "mixed" tickets are sold for long journeys, entitling the holder to first-class in other countries and second in Germany.

In some countries, but not in all, there is a difference in fares, according to the speed of the train by which you take passage, so that a given distance costs less by a way-train than by an express. In France and Italy the quickest trains are generally made up of first-class carriages only, so that the economical voyageur must content himself to move more slowly than his first-class rival. The fares by mixed trains (freight and passengers) are often only about a third of those of the first-class expresses. This is particularly the case in Austria and all the South German States.

The allowance of baggage varies greatly. In England it is one hundred pounds, but the weight is not always taken, and even if it is considerably in excess, a shilling in the hand of the man who weighs it will cause a sudden diminution of its avoirdupois, so as to bring it within the limit. This is particularly the case on the roads where notices are posted forbidding the employés of the companies to receive gratuities, under penalty of dismissal. In France and Spain the allowance is thirty kilogrammes (about sixty-five pounds). In most parts of Germany it is fifty pounds, and sometimes sixty, and in Bavaria, Italy, and most parts of Switzerland there is no allowance, and every pound of luggage must be paid for. In Austria the traveler, no matter what class ticket he holds, is allowed fifty-five pounds. In Russia fifty-five, in Sweden sixty-six pounds to first-class and forty-seven to second-class, and in Denmark fifty-five pounds. The rates for excessive luggage are pretty high, and in the countries where no allowance is made the rate of transportation is worse than in any other.

The sale of tickets ceases from five to ten minutes before the departure of a train, and the registration of luggage not less than fifteen minutes. The traveler first buys his ticket and then goes to the baggage agent, who stands in a little office close to the baggage-counter. The baggage is weighed and the weight declared by one of the attendants; the agent takes the ticket, stamps it to show that it has received its baggage allowance, then fills out a receipt stating the number of trunks, their weight, and the amount paid (if any). Where there is no excess there is usually a charge of ten centimes (two cents) for the receipt; the paper should be carefully guarded, as its production is necessary at the destination to secure the delivery of the baggage. The attentive traveler who closely scans his receipt will find that there is a column for dogs, and if he investigates the train he will discover a compartment for those animals, with grated doors.

On most of the English roads no receipt is given for baggage, and the traveler must take the chances of its loss. A label showing its destination is pasted on your trunk, and when you are at the journey's end you must go to the platform where the contents of the van have been discharged, and pick out your property. Attempts have been made to introduce the American checking system in England, but the English are too conservative to take up with such a Yankee notion.

Ticket and baggage arranged, the traveler is permitted to go to the waiting-room. There the intending passengers (no others are admitted) are huddled together till within a few minutes of the departure of the train, and very often the room is overcrowded, and cheerless in the extreme. Passengers are not allowed on the platforms till everything is ready, and sometimes there is hardly time for all to get comfortably seated before the train moves. Latterly some of the roads have made a reform in this matter; the *Paris, Lyon & Mediterrance* was the first to relax the rules and allow passengers to go direct to the platform, after passing the supervisor of tickets, instead of shivering or crowding in the waiting-room. On some lines the porters are not permitted to enter the waiting-rooms, and passengers must carry their own satchels and other impedimenta, while on others the porters can go direct to the carriages, and secure desirable seats for actual or expected return in cash.

On account of the high tariff for extra baggage, travelers on the Continent usually carry more in their hands than would be the case with the same people in America. Parcels may be stowed under the seats or in the racks overhead, but no one is allowed to have anything that will be an inconvenience to others in the same compartment. This rule is not rigidly enforced, as will often be seen; the old woman with six bandboxes and three bundles is as common in Europe as she was traditionally in America, and very often it is impossible for eight passengers to dispose of all their " traps " without holding some of them on their knees.

Railway fares are much higher on the eastern side of the Atlantic than on the western, and those of England are dearer than the fares on the Continent. The English fares are threepence, twopence, and one penny a mile for the respective classes; *i. e.*, about six cents, four cents, and two cents of American currency. In France the rate is calculated at twelve centimes, the kilometre which is equivalent to very nearly twenty centimes (four cents), the mile. This is for first-class; third-class is half the price of first-class, and second-class midway between the two. Italian fares are a trifle higher than those of France, while those of Belgium, Bavaria, Sweden, Norway, and Germany are lower. A rough calculation of the cost of travel by railway may be made by allowing four cents to the mile for first-class, and the corresponding rates for the other classes. Another mode of ready reckoning is to allow five francs (one dollar) per hour for the time required for transit from one city to another by first-class ordinary trains, and six francs an hour for the fast expresses. For example, the fare from Paris to Marseilles is one hundred and six francs, twenty centimes, and the distance is eight hundred and sixty-three kilometres, or five hundred and thirty-nine miles. There is a train called the " Rapide " that runs through in fifteen hours, and makes only eight stoppages; the ordinary express takes a trifle over twenty hours for the same journey, and the so-called " Directe " train requires twenty-three hours. The direct train contains carriages of the three classes, but the express and " Rapide " are exclusively first-class.

Any one who is curious in arithmetic can apply the rules given above, and will find that they bring the result near enough for rough estimates.

Return tickets are sold at various discounts from the full rates, generally about twenty-five per cent. less than the double fare. They are sometimes good only for the day of issue, but are usually available for two days, and in some countries for four or five. On some lines they do not issue return tickets for express trains, or for trains exclusively first-class. The holder of a return ticket (first-class) often feels that he is harshly treated when refused a place on a train of first-class coaches only, and if he cannot speak the language, it is impossible to make him comprehend the rules of the company.

Circular tickets are issued at a great reduction from the single fares, but they are subject to certain restrictions that go far toward counterbalancing the saving in money. A circular ticket is limited in time, according to the localities it covers; it may be available for only one week from the date, or it make be good for three months, or even longer. The journey can commence at any point of the route, but once begun it must be continued in the same direction, and on the route indicated, and if it is not completed within the time specified, no money will be returned for unused coupons. If the traveler halts at any intermediate station not indicated on the itinerary, he must pay his fare to the next indicated station on resuming his journey, and he is also required to have his ticket stamped by the proper official when he arrives at a station where he is to stop.

These circular tickets are highly popular, and have been the means of creating a great deal of travel by reason of their cheapness. A tourist who selects his route and finds a circular ticket that covers it will make a large saving over the single fares from one place to another. To illustrate: the writer once bought for one hundred francs a circular ticket (first-class) with the following itinerary: Paris, Vichy, Lyons, Grenoble, Aix-les-Bains, Culoz, Besançon, Dijon, Paris, with the option of returning from Grenoble by way of Lyons, Macon, and Dijon to Paris, instead of passing by Besançon and Dijon. The single fares from place to place would have aggregated something over two hundred francs for the journey. In many instances the saving by a circular ticket is considerably more than one-half.

The circular tickets issued by the railway companies should not be confounded with those sold by private individuals in London, Paris, New York, and other cities. The railway companies sell their own tickets at their own offices or agencies; it frequently happens that the most direct of the lines will have nothing to do with the "tourist agencies," so that those who patronize the latter establishments find that they are sent by roundabout ways from one great city to another.

At all the principal ticket-offices on the railway lines there is a table of fares near the window; it is printed in large letters and figures so that there is little chance of a mistake. And in most countries there is an additional security to the traveler; the fare is printed on the ticket in plain figures, so that the most laudable intentions of the seller to cheat the stranger may be frustrated, provided the latter knows enough to count his money.

In Northern Europe, especially in Russia, the carriages are warmed by stoves, though sometimes the first-class passengers are the only ones having the benefits of heat. In Central and Southern Europe long cylinders of sheet iron containing hot water are thrust into the compartments at intervals more or less regular; by means of these cylinders the traveler can keep his feet comfortable, and if the weather is not too frosty, they give all the heat to be desired in the compartment. In cold weather the railway traveler should be well provided with wraps, as the night air has a penetrating familiarity, especially when the wind is blowing.

Eating-rooms, or "buffets," are abundant, and generally good. The best are on the long lines where there is a large amount of through travel, so that a good patronage is secured, and the trains halt there at convenient hours for meals. The table d'hote system prevails, but there are always plenty of small tables where those who do not want a "square meal" can be accommodated. The price of a table d'hote breakfast varies from two francs, fifty centimes, to four francs, and that of a dinner from three francs to five francs, wine included. On most of the lines the keepers of the restaurants are required to post a notice in a conspicuous place, showing the prices of meals, so as to prevent any possible cheating; any complaint addressed to the management of the road is pretty certain to receive attention, as the companies are desirous of having the best possible service.

A table d'hote breakfast or dinner on the great lines, especially on the Paris, Lyon & Mediterranee, is the perfection of railway feeding, and the most rapid eater the world ever saw cannot complain of the dilatoriness of the waiters. The conductor generally telegraphs the number of passengers on the train, so that the restaurateur knows pretty nearly how many will patronize him; as the train rolls into the station, the first dish of the course is placed on the table, and you have only to drop into a chair and begin eating. Before you are through with the first course the second is at your side, and the third is there before you can possibly finish with the second. Thus the meal is served, and when it is near its end the cashier passes around and collects the stipulated money. The time allowed is from fifteen to thirty minutes; five minutes before the moment of starting, a bell rings or a gong is struck, or perhaps a horn in blown, and the signal is repeated four minutes later, and when you hear the second signal there is no more chance for delay, as the train, like time and tide, will wait for no man. The form of the signal, and also the period of giving it, are not the same in all countries, and the verdant traveler will do well to watch the motions of his neighbors, and be governed accordingly. The buffets are divided into the first, second, and third class at the great stations, and there are waiting-rooms with the same distinctions. In France the smaller stations are known as "stations," and the larger ones, especially at terminal points, are called "gares." "Bahnhof" in Germany, and "stazione" in Italy means the same as "station" in England and "depot" in the United States.

On some of the roads meals are served in baskets, so that they can be eaten while the train is in motion. An hour or more before you arrive at the restaurant station, the conductor, or some other employé of the company, takes your order for a breakfast or dinner according to a bill of fare which he presents. The order is telegraphed forward, and you are told to ask for a certain number, by which it has been indicated. When the train reaches the station a basket containing what you have ordered is handed in through the door of the compartment, and the train moves on. The baskets are specially made for the business, and contain compartments for everything needed in the meal, together with the inevitable bottle of wine. You eat at your leisure, and at a stopping place an hour further on the basket is removed and sent back to the place whence it came. The plan has certain merits, and likewise certain defects; to eat without hurry and without delay is certainly a great advantage, but it is not altogether comfortable to breakfast or dine from a wicker basket that rests on your knees, and it frequently happens that the pepper, salt, or some other necessary trifle, has been overlooked.

A private lunch-basket is as desirable on a European railway as on an American one, and may be stocked to suit the owner's taste. On a long journey provide yourself with a bottle of water, as there is no water-cooler on the train, and you might suffer from thirst without the means of alleviating it. The advocates of principles opposed to the total abstinence theories of Father Mathew will not forget their pocket-flasks with stimulating contents.

Measures of distance on the railways in the British Dominions are in English miles, as in America. In France, Switzerland, Italy, Spain, and Belgium, they are in kilometres; in Russia, in versts, and in Germany in German miles. The kilometer is five-eights of an English mile, and the verst very nearly the same; the German long mile equals five and three-fourths English miles, and the German short mile is about three and a half English. The rapid spread of the metric system of weights and measures will probably make the kilometer the unit of all railway distances on the Continent in the next decade. Trains are run by the time of the capitals of their respective countries, without regard to the longitude, and you will often find the local clocks a long way ahead or behind those of the railway station.

On arriving at a continental railway station there will be an abundance of porters to carry your hand-baggage to the hotel omnibuses that wait outside for passengers. You have only to indicate the name of your hotel and the

porter who takes charge of you will lead the way to its
carriage. You hand the receipt for your heavy baggage
to the porter, after depositing the light impedimenta in
the omnibus, and follow him to the *salle des bagages*, where
you have a period of waiting, more or less tedious. When
the trunks are ready for delivery you point out the pieces
which the porter has gathered according to the numbers
on them, and the formalities of the octroi begin.

The octroi is a continental institution, distinct from the
custom-house, but greatly resembling it, whereby every article of food or drink entering a city pays a tax. The officers of the octroi rarely request a traveler to open his
trunks, as they know very well he is not likely to transport mutton-chops, cheese, or wine, at the high rates
charged for railway luggage. But they are sure to ask
whether you have anything liable to the octroi, and when
you answer in the negative you may depart. The porter
mounts your impedimenta to the top of the omnibus, and
receives his fee—five cents for each heavy parcel, and
five or ten for all the light ones together—you take your
seat, and when all is ready you rattle away to the hotel.
There are plenty of cabs and two-horse carriages to be
had at the stations, if you do not wish an omnibus, but
they are more troublesome than the other vehicles in consequence of the acquisitive tendencies of the drivers, and
the stranger ignorant of the language had better reject
them. In some cities, notably in Berlin, you have no
choice in the selection of your carriage, but must take the
first that is offered. As the drivers come to the station
before the arrival of the train each of them hands to an
official a metal check bearing his number. These checks
are strung on a cane or rod, and when the train arrives
the rod is reversed, and the numbers come off in the order in which the cabbies presented themselves. The sys-

tem is a fair one for the drivers, but bad for the public, as it often happens that a party of three or four persons will find themselves assigned to a two-seated cab; in such case they must keep it, and if they cannot stow themselves into it somehow they can take an additional vehicle.

In most of the large cities of Europe the railway companies have an omnibus system not unlike that of the western cities of the United States. On arriving at the station you can engage an omnibus, if you happen to be three or more, and it is as much under your control as a private cab would be. These vehicles are of all sizes, carrying from four up to thirty-two persons, and there is a gallery on the top for baggage. You can telegraph ahead if you want to make sure of having an omnibus at the station; address your despatch to the *Chef de gare*, and say for how many persons you desire the omnibus.

These omnibusses are specially useful for family and other parties of three or more who are about leaving a city and are not stopping at a large hotel. Go to one of the company's agencies the day before, and say by what train you intend to leave and the number of your party, and the omnibus will be at your door at the proper time. The cost of a vehicle of this sort is less than for a carriage of the same capacity, and the printed tariff leaves no chance for a mistake.

CHAPTER XIII.

STEAMBOAT TRAVEL IN EUROPE.

Compared with the United States the continent of Europe has a small amount of inland navigation. Russia contains more rivers where steamers may run than all the rest of Europe, and until within a few years her steamboat interest was greater than that of her railways. The Rhine is the most important stream of Western Europe, and the Danube has the greatest navigable length of any river outside of Russia. The Danube has a serious impediment at the Iron Gates, where a succession of rapids and a channel full of rocks prevent the passage of boats. From the days of the Romans to the present there has been talk of a canal around the Iron Gates, and there are the remains to-day of a canal that was begun by one of the Roman emperors, but never completed. From the head of navigation at Ulm to its entrance into the Black Sea the Danube has a course of more than seventeen hundred miles, while the Rhine can only claim a navigable distance of less than five hundred. The Rhone and its tributary, the Saone, are classed as navigable streams, but their currents are so swift that their steamboat interest has never been an important one, on account of the great cost of making an ascending journey. Many of the smaller rivers of Europe are navigated by freight-boats only; as a general statement it is fair to say that the inland navigation available to the tourist is comprised in the Rhine and Danube rivers, and the Swiss and Italian lakes. In Russia he will find the Volga, the Don, and the Dneiper rivers worthy of attention, and, if he is on the lookout for more streams, he may venture on the Vistula, and one or two others of lesser consequence.

All the Swiss lakes are well equipped with steamboats, and the service is prompt enough to suit the most exacting. On the lake of Geneva, for example, there are half a dozen boats each way, daily, the whole length of the lake, some of them stopping at every landing, and others making only two or three halts. The boats are long and narrow, and present a most insignificant appearance when compared with the steamers of the Hudson and Mississippi; the after part is reserved for the first-class passengers, who can sit under an awning on deck, or retire to a cabin below. The second-class is forward, and in fine weather is preferable to the first, since the latter has all the benefit of the smoke and cinders as they blow aft. The boats on the Swiss lakes are for day service, and contain no sleeping-cabins, but there are sofas and couches on which an invalid may recline, provided the craft is not too much crowded. Meals are served *a la carte*, and sometimes at a fixed price; the latter are not to be recommended on the majority of the boats, though they are cheaper than meals *a la carte*.

Tickets are bought at the clerk's office, and the traveler is advised to visit that locality and settle his fare as soon as he goes on board. No receipts are given for baggage, and if there is an excessive amount it is charged for. There is an attaché of the boat who looks after the baggage—expecting a fee as a matter of course—but even with his watchfulness it behooves the stranger to keep an eye out for himself, or he may find on reaching his destination that his trunk has gone ashore by mistake at some other landing. In selecting a seat on deck take one on the side of the boat opposite the sun, so at to avoid the reflection on the water, and whenever you leave your seat for a moment put a satchel or some other article in it. Fashionable travelers on the Swiss lakes are not always respectful of the rights of others, and will drop into an eligible locality the moment it is vacated, even though they know your absence will be exceedingly brief.

The description of the Swiss steamers will apply in general terms to those of the Italian lakes. The boats are for day service only, and their models are very nearly those of the Swiss. Most of the attachés of the boats, especially the waiters in the cabin, speak French, and occasionally one may be found who can grapple with English. Some of the boats are much finer than others, and the traveler will do well to make enquiries before taking passage. When embarking at an intermediate landing buy a ticket immediately, or you may be charged for the whole distance from the steamer's starting point. This custom is not altogether unknown in other countries; there have even been occasions when it cost less to go from New York to Albany than to a point half-way between those cities, as many an individual can testify.

For a long time the steamers on the Rhine were of the model already described, and the accommodations for passengers were decidedly limited. But with the increase of travel there has been a great improvement, and now there is a line of " American steamboats " plying the river so famous for its crumbling castles and historic associations. The steamers of the American rivers have been taken as models for these boats, and some of them are finely fitted up and contain many features of real comfort. They are fast winning the favor of the Germans, and, of course, are patronized by Americans and English to the neglect of the old boats. The traveler should make sure of the name and character of a boat before buying his ticket and embarking, or he may find himself delegated to an antiquated tub, with limited accommodations and snail-like speed, when he had expected to be on a floating palace.

The tariff of fares is carefully arranged, and is posted at the window of each ticket-office, so that there can be no doubt as to the proper sum to be paid. In most instances tickets are sold at the offices on the docks, but it is well not to purchase at an intermediate landing until the boat is in sight; boats are liable to detention from various causes, and, if a tourist is in a hurry, he can take the railway, which follows the bank of the Rhine, or very near it, all the way from Dusseldorf to Mayence.

On the Rhine steamers meals are served *a la carte* and at fixed prices, but there has been a tendency of late years to abolish the fixed-price system and serve only *a la carte*. On most of the boats there is a table d'hote breakfast or dinner at certain hours, and a notice thereof is given by the ringing of a bell. The waiters are fond of delaying the collection of a passenger's bill till just as he is going on shore; by so doing they have a better chance of imposing on him than when his memory is quite fresh as to the items with which he can be properly charged.

Baggage is not checked unless an extra price is paid, but there is a free allowance of one hundred pounds for each passenger. The charge for guaranteeing the safety of baggage varies from two to ten cents a parcel, according to its size and estimated value; when this amount is paid the company is responsible for loss, and will indemnify the owner according to a fixed tariff. Everything goes by tariff on the Rhine, except the fees to the waiters, and the current of the river, and the wind.

On the Upper Danube, from Ulm to Linz, and from Linz to Vienna, the steamers are small and the accommodations limited, but on the lower part of the stream there is a different state of affairs. The Danube Steam Navigation Company has some large boats elegantly fitted up, and though they are deficient in several things they remind the American of home. The sleeping accommodations are rather limited, as there is only a common cabin with two or three tiers of berths, unless a high price extra is paid for a private room. The dining-saloon is airy and well lighted, and the table generally excellent. There are two, and sometimes three, classes of steamers; the fastest is the "Accelerated," which makes only the few principal landings, and leaves the other boats to perform the details of the service. On the "Accelerated" boats meals are included in the fare, and the payment for them is compulsory, while on the other steamers the traveler pays only his passage, and the meals are an extra that he may take or leave alone. There is a Hungarian line with its headquarters at Pesth, and on the lower part of the Danube there is a Turkish line that has periodical fits of suspension, and once in a while disappears for months at a time. There is a considerable amount of travel between Central Europe and Constantinople by the Danube route; a traveler from Vienna goes as far as Rustchuk by the river, and then proceeds (in about eight hours) to Varna by rail. From Varna is a run of fourteen hours by steamship through the Black Sea, and down the Bosphorus, till the domes of Saint Sophia's Mosque rise to view.

The steamers on the Russian inland waters leave much to be desired in the way of personal comforts, and the most that can be said of them is that they are better than no steamers at all. On some of the rivers, especially on the Volga, there are some boats that are fairly equipped, but the cooking is not the best in the world, and the passenger must expect to do a good deal of roughing it. The first-class travel is not sufficient to pay for anything like a good service and liberal table, and if one is on the hunt for luxuries he will keep away from the steamboat service in the land of the Czar.

On the Siberian lakes and rivers there is a steamboat service of very limited character. The great rivers, with the exception of the Amoor, flow into the Arctic Ocean, and consequently their only business is a local one. There are only two or three steamers on the Obi, and the same number on the Yenesei; the commerce of the Amoor maintains from twenty to twenty-five steamboats, and there are less than half a dozen on Lake Baikal and its outlet, the Angara. All these steamers are small, compared with American boats, and their accommodations leave much to be desired. The first cabin is usually an open room, with wide sofas running all around it, and on these sofas the traveler makes his couch with his own bed-clothing, none being provided by the boat. The ticket does not include food, and the table is supplied by the captain, at an expense of about a dollar a day for each passenger. A traveler across Siberia must expect hard fare and poor accommodations, and find the compensation for his privations in the novel scenes the journey affords.

CHAPTER XIV.

SEA-GOING STEAMERS IN EUROPEAN WATERS.

The name of steam lines in the waters adjacent to Europe is more than legion, and the enumeration of them would occupy several pages of this volume. Bradshaw's Continental Railway and Steamboat Guide contains a list of these lines, corrected from month to month, according to the changes that have occurred; the information is conveyed in skeleton form something like the following:

"Malta to Tripoli.—By a French steamer, three times a month. Twenty-two hours. First-class (including food), £2, 8s."

"London to Honfleur.—The Villa de Lisbon and the Villa de Paris twice a week."

All the great steamship companies issue pamphlets (gratuitously) containing the information needed by travelers. These can be obtained by writing to the office of the company, or by personal application, and it is advisable for a traveler who expects to wander away from *terra firma* to provide himself with a stock of these documents. They are of essential advantage in laying out a route, and by a little study a tourist may often save much time and money. Take the following as an illustration:—

In 1873 the writer was at Vienna to attend the great exhibition of that year. At the close of the affair he projected a journey to Syria, Palestine, and Egypt, and persuaded a friend to accompany him; the time of each was limited, and it was desirable to make the trip as expeditiously as possible consistent with doing it thoroughly. Information concerning the facilities of eastern travel was difficult to obtain, and it was concluded to postpone final arrangements until reaching Constantinople. There were three companies engaged in navigating the waters of the Levant, but no one of them would give the least information about another. "You can buy a through ticket by our line," said the agent of each, "and then you may stop over at each port till the next ship of our company comes along." This seemed fair enough, and is what is done by the majority of tourists, but it was thought possible to improve on the plan.

The handbooks of the companies, French, Austrian, and Russian, were obtained, and with these books before them the twain sat down one evening in the hotel. It required a couple of hours to arrange a route, but by dint of hard work it was accomplished. The result was something like the following:—

Leave Constantinople by Austrian Lloyd steamer of the —th, and go to Syra, one of the Greek Islands. There connect with a steamer of the same company for Athens.

Spend eight days in and around Athens, and return to Syra by an Austrian Lloyd ship.

Spend a day at Syra, and then take the fortnightly French steamer for Beyrout. It stops two days at Smyrna, and part of a day at each of half a dozen points including Rhodes, Alexandretta, and Latakieh, so that a fair view of those places can be had.

Eight days after the arrival of the French steamer at Beyrout, an Austrian one will touch there. This time will suffice for a journey to Baalbeck, and Damascus, and the return to Beyrout, so as to catch the Austrian steamer, and proceed to Jaffa, the port of Jerusalem.

Eleven days later a Russian steamer will touch at Jaffa, on her way to Egypt. Eleven days will be enough for Jerusalem, Bethlehem, the Dead Sea, and the river Jordan, together with the return to Jaffa, to catch this Russian steamer.

The plan was carried out to the letter. There was plenty of time for seeing everything, and no loss in waiting for ships in the different ports, save in a single instance that had no serious consequences. The scheme had a decided advantage over the ordinary plan of buying a ticket by a single line, and depending only on the ships of that line. In the latter instance you are compelled to wait for a fixed period, while by traveling independently, and knowing the movements of all the ships serving the ports in which you are interested, there is often a material saving of time.

In addition to the regular lines, there are many independent steamers trading along the coast of the Mediterranean and through the north seas, and by scanning the advertisements, or enquiring at the steamship offices, the traveler will often find something decidedly to his advantage. For example, the writer was once in Singapore, at the Straits of Malacca, intending to go to Java. There is a steamer once a week from Singapore to Batavia, the capital of Java, and the vessel for that particular week was a French one that had only sixteen berths in her cabin; it was whispered around the hotel that she would be terribly overcrowded, as she had nearly fifty passengers booked, and perhaps more. By enquiring at the shipping offices it was ascertained that a Dutch steamer had been at Singapore for repair, and would return the same day and hour as the French one, but she had not been advertised, and nothing would have been known of her in the ordinary way. The writer and his friend secured passage on the Dutch steamer, and had a pleasant voyage; she had the same accommodations as the French ship, and only seven persons to occupy them, while the latter had fifty-two! They were packed somewhat after the manner of sardines in a can, and had a hard time of it, while every passenger on the Dutch ship had a room to himself, and all the space he wanted at the dinner table.

The rules and regulations on the steamers in and around European waters vary somewhat, according to the nationalities of the companies. The American traveler will run across what will be to him a curious custom, on some of the Mediterranean lines; the supplying of food, and the service of the table generally is not undertaken by the company, but is leased or farmed out, the same as a hotel-keeper in New York leases the space for a cigar or newspaper stand. The consequence is that the table will vary considerably on different ships of the same company, in proportion as the steward is liberal or the reverse. It also happens frequently that the captain and steward are not on friendly terms, as the latter does not run the table in accordance with the ideas of the former; the steward is not responsible to the captain, and cannot be removed by him, and as long as the contract is a favorable one for the company, and the passengers make no complaint, the managers of the concern are likely to uphold the steward as against the captain. On most of the French and Italian lines it is useless to make any complaint to the captain concerning the table, and the steward will laugh at you for so doing. But if you write your objections in the official complaint book, the situation is changed at once.

This matter requires a little explanation. On all Italian mail steamers, and on some of the French and Austrian ones, there is a book accessible to the passengers for the express purpose of receiving their complaints. The pages are numbered consecutively, and they are stamped by the chief maritime officer of the port where the ship is registered, and at the completion of every voyage the book goes to that functionary for examination. If there is any complaint it is investigated, and receives the proper punishment, at least such is the general belief. The service of the table of an Italian steamer has been changed from bad to good by the mere threat of writing a complaint, and on one occasion, when the matter had been written out, the captain and officers subsequently begged the complaining passenger to add a postscript to the effect that the cause of his growl had been removed, and he was willing to withdraw his remarks. They had bestirred themselves to make things pleasant, and so he complied with their request, but not till the steamer was in sight of port, lest their vigilance might relax. It is a pity that the same system is not in vogue on some of the trans-Atlantic steamers, as it would have a good effect now and then on the discipline of the servants.

One great inconvenience of travel in the Mediterranean, and also at many ports on the eastern and northern coast of the Continent of Europe, is the necessity of landing or embarking in row-boats. The boats are rarely supplied by the company owning the steamers, but must be secured by the passenger, and as the boatmen are rapacious, and more or less dishonest (generally more), the negotiations are not pleasant. Besides it is no joke when the sea is rough, and the distance long, to be tossed in a skiff between shore and steamer, or steamer and shore, especially if one is inclined to sea-sickness, and not over-confident in the safety of the craft that carries him. The operation of landing or embarking when the waves are tossing, has an element of risk about it, and many a person has been dropped into the water in stepping from a skiff to the gangway stairs, or from stairs to skiff. The steamship companies shirk the responsibility of transfers in harbors where they connect with ships of their own lines; in the voyage just mentioned, from Constantinople to Syra, and from Syra to Athens, the tickets were purchased through from the Golden Horn to the Piraeus, but on reaching Syra the party was told it must pay its own expense for transferring to the branch vessel that was waiting for them. Gouty, feeble, and timid persons are warned that a tour of the Mediterranean is not to be undertaken lightly, by reason of this impossibility of landing directly at a dock. Of all the ports of the Mediterranean there are not half a dozen where the steamers lie at docks, so as to render the small boat unnecessary.

For general advice concerning the business of going down to the sea in ships, the reader is referred to a previous section of this volume. The precautions against sea-sickness are as good (or as useless) in the one case as the other, and the stewards and other employés of the ship are much alike, whatever their nationality. On the French, Italian, and Austrian steamers, the chief steward has the assignment of rooms instead of the purser; the latter functionary is rarely seen by the passenger, and is supposed to be busy with his accounts of the freight. Consequently the chief steward is the proper personage to evince any friendly disposition for, and he is generally open to arguments of a financial character. A five-franc piece will render him attentive, for ten francs he is obsequious, and for twenty he may possibly harbor the proposal to throw the captain overboard, and put you in chief command.

For parties containing ladies it is well to remember that English, French, or Austrian steamers on the Mediterra nean and Black Sea lines, are preferable to other nationalities, as they generally carry stewardesses, while the others do not. There are exceptions to this rule on some of the Italian ships on long voyages, but they are decidedly rare. In the matter of cleanliness, the various nationalities may be ranged in the following order:—English, French, Austrian, Russian, Italian, Spanish, Greek.

The Turkish and Egyptian steamers are hardly worth including in the list as they have at best very poor accommodations for occidentals of the sterner sex, while they are totally unfit for ladies to travel on.

In Northern Europe the German, Dutch, Swedish, Norwegian, and Russian ships are pretty nearly alike, and if there is any difference it is in the order named. All the northern nations are good sailors, and the captains are competent navigators; the Latin races are less reliable in this respect than the Teutons and their kindred, and the Orientals are the worst of all. Of the Latins the French are the best, and especially those from Marseilles and its vicinity. The Italians were once hardy navigators, and the mariners of Genoa, Venice, and other maritime cities of Italy have a noble record; but in these latter days they have degenerated very seriously, and their triumphs on the sea are not of great renown. The best of Italian seamen and sailors come from Genoa, Sardinia, and Corsica,—the latter, though belonging to France, may be classed as Italian, since the people are of that lineage and speak the language of the peninsula. In the same way the Austrian Lloyd steamers belong properly to the Italian classification, since Trieste, the headquarters of the company, is essentially Italian, and it is not unusual to find captains and other officers of the company who speak no other language, although German is the tongue of the country under whose flag they sail.

The Spanish sailors are a sad travesty on the men that four hundred years ago traversed the Atlantic with Columbus, and during the three following centuries made the Spanish name respected and feared on the seas all over the globe. A Spanish steamer generally abounds in fleas and dirt, and the cuisine leaves much to be desired; if you call the attention of the steward to creeping or jumping things in the berths he will gravely inform you that such a thing was never known before on the ship and you must have brought it on board when you embarked.

The Turk is too much a fatalist to be a good sailor. He is not deficient in bravery or intelligence, but in a place of peril he is very apt to fold his arms and say "Inshallah" (God wills it), and let events shape themselves. Therefore it is well to avoid a Turkish or Egyptian ship whenever another nationality can be found, not only on the score of cleanliness already mentioned, but on that of safety.

CHAPTER XV.

SEA AND OCEAN STEAMERS IN VARIOUS PARTS OF THE WORLD.

There is now hardly any part of the world touched by salt water that cannot be reached by steamer; wherever there is sufficient commerce to give promise of remuneration a steam line is sure to be established. Most of the European governments support lines of steamers by subsidies in the shape of mail contracts; in this way they have built up a mercantile marine, comprising thousands of ships that plow the waves in all directions and spread their flags wherever the breezes blow. Commerce has been developed by the steamship, and one after another the subsidized lines have created a trade that has enabled them to take care of themselves, or will thus enable them as the years roll on. The steamer is one of the links to unite the nations, and the familiar intercourse that it creates is a sure promotor of universal peace.

Of transatlantic lines there are many; it is impossible to give the exact number for the reason that new ones may be created or old ones suspended during the time this volume is passing through the press. On the American coast the ports of Montreal, Quebec, Halifax, Portland, Boston, New York, Philadelphia, Baltimore, Charleston, Savannah, and New Orleans are served by transatlantic steam lines; New York alone has a dozen (roughly stated) and several of the others have each two or three. The ports on the other side of the Atlantic that are thus connected with the United States are Liverpool, London, Glasgow, Belfast, Bristol, Hull, Southampton, Hamburg, Bremen, Rotterdam, Antwerp, Havre, and Bordeaux. The Liverpool steamers touch at Queenstown, both going and returning, so that the latter port has an almost daily communication with America by steam without herself owning a single ship. There are lines between New York and the ports of the Mediterranean, with a service more or less regular. In the fruit season there is more activity in their movements, and their numbers are greater than when the oranges have ceased to be gathered and the lemon has been squeezed. Occasionally there is a steamer for ports on the Baltic, and not many years ago there was a line to Stettin and another to Amsterdam. They may be revived any day, and new lines may come into existence while yet we are talking about them.

Thus far there are no regular lines of steamers between the Atlantic coast of the United States and the ports of Asia. One of the New York and Liverpool companies has a line to Bombay and can send passengers and freight all the way by its own ships, with a transfer in Liverpool. In the tea season steamers come from China to New York by way of the Suez Canal, bringing cargoes of the herb that forms our breakfast beverage, but they do not return by the way they came; from China to New York they make a direct voyage, but on the return journey to the Land of the Celestials they take cargoes for Liverpool, London, or any other port that offers. Most of these ships are specially designed for freighting purposes, and their passenger accommodations are limited; some of them are noted for their speed, though they rarely make as rapid progress as the crack vessels of the transatlantic lines.

The great majority of the steam lines everywhere are under the English flag; of the transatlantic companies only one is American, but not all of its ships are of American build. Of the two great companies that connect Europe with the far East one is French and the other English; there are two smaller companies connecting England with China, both of them English, and there are occasional irregular ships, all of the same nationality. Without attempting statistical exactness it is safe to say that of the ocean steamers that link the different parts of the world together at least nine out of every ten are British.

We have already glanced at the steamship service in waters adjacent to Europe; let us now look away to the East.

There is an average of fully four steamers a week from Europe to Alexandria, Egypt, and in the winter season the number is greater. The lines are English, French, Austrian, and Italian, with a semi-monthly Russian and an occasional craft of some other nationality. Some of these steamers end their journey at Alexandria and return thence to Europe, while others proceed to Asia by way of the Suez Canal. The steamers touching at Alexandria form but a small part of those that use the Suez Canal; the traffic through that artificial highway has steadily increased, from year to year, until it now amounts to 120 ships a month, or four per day. Nearly all the craft that pass through the Canal are steamers, as it has not been found profitable for sailing ships to make the voyage up or down the Red Sea, with its treacherous winds and dangerous navigation. It is probable that within the next decade the number of steamers passing the Canal will be not less than 200 per month, and many persons familiar with the subject predict an increase still greater.

From Suez the steamers follow the narrow track of the Red Sea, where the sun pours down its pitiless rays and causes the panting traveler to absorb copiously of beverages that cool if they do not inebriate. From the Straits of Bab-el-Mandel (Gate of Tears) the routes diverge; one tends northward and eastward to the Persian Gulf and the rivers that flow into it, while another heads almost due east to Bombay. The route of the Persian Gulf is served by an English company, while that of Bombay can boast of three or four English lines, an Austrian line, and an Italian one, not to mention the many irregular steamers on the hunt for chance cargoes and passengers. A hundred miles from the entrance of the Red Sea is the verdureless Rock of Aden, where British enterprise has established a port and coaling station. Most of the regular lines make a halt there, and it has been found in practice that Aden is an important point of divergence. Some of the English companies have a service down the east coast of Africa as far as the Cape of Good Hope, and the French have a line to Seychelles, Mauritius, and Reunion.

The majority of the steamers going east from Aden head for Pointe de Galle, at the southern extremity of Ceylon. Here they diverge again, some going to Calcutta, some to Australia, around its southern coast, a few to Burmah, and the rest to Singapore, at the Straits of Malacca.

From Singapore there are various routes for the ships that have followed each other from Pointe de Galle. Northward go some to the capital of Siam, less northerly others to Cochin China, and others to Hong Kong, Shanghai, Yokohama, and the different ports of the Celestial Empire, and the Land of the Mikado. Others turn southward from Singapore to Java, and there is a line between Singapore and Australia, by way of Java and Torres

Straits, following the northern coast of the great island instead of its southern one. Irregular ships go to Borneo and around Sumatra, and there is a Spanish line that unites Singapore with the Phillipine Islands.

From Japan and China to Europe there is a regular mail service each way once a week, and the arrivals and departures can be relied upon very nearly like those of railway trains. One week it is performed by the French steamers, and the next by the English, and so it goes on, from the year's beginning to the year's ending. The smaller lines of steamers add materially to the opportunities for a traveler between Europe and the far East, and it may be fairly stated that at all times of the year there are two steamers a week each way, while during the tea season there are double that number. When the new crop of teas comes in there is generally a race between two or more steamers from China to London; the shortest passage thus far recorded was made in thirty-seven days from Shanghai to the docks at London by one of these tea steamers, and her competitor was only a few hours behind her.

An English company skirts the coast of India and Ceylon from Bombay to Calcutta with weekly steamers each way; it sends its ships northward from Bombay to Kurrachee, Bushire, and up the Tigris as far as Bagdad, and from Calcutta it sends them to Burmah, the Straits of Malacca, and Singapore. There is a Chinese line from Rangoon to Singapore, touching the principal ports of Burmah and the Straits, and there is a Chinese line and a Siamese one also, connecting Singapore with Bangkok every four or five days. The Dutch owners of Java have a line from Amsterdam to Batavia twice a month each way, touching Gibraltar, Naples, and Suez, and they have several lines around the Java seas, to communicate with the Spice Islands, and enable them to keep a watchful eye over their possessions. About once a month they send a steamer to Melbourne and Sidney by way of Torres Straits, and they send a ship every week around the coast of Sumatra. The coast of China is well served by English lines, and in the last few years by a Chinese one, composed of ships purchased of foreigners. In the same way there is a Japanese company that navigates the waters around the Mikado's Empire, aud also connects the Japanese ports with Shanghai and Hong Kong. The Yang-tse, the great river of China, is navigated by a Chinese company and an English one, the former being equipped with steamers built in the United States, and the latter with boats constructed in England, after the American model.

The ports of Australia and New Zealand are connected by local lines, and there are two or more lines of steamers that ply between Australia and England; from England to Australia the route is by the Cape of Good Hope, but on the return voyage the ships go through the Suez Canal, in consequence of the peculiar course of the trade-winds. On their outward passage they touch at the Cape of Good Hope, and thus come in competition with the lines that have been established between England and South Africa. The regular service is weekly, and performed by two companies, making alternate departures.

Coming back to Europe, we will turn our eyes toward the west once more. There is an English line running to the West Indies, touching the principal ports as far as Aspinwall, where they connect with the steamers of another English line from Panama to the Straits of Magellan. Three French lines perform nearly a similar service, one going from Saint Nazaire to Aspinwall, a second from Saint Nazaire to Vera Cruz, and a third from Havre and Bordeaux to Aspinwall. All these lines touch at ports on the way, and one of them has a branch to Cayenne; the departures each way in each direction are monthly, while that of the English one is fortnightly. Another French line goes to Brazil and La Plata, touching at the French colony of Senegal, on the African coast, and there are two Italian lines from Naples and Genoa that cover the same route, but without visiting Senegal. There are two other French lines to the east coast of South America, and two or three English ones, so that the traveler in either direction will have plenty of ships to choose from. Then there are local lines all along the coast, and there is an English line through the Straits of Magellan, and up the west coast of South America as far as Callao, not to be confounded with the one already mentioned from Panama southward. Besides these there is a Spanish company plying between Cadiz and Havana, and a Portuguese one from Lisbon to Brazil.

We have almost girdled the world in our observations of steamships, and may now return to New York. The advertising columns of the leading dailies will tell all about the numerous local lines that skirt our coast as far South as Vera Cruz and Aspinwall, and they may or may not tell us of a line from New York to Rio Janeiro flying the American flag. Several lines of this kind have been established, but they have never been of long duration, as the cost of maintaining them is greater than the receipts, and the United States government refuses to adopt the English policy of sustaining steam lines by permanent mail contracts. As this page is being written such a line is in full operation; its permanency is to be most devoutly hoped, but hopes will not always pay the expense of running a steamship. An English line connects New York with Brazil, but does it in a roundabout way; the steamers go from England to Brazil, carrying cargoes of English manufactures, thence they take cargoes of coffee and other South American produce to New York, and at the latter port they load for home with whatever freight is offering.

Between San Francisco and Japan and China there are two lines of steamers; both are under American management, and the ships of one are of American build while those of the other are leased from English owners. The service is semi-monthly, divided between the two companies, and the broad Pacific is traversed in about twenty days. There is a coasting line from San Francisco to Panama, and there are two coast lines going north to Oregon and British Columbia. An American line runs from San Francisco once a month to the Sandwich Islands, and the Feejees to New Zealand, and there connects with the local steamers to Australia.

Here we are at the point we reached by steamer from Europe, and may pause awhile to consider other matters. We have seen the North Star and the Southern Cross, the pine and palm; blasts from high latitudes have chilled our limbs, and we have been faint and suffering under the terrible heat of the equator. But our tireless steamer bears us on and on, indifferent whether it breathes the airs of the tropics or the poles; its pulseless limbs are never wearied so long as we supply its digestive and respiratory organs with their needed aliments. The steamer has destroyed the poetry of the ocean, but it has been a material force in bringing peace on earth and good will to men.

CHAPTER XVI.

BY STAGE-COACH, DILIGENCE, AND POST.

The world moves rapidly, and the greater part of its motion, from a traveler's point of view, is by steam. On land and on sea the steam engine is the great propelling force; the railway train has usurped the place of the stage-coach and diligence, and the white wings of the sailing ship have been shrouded by the smoke of the steamer's funnel. The sailing ship and the stage-coach still exist, but their importance is gone, and, from present indications, there is no likelihood that they will ever return to their former greatness. On a few routes in England coaching has been revived, but only as an amusement, and there is no prospect that it will gain more than a slender patronage. The sailing ship is not a remunerative possession in competition with the steamer, and the persons who take passage in it wherever there is opportunity for the more expeditious form of travel are few and far between.

Before the general adoption of the railway in the United States, the mail-coach was in the height of its glory; all over the settled portion of the country the crack of the driver's whip resounded, and the vehicle, gaudy with paint, and dusty with what it had gathered from the road, was the admiration of all who saw it. The veterans who guided these conveyances were famous in their line as victorious generals, and it was the proud ambition of many a noble youth to be a first-class stage-driver on a great route. Early in the century, and down to 1840, the triumphs of these jehus were mainly in the Atlantic States and over the Alleghanies, but with the extension of the railway, the stage-coach became a star of empire, and took its course westward. The last great route of the stage-coach was covered by the completion of the Pacific Railway, and now its services are confined to localities that have not been reached by the iron horse.

The Pacific States have several important stage lines of a local character, and some of them have acquired a national reputation. Every visitor to California can tell about the drive to the Geysers, or the road to the Yosemite Valley, where teams of six and eight horses are driven at full speed around sharp turns, and a mishap might send coach and passengers whirling a thousand feet down the mountain side. Those who have journeyed north from California to Oregon are familiar with the mountain ride of three hundred miles between the termini of the railways of the two states, and there are several interior places of importance where the railway has not yet penetrated. The newer states and territories have a considerable number of stage routes in operation, and in the summer season the whip of the stage-driver is heard among the mountains of the eastern states, and in other pleasure-resorts where the denizen of the city seeks coolness and relaxation.

For traveling by stage-coach in America the preparations are not numerous. If the journey is to be one of several days you will need a strong constitution, as the luxuries of a palace-car, or an ocean steamship, are not to be found on the horse-propelled vehicle. Have a suit of clothes as near the color of dust as possible, and, if your sex is masculine, cut your hair and beard so that your head will resemble that of a pugilist, or the back of a bull-dog. C_y very little baggage, the least you can possibly get along with, and don't keep it where it will get in your way. Find a rear seat in the coach, and, if in winter, try to have it on the side favored by the sun. Of course you will try for a corner seat, and, if you get it, you will be all right. These things accomplished, resign yourself to fate and the care of the driver.

On a long ride by stage-coach you will naturally wonder how you are to sleep. For the first twenty-four hours you have a hard time of it, and your first night's sleep will be principally made up of wakefulness. But Nature will assert herself; the second night is quite comfortable, while on the succeeding nights you find yourself sleeping as well as in your bed at home, at least so far as obtaining relief from weariness is concerned. If you have never tried it you will be astonished to find how little you are fatigued after a ride of five or ten days.

In regions where there are highwaymen, facetiously termed "road agents" by the Californians, carry as little money as possible, and leave your valuable gold watch behind. You may have a revolver if you like, but it is generally of very little use, as the robbers come on you in such numbers, or under such circumstances, that your weapons cannot be employed. Generally the first intimation of their presence is the protrusion of several rifles or pistols into the windows of the coach, with a request, more or less polite, for you to hand over your valuables. When you have no alternative but to hand over, do so with alacrity, and lead your assailants to think it the happiest moment of your life. If you are compelled, as often happens, to step outside the vehicle and hold your hands in the air while standing in line with the other passengers, try and hold them a little higher, and be more in line, than anybody else. Where resistance is useless do not make the least attempt to oppose your uninvited interviewers, as they are a fastidious set of gentlemen, and regard with suspicion any movement of your hand towards your hip-pocket. The traveler who accepts the situation, and conducts himself philosophically under such circumstances, runs very little risk of bodily harm; the robbers are after his valuables and not his life, as it is not the least use to them, and they are unwilling to take it except in self-defense, or to aid their search for his personal property.

American highwaymen have not yet learned the art of carrying travelers away and holding them for ransom. This accomplishment is of Italian origin, and flourishes in Italy, Sicily, and other parts of Southern Europe. It was introduced into Mexico by the Italian emigrants who went there with Maximilian, and prevails to some extent in South America.

Accidents on stage-coaches are much more rare than one might expect when the occasional badness of the roads and the apparently reckless driving are considered. The fact is the driving is more reckless in appearance than in reality; the stage companies generally employ men who understand their business, though they may not be altogether Chesterfieldian in their manners. If you have any doubts as to the merits of the man who is to conduct you they can be generally settled by consultation with the agents of the company; the story they tell you may not be true, but there will be a vast amount of comfort in it.

A great many stories, mostly apochryphal, are told of stage accidents in the far west. One is to the effect that a driver once informed a timid traveler that nobody was ever hurt on his stage, though a good many had been killed. The stranger naturally asked an explanation, and received the following:

"There used to be a good many accidents," said he, "and lots of people were killed or wounded. The killed ones didn't make any fuss; the company just settled with their relatives, and that was the end of it, but them that was hurt made a good deal of trouble. They were always bringing suits for damages for large amounts, and generally getting 'em, and so I made up my mind to put a stop to it. When we have an accident nowadays I just take a linch-pin and go round and finish up all the wounded ones, and we find things going on much better."

For a short ride in good weather an outside seat is preferable, especially where there is fine scenery along the route. The place by the driver is usually the post of honor, and if that worthy is talkative, as he generally is, a good deal of information can be gleaned from him. He is usually unaffected by temperance principles, and a pull at a flask will serve to loosen the cords of his tongue.

The American coaches are of varied size and construction, according to the character of the roads where they are used. The old-fashioned stage-coach usually had a capacity for carrying twenty-one passengers, twelve inside and nine out, and was suspended on leathern braces. The form is still retained in the so-called Troy coaches and Concord coaches, but in many vehicles steel springs have taken the place of leather. A form of coach largely used in the far west is the "mud-wagon," which can traverse routes impassable for the larger and heavier carriage, and is specially preferred where the roads are bad. On some of the California routes, when the roads are moulting in the spring, there is often a depth of several inches of mud, and only the lightest vehicles can pass through it.

The diligence in Europe corresponds to the stage-coach in America; like the latter it has seen its sphere diminished by the construction of railways, and like it, too, it reflects the institutions of the countries where it exists. On the American coach there is no distinction; all seats have an equal price, and the first-comer has the choice. On the diligence there are grades and classes, and the seats are numbered and reserved like those of a theatre. The most costly places are in the *coupé*, which is beneath the driver's seat, and has windows in front above the level of the horses' backs; then comes the *banquette*, which is behind the driver, and is an excellent spot in fine weather, but disagreeable in a storm. The *interieur*, as its names implies, is an inside affair, and affords very little view of the road, and the *rotonde* is at the back of the *banquette*, and cheapest of all, as it is also the poorest. Particular places may be secured for days ahead; on some of the Swiss diligences you may take your place thirty days in advance by payment at the office, or by enclosing the price of the fare with your card and a memorandum of the day and hour of departure.

Diligences are in use all over Europe to reach towns and villages that are not accessible by rail. Their fares are regulated by government, and the hours of departure and arrival may be relied upon as exactly as those of railway trains. At present the greatest country of diligences is Switzerland; they are to be found on many roads of that mountainous region, and on some routes they have a heavy patronage. Between Geneva and Chamouny, a distance of about fifty miles, there are sometimes a dozen diligences each way daily in summer, all of them filled with passengers. The diligences on this route are a solution of the problem, often declared impossible by American stage-drivers, of making a coach where all the seats are outside ones. The body of the vehicle contains the baggage, and the seats are in rows on the top, over which an awning is spread. The only exceptions to the rule of putting all the seats outside is in the *coupé*, which commands a higher price than the *banquette*, but in fair weather is far less desirable. The old-fashioned diligence with *coupé, interieur, banquette*, and *rotonde*, is not much used on pleasure-routes, as very few of the seats are desirable for tourists.

For a long journey the *coupé* is the most comfortable part of the diligence; it contains three and sometimes four seats, but one or two persons may secure it by paying for the whole space. The French in Algeria have introduced the diligence, and the writer has pleasant recollections of some night rides in a capacious *coupé*, while journeying with a friend to and from the Desert of Sahara. The *coupé* or any other part of the vehicle, once engaged, it cannot be invaded by any other person, and not even a Prince, Grand Duke, or any other titled individual would dream of taking it from you.

Posting is still in vogue in some parts of Europe, especially in Russia. Where the system exists it is under control of government, and the supervision is usually pretty strict. One may travel by post in many parts of Switzerland; he may have his own carriage or he can hire one from the government or from a private individual. One hour's notice is required for hiring a conveyance of this sort, and the changes at the relay stations generally take from 15 to 30 minutes. As in stage coaching, or any other travel by horse-power, the less baggage you have the better.

The country *par excellence* of posting is the Asiatic portion of Russia, commonly called Siberia. European Russia was formerly traversed by post routes, but the construction of railways has caused most of them to be discontinued. In Siberia there are as yet no railways, the country is large and the roads are excellent. All these conditions are favorable to the posting system, and by means of it you may travel from the Ural mountains to the Sea of Okhotsk without a break. The writer once journeyed by post from the head of navigation on the Amoor River, in Siberia, to Nijne Novgorod, in European Russia, a distance of nearly five thousand miles. Fourteen hundred miles of this was accomplished in a wheeled carriage (called a *tarantass*) and 3,600 in a sleigh. A brief account of this journey will describe the Russian posting system.

The first requisite for the road is a *Padarojnia*, or road pass, which is issued by the government authorities, and without it no one can pass a single station of the route or obtain horses. The document states the name, residence, and destination of the bearer, the number of horses to which he is entitled, and the grade of his pass. There are three grades of road passes, the first for government couriers and high officials, the second for lesser lights in the official firmament, or for distinguished civilians, and the third for the common civilian. Horses are kept waiting for the first, and are generally forthcoming for the second, but the holder of a third class Padarojnia will often wait for hours before he can be supplied, unless he is willing to pay an extra fee to the station master for expeditious service.

Baggage must be in flat and broad valises of soft leather, and all hard boxes and square parcels should be thrown away at the start. These broad valises, or *chemidans*, are spread on the bottom of the vehicle; straw or hay is laid over them and the whole is covered with a heavy coarse quilt. You sit, recline, or lie at full length on this soft flooring; no seats are in the vehicle, and one very soon learns that he is far better off without them. A couple of thick and strong pillows are necessary to hold you in your corner and save you from the frequent thumps you would otherwise receive.

You can travel in the vehicle (*telega*) belonging to the government stations, but in this event you must change at every station, a performance that speedily becomes a nuisance, especially in a cold night. It is best to hire a tarantass to be taken through, or, if you cannot hire one, you had better purchase it outright and sell for what you can get at the end of the journey. The tarantass is mounted on a pair of stout and flexible poles that serve as springs, and sometimes they are so long that the two axles are at least twelve feet apart. It has a hood like an old-fashioned chaise, and is equipped with a boot and an apron, so that it can be quite shut in at night or in a storm.

To protect him from the cold the writer had a suit of thick clothing, covered with a sheepskin coat that buttoned tight around the neck and descended to the ankles. Over this he had a deerskin coat with the hair outside; it reached to his heels, trailing like a lady's dress when he walked, and was large enough inside for a man and a boy. The collar was a foot wide, and the sleeves were six inches longer than the wearer's arms; they were very inconvenient when he wanted to pick up anything, and when the collar was turned up and brought around in front it suggested the idea of a man without a head. For wraps he had a robe made of nine sheepskins, sewed together and backed with heavy felting; the robe was about three yards square and as impervious to cold as the side of an ordinary house. Then he had a fur cap fitting close to the head, fur gloves for his hands, and a mitten of sable skin for his nose. He discarded the ordinary boot of civilization and wore, over his ordinary socks, a pair of socks of squirrel skin with the fur inside. Over these he had sheepskin stockings reaching to the knees, with the wool inside, and over these he had deerskin boots that rose to the bifurcation of his legs, and were held in place by thongs. Thus equipped one may bid defiance to the low temperature of a winter journey across Siberia.

At Irkutsk, the capital of Eastern Siberia, he remained a month, till the snows fell and the winter roads were good. Then he bought a sleigh (*kibitka*), constructed after the general pattern of the tarantass, save that it was on runners instead of wheels. With a slight expenditure for repairs he carried this sleigh through to Nijne Novgorod (3,600 miles), or rather was carried by the sleigh. A Siberian journey may begin at any hour of the day the traveler chooses, and is continued day and night till it closes. The usual custom is to order the post horses to be brought around about 10 P. M.; the day and evening have been spent in feasting and farewells, and towards midnight the departing traveler nestles down among his garments and thick wraps, and is ready to go to sleep while the team dashes over the road at a rattling pace. Sometimes he is escorted to the first station by a party of friends, and in this case they set off all together about sunset and make an evening of it.

The horses are changed at distances varying from ten to twenty-five miles; they are paid for at each change, and the traveler must be provided with a bag of copper coin, so that he will never be at a loss to make out the exact amount that may be due. The driver expects a small gratuity, and he generally earns it by driving at a lively gait; a placard is hung in every station, showing the distance to the stations on each side, and the price per horse, so that the best intentions of the station master to cheat the wayfarer are frustrated. Everything included, cost of padarojnia, hire of horses, and gratuities to drivers, the expense of posting in Siberia is about four cents a mile; two persons may occupy a kibitka, and some of these vehicles will hold three, and the number of persons makes no difference in the cost except when it is so large as to call for more horses.

The station master is required by law to furnish travelers with hot water and bread, at a fixed price, and he may sell anything else that he chooses. Eggs can generally be had at the stations, but no other article of food can be relied on. The traveler will carry his own tea, coffee, brandy, and edibles generally; in winter the frost preserves them perfectly, and he is under no apprehension that his perishable provisions will perish. Soup is carried in cakes like small bricks; roast beef resembles red granite, and must be carved with an axe. There is always a fire in the travelers' room at the stations, and no difficulty in preparing one's dinner, which is seasoned with that best of all sauces, a keen appetite.

The sleigh glides merrily over the smooth roads and bounds the reverse of joyously where the way is rough. As long as the harness holds together and the team is in motion the driver pays no attention to the passengers, but lets them rattle about as they will. Occasionally there is a spill, but it rarely amounts to anything more than a disagreeable shaking up and a scattering of one's property along the road. To guard against a mishap of this sort it is customary to lash the baggage into its place by passing a strong cord over it a half-dozen times or more.

On and on you go, changing horses at the stations, and alighting two or three times a day for meals. In the cities and large towns you may halt a day or two for relief from the monotony, and for any repairs that your sleigh may need. The road is long; there are 209 changes of horses between Irkutsk and Nijne Novgorod, and some 90 odd between the head of the Amoor and Irkutsk. It gets tiresome after a while, and you gladly hear the whistle of the locomotive which tells you that your long ride is at at end.

The winter is by far the best season of the year for traversing Siberia. In summer the roads are dusty, the delays at the river crossings are frequently long and vexatious, mosquitoes and flies fill the air, provisions will only keep fresh for a day or so, and the tarantass is a heavy vehicle to draw. The frost seals the rivers, shuts up the the flies and mosquitoes, lays the dust, extinguishes the malaria of the marshes, and preserves your animal food for an indefinite period. If you intend taking the longest and most exhilarating post ride in the world, by all means make up your mind to try it in winter.

The whole of Asiatic Russia enjoys the benefits of the posting system, and one may go by the government roads to the shores of the Arctic ocean in the north, or to the country of the Kirghes and Turcomans on the south. Whenever a new region in Central Asia is conquered and brought under the Russian rule, a post route is opened and stations are established, so as to afford certain and quick communication. The post route is to Russia what the railway is to the United States in developing new territory, and carrying to it the blessings, as well as the curses, of civilization.

CHAPTER XVII.

TRAVELING WITH CAMELS AND ELEPHANTS.

Next to the horse the camel is the beast of burden available for travelers, and in some parts of the world he is a most important animal. He has long been known as "The Ship of the Desert," and without his aid the sandy wastes of Asia and Africa would be well-nigh impassable.

The regions where the camel is in use are practically comprised in Persia, Tartary, Arabia, Northern Africa, and portions of China and India. There are several varieties of camels that differ from each other, like the various kinds of horses; the finest and best of the race is the one called the dromedary, which bears the same relation to the ordinary camel as the carefully-bred trotter does to the common horse. The pace of the common camel is about three miles an hour, and his day's journey is from twenty to thirty miles. At this rate he can carry from five hundred to nine hundred pounds of burden, and for a short journey a strong camel can be loaded with one thousand pounds. The swift camel or saddle dromedary has been known to make ten miles an hour, though his ordinary pace will not exceed seven or eight. He will travel fifty miles a day for days together, and, on emergencies, he will accomplish one hundred miles or more without resting. Mohammed Ali Pasha, who ruled over Egypt in the early part of this century, once rode on a dromedary from Suez to Cairo, eighty-two miles, in less than ten hours. He made only a single halt of about half an hour; the driver of the beast ran at his side for the entire distance, and died the next day from the exertion.

The stomach of the camel is so arranged that it can hold water enough for a week's supply; the animal is thus enabled to traverse the desert where the wells are often several days' journey from each other. His foot is a spongy mass that flattens to a great breadth when placed on the ground, and enables him to walk on the yielding sand, and his hump is a store of fat that sustains him in the privations of the desert. Attempts have been made to employ the camel on the arid wastes of the south-western parts of the United States, but none of them have been more than experimentally successful.

The motion of a camel is far from agreeable to the novice; even the slow walk is unpleasant and wearying, and when it comes to the trotting camel, or swift dromedary, the exercise is like being tossed violently in a wooden blanket, and allowed to fall heavily every other second. The rider's head and shoulders are thrown forward and then back with a jerk, and as the jerks average about thirty-eight to the minute each way, they become monotonous after a while. The novice who reads this book is advised not to try a trotting camel till he has become thoroughly accustomed to the dignified walker; the latter will give him all the amusement he wants for a week or so, and perhaps longer; and if he accomplishes twenty-five miles a day on his humpbacked steed he should be satisfied. The first day he will feel somewhat shaken up, but unable to locate his pains; the next day he feels as though his backbone had been removed, and the third day he finds it has returned, but is converted into glass. After that his pains will subside, and a week will find him acclimated.

The riding saddle for a camel is a sort of dish with a

pommel, and the practiced rider crosses his legs around this pommel, and thus holds himself in place. Stirrups are sometimes added, but they do not properly belong to the equipment of a camel. A very good seat may be arranged by taking the common pack-saddle, slinging the saddle-bags across, and then piling on rugs and wraps enough to form a soft and wide seat. The whole should be firmly lashed to prevent slipping; stirrups may be added either at the pommel or at the side, and when thus arranged the rider may mount to his place. He may ride in any way he likes, either astride or sidewise, and he soon finds that he can change his position without difficulty or danger.

A gentleman who has had much experience in camel riding gives the following directions:—

"Place a light box or package on either side of the pack-saddle, sufficiently closely corded to form one wide horizontal surface. On this lay a carpet, mattress, blanket, and wraps, thus forming a delicious seat or couch, and giving the option of lying down or sitting, either side-saddle or cross-legged. Sheets, pillow, rug, etc., may be rolled up and strapped to the back of the saddle, and form an excellent support to the back or elbow. The object of the light box or package is to a certain extent answered by a pair of well-stuffed saddle-bags."

The traveler on a camel in the hot regions of Africa should have a good supply of white clothing and a pith hat, or *sola topee*, to protect his head from the broiling sun. But he should always have a suit of tolerably thick clothing, for the night-air is cold, even in the tropics, and a heavy overcoat will often prove useful. Water is carried in barrels, or goat-skins; of late years boxes of galvanized iron have been used very successfully, the first man to try them being Dr. Rohlfs, the celebrated explorer of Northern Africa. In addition to this, every man carries a small water-skin, called a *zemzemeeyah*, at his saddle-bow, for use during the day, and as a reserve in case he strays from camp.

The outfit for a journey by camel will depend much on the locality to be visited, and the time consumed, and consequently no general rules for it can be laid down. Whether it be the African deserts of Lybia or Sahara, or the desert of Arabia, the traveler must carry the most of his provisions with him, and be prepared to rough it a good deal. With an enormous train of camels it is possible to transport many of the luxuries of life, including spacious tents, carpets, bedsteads, and other furniture, but if you cannot be comfortable without all these things you had better stay at home. The usual allowance for travelers in the Arabian desert is a tent for every four or five persons, and an extra tent for a dining and sitting-room. The expense varies from five to eight dollars a day for each person, and depends a good deal on the size of the party and the style of traveling. At all the starting-points it is easy to find a dragoman who will undertake the whole business, but his recommendations should be critically examined, and the contract drawn with judicious care. The dragoman is too often a slippery party, who seeks to enrich himself at the expense of his employer. A good one is a treasure, but a bad one is a source of never-ending trouble.

In Northern China the camel is largely used, especially on the desert of Gobi. Travelers between Pekin and Kiachta, on the frontier of Siberia, generally ride in camel carts, or at all events have them in reserve, while they promenade on their saddle ponies. Formerly all the tea that entered Russia was imported overland, and in the tea season long files of camels, laden with the delicious herb, could be seen entering Kiachta at any hour of the day. Since the opening of the Russian ports to importations by sea the camel traffic has largely diminished, but there are still a goodly number of these patient animals traversing the desert of Gobi, and the regions to the west of it. The camel is an important reliance of Russia in her military conquests in Central Asia, and the failure of an expedition is often chargeable to him.

For riding purposes the elephant is preferable to the camel, as the motion is far less disagreeable, and the broad back of the beast affords a comfortable seat. The driver sits on the neck of his steed and manages him with an iron goad that has a hook at the end, as well as a straight point. The traveler has nothing to do with directing the elephant beyond giving his instructions to the driver before starting; if the ground is wooded he must keep a sharp watch for the limbs of the trees, or run the risk of being brushed from his place. The writer's first experience with elephant riding was at Benares, in India; a magnificent elephant, belonging to a native prince, was furnished to him for an excursion, and he returned from the adventure without any of the disagreeable aches that accompanied his novitiate with the camel. The howdah, or saddle, was like a small carriage, capable of seating four persons; it was held in place by several thongs and cords, and was reached by means of a ladder placed against the animal's side. A more primitive equipment is a pad-saddle, which is described by its name; it is simply a broad pad, like a well-stuffed mattress, and is held in position the same as the howdah. An elephant can easily carry all the passengers that can cling to him, as his ordinary load is anything less than two thousand pounds.

When troops are on the march they have a form of saddle that will carry eight men, and some of the largest will hold ten! It consists of two benches or settees placed back to back and resting on a small platform that gives support to the feet. In riding in this way the traveler looks to one side, the same as in an Irish jaunting car, and if he wants to see anything on the opposite side he must give his neck a twist, more or less inconvenient.

There are two species of elephant, the African and the Asiatic; the former is much the more fierce and not often domesticated, though it is pretty clearly demonstrated that the first elephants ever tamed and used by man were from Africa. The Asiatic elephant is employed in Siam, Ceylon, Burmah, and India as a beast of burden, and in a few other countries. The traveler in India will often see dozens of these beasts at the railway stations waiting to receive their burdens of bales and boxes, and sometimes he sees them at work on the roads. The great expense of feeding them makes them an expensive article of luxury, and it is not likely they will ever come into general use. A good elephant will carry a ton of cargo and march fifty miles a day over ordinary roads; he gets along very well on level ground, but sometimes topples and falls backward when trying to climb a steep hill with a burden on his back.

One caution the elephant rider should bear in mind. It is a peculiar trait of this animal to take fright from slight and often absurd causes, and sometimes he gets beyond the control of his driver. In such a case do not seek safety by slipping or jumping from his back; you may escape injury from the fall but will be in danger of being trampled to death by the elephant or pierced by his tusks. Even while he is going quietly along the road you should be careful not to fall by accident to the ground, or attempt to jump there, as he is very apt to turn and attack you.

The most docile elephants are nearly as dangerous in this respect as the ferocious ones; while the writer was in India an engineer officer was one day riding a favorite elephant that had been in his possession for years and was much attached to him. By some accident he slipped from the saddle and fell to the ground; the elephant immediately turned, and in spite of the efforts of the driver to stop him, pierced his master with his tusks, killing him almost instantly.

Another peculiarity of the elephant is to become suddenly insane from no apparent cause. The animal may be walking quietly along the road, or standing in his stable, when, without a moment's warning, he raises his trunk in the air, bellows loudly, and rushes upon the nearest man or beast with an effort to annihilate him. The paroxysm may be over in a few minutes or it may last for hours; while it continues, the beast is full of malice, and it is dangerous in the extreme to approach him.

CHAPTER XVIII.

TRAVELING WITH REINDEER AND DOGS.

Comparatively few of the readers of this volume are likely to have any practical use for information concerning the modes of traveling with reindeer and dogs, and therefore the subject will be treated very briefly. The use of these animals for riding or driving purposes is confined to the Arctic Circle, and regions adjacent to it, rarely going below the fiftieth parallel of north latitude.

In Lapland, and in some portions of Northern Siberia, the reindeer is employed to the exclusion of the dog, while in Greenland and that part of North America bordering the Arctic Ocean the dog is the only beast of burden. The American and Greenland dogs are of the variety known as Esquimaux, and closely allied to the familiar and treacherous Spitz. In Kamchatka and Northeastern Siberia both dogs and reindeer are employed for drawing sledges, and the reindeer for a saddle animal. The Kamchadale dog is quite like the Esquimaux in appearance, character, qualities, and uses, and the description of one will answer in general terms for both.

The sledge used for the reindeer in Lapland is a sort of box, not unlike a coffin in general appearance, and it has the faculty of overturning very easily. The animal is harnessed with a broad collar of deerskin, and a stout thong extends between his legs to the front of the sledge.

A single rein is fastened to one of his horns, and by means of this he is guided. Sometimes there are two thongs or traces, one on each side of the deer, and when two deer are employed together they are harnessed side by side. In that case a rein is fastened to the horn of each.

In Kamchatka and Siberia the sledge is higher and broader than that of Lapland; the latter has frequently but a single runner, like a broad plank turned up at the ends, while the former has a pair of runners, each about six inches wide. Generally the occupant of the sledge is his own driver, especially if he has but a single deer, but with a fine turnout of a pair of trotters the driver sits on the forward part of the vehicle while the passenger is wrapped in his furs and takes things comfortably. The ordinary deer is not a fast animal and his speed does not exceed five or six miles an hour, but the fancy team is quite another thing. It has been known to make fifteen or sixteen miles an hour and to travel a hundred and forty miles without any rest beyond a few brief halts. A ride behind a fast reindeer has the disadvantage that the driver and passenger are pelted with balls of snow, thrown by the animals hoofs, unless the weather is so cold that the snow will not unite.

In Northeastern Siberia the reindeer is much oftener used under the saddle than with a sledge. The saddle is placed directly over the animal's withers, as the back is not strong, and will give way under the weight of an ordinary man; it is nothing but a flat pad without stirrups, and the rider, who is passing his novitiate, has no easy task. The first time he gets on he generally tumbles off on the other side at once, and even after he has succeeded in balancing himself the first step of the deer is pretty sure to send him to the ground. It is customary to carry a long stick with which to preserve the balance, and some riders provide themselves with two sticks, one on each side. The stick is absolutely necessary in mounting, as the deer is liable to be thrown down if mounted as one would mount a horse.

A hundred pounds is considered a sufficient load for an ordinary deer, and it is only the very best of the animals that can sustain the weight of a good sized man. Nature has made the inhabitants of the country of small stature and slender figures, probably in an effort to adapt them to the carrying capacities of their beasts of burden. A native rides one deer and leads a pack train of any number up to a dozen, the halter of one being fastened to the tail of his predecessor. The one that he rides is guided by a halter around the neck, and a line which is fastened to the nose in case the animal is without horns.

In Kamchatka and the Arctic Regions generally, where dogs are employed for drawing sledges, they are broken to their work while quite young. Their training begins when they are six months old, but they are not put to actual labor till three years old, unless in times of great distress and a scarcity of dogs. One mode of training is to fasten them to posts or trees, with thongs of green skin, and then place their food just beyond their reach. By reaching for it they stretch the green thong; in this way they learn to pull steadily for some minutes at a time, and the muscles of their necks are strengthened. Occasionally they are harnessed to carts or sledges and made to run for short distances, and are thus gradually trained to the work they are to perform.

Dogs are driven without reins and generally without a whip. The driver has a stick, called an ostoll, with one end pointed with iron; this he uses for stopping his team when he wishes to bring it to a halt, and checks its speed when descending hills. Occasionally he punishes a refractory dog with it, but not often as the hard stick is apt to inflict permanent injury on the slender bones of the animal. The most important dog in the team is the leader, whose position is indicated by his name. He is selected for his superior intelligence and docility, and his training requires much care and attention. An ordinary team dog is worth from eight to twelve dollars, while fifty or even a hundred dollars may be refused for a good leader. The leader obeys the voice of his driver and turns to the right or left, according to directions. When the team is weary and moves at a slow pace, the leader has been known to put fresh life into their movements by suddenly pretending to have fallen on the track of an animal, by putting his nose to the ground or snow and barking violently. Away they go in pursuit, and only the leading dog and the driver are aware of the ruse that has been played.

A team may consist of any number of dogs up to twenty, but the large teams are only used for carrying freight, and rarely travel faster than a walk. A team of running dogs for traveling purposes usually consists of five or seven; the number is almost always odd, as it consists of one or more pairs of dogs and a leader. The sledge is long and narrow, and the size and shape are varied, according to the way it is to be used. The driver sits sidewise on the sledge and clings to it with one hand, while he manages his ostoll with the other. The traveling sledge is as light as possible, and just large enough to support the driver and a very little cargo. It is made of wood, fastened together with thongs of deerskin, and the runners are usually shod with polished bone.

A good team will travel from forty to sixty miles a day with favorable roads. Sometimes a hundred miles may be made in a single day, but such performances are rare. The news of the declaration of the Crimean war was carried from Bolcheretsk to Petropavlovsk, one hundred and twenty-five miles, in twenty-three hours without change of dogs. A good team can average forty miles a day, and even fifty miles for a week or more, but they must be lightly laden, and have favorable roads.

The comparative merits of dogs and reindeer in the countries where both are used may be set down as follows:—

The reindeer seeks his own food; he lives on moss that grows beneath the snow, which he scrapes away to reach it. Thus he may travel any length of time and be in good condition, provided he has sufficient time each day for feeding.

The food for dogs must be carried on the sledge, unless the traveler is certain of finding it along his route. The maximum supply that can be carried by a team for its sustenance is for one week. Consequently where dog food cannot be procured every five or six days those animals are useless.

A forced journey can be made with dogs, but not with reindeer. Dogs may be driven till utterly exhausted, and they will travel an entire day, or even more, after their food has given out. But when the reindeer is weary and hungry he stops and lies down, and no argument that his driver can use will induce him to move on. He may be pounded with sticks, or prodded with goads for hours, but all to no purpose. He wants his food and will have it at whatever risk. When a reindeer team thus halts there is no alternative but to turn the animals out to feed, and wait till they have eaten all they wish.

CHAPTER XIX.

TRAVELING WITH MAN-POWER. PALANKEENS, JINRIKISHAS, AND SEDAN-CHAIRS.

To be carried on the shoulders of his fellow-man is not often the lot of the American; the most frequent form of this species of locomotion in the United States is decidedly uncomfortable and degrading, and is known as "riding on a rail." The costume for an expedition of this sort is inexpensive and ungraceful, though fitting closely; it usually consists of a veneering of warm tar applied to the skin of the tourist, and immediately afterwards he is rolled in a bed of feathers. Thus equipped he is mounted on a pole, generally a fence-rail, without saddle or bridle, and borne on the shoulders of those who supplied his wardrobe. There is no mode of traveling known to civilization where the accommodations are so wretched, and the mental and physical discomforts so great, as in riding on a rail after the American system. The only thing in its favor is its cheapness, as it is generally quite gratuitous.

In Europe, before the adoption of wheeled vehicles, those who could afford the luxury, were carried in chairs by two or more porters; the conveyance was said to have originated in Sedan, France, and thus became known as the sedan chair. It was introduced into England about the time of King Charles First, and speedily attained great popularity. It was gradually displaced by the wheeled carriage, and disappeared from the cities of Continental Europe, one after another; it lingers in Constan

(179)

tinople with other relics of past ages, and may be seen occasionally at the European watering-places, where it is used to convey invalids to and from the baths and springs. Before the construction of the railway on Mount Vesuvius chairs were employed to carry visitors up the steep incline, and they cán be seen now and then among the Swiss mountains. To see the *chaise a porteurs* in all its glory it is necessary to visit Asia.

The first vehicle of this sort that meets the traveler's gaze as he journeys eastward from Europe is the palankeen, or *palkee*, as it is usually called in India. It is a conveyance peculiar to India, and consists of a box about seven feet long by four wide and three high. It is entirely of wood, roof and all, and there is a sliding door in each side, while the interior is equipped with a hard mattress and bolster. There is a pole three or four feet long at each end, which rests on the shoulders of the bearers, and is generally made secure by iron braces. To enter this contrivance you back into it till you can sit on the mattress, and then by a skilful swing you bring head and feet inside at the same moment. Then you lie down at full length and the coolies move off. You are expected to lie still, so as not to disturb the equilibrium, and in the enervating climate of India you are quite willing to be motionless. The bearers have a peculiar swinging step that saves you from any jolts, and the motion is quite luxurious.

Formerly in the cities of India the foreign residents made great use of the palankeen, and every person of respectability was supposed to keep one, together with the appropriate number of bearers. Of late years it has been largely superceded by the horse carriage, of which there are two or three varieties, and the palkee-bearers have been forced to seek other employments. Four bearers are necessary to carry the palkee, and four more run alongside to take their share of the burden when the first are weary. At night a torch-bearer is necessary to light the way, and to do the thing in style, there should be four torch-bearers, two in front and two in the rear. Formerly the palkee was the only means of traveling in the interior of India, but the carriage road, and later the railway, have made the "palkee dawk" (palankeen express) among the things that were.

For traveling on the high roads through the interior each palankeen required sixteen bearers, and if the traveler had more than a very little baggage he was compelled to hire from eight to twelve men to carry it. The torch-bearers and other attendants generally brought his retinue up to thirty-five or forty men, and sometimes even more. There were stations on the road every ten miles where relays were obtained, and there was always more or less delay at these stations, so that the palkee was not a rapid means of travel. The "lightning dawk," as the natives call the locomotive, has beaten it quite out of sight.

A cheaper vehicle for country travel is the dhoolie, a sort of chair with a covering of canvas or muslin; it is lighter than the palkee, and requires only twelve bearers instead of sixteen. An English statesman of considerable renown once spoke in Parliament of the ferocious dhoolies that carried the wounded from the battle-field on a certain occasion; he was under the impression that the dhoolie was a blood-thirsty native rather than an inoffensive chair.

What the palankeen was to India the sedan-chair is to China. As the traveler finds it at Hong Kong or Canton it is a bamboo chair with a ventilating top, like a Venetian blind, and it has curtains at the side that may be rolled up or let down at will. It has a floor for the feet, and rests for the arms, and altogether the Chinese chair is a very comfortable vehicle. Long poles are fastened to the sides, parallel with each other and projecting three or four feet in front and rear, and by these poles the concern is carried. The chair is placed on the ground for you to enter it, and you have none of the difficulty experienced in getting into a palankeen. You simply sit down as in an arm-chair at home; when you are seated, the bearers seize the poles, and, at a signal from their leader, swing the burden to its place on their shoulders. They move at a swinging pace, and usually, but not always, keep step in unison. Every ten minutes or so they change the pole from one shoulder to the other, and about every half hour they halt and put the chair on the ground for a few minutes. You may retain your place during this halt or get out and stretch your limbs, just as you please.

In all the cities of China the chair is in use, and in most, if not all of them, the streets are so narrow that carriages could not possibly move about. For a short ride two bearers are sufficient, and the chairs for hire in the streets of Hong Kong rarely have more than two. But for an excursion into the country, or to the summit of Victoria peak, overlooking Hong Kong harbor, four bearers are necessary. There is a regular tariff for chairs, just as there is for cabs in London or Paris. A short course costs ten cents, and a longer one in proportion, and a chair with four bearers for an entire day, in making the circuit of Canton, may be had for a dollar. Labor is cheap in the far East.

Two-wheeled cabs, drawn by a single horse, take the place of the chair to some extent in Pekin, but there are many streets where the cabs cannot circulate. In Shanghai the wheelbarrow is a rival of the chair; it is cheaper and more uncomfortable, and its use is almost entirely confined to the natives. It has no springs, the pavement is rough, the man between the shafts is generally far from strong, and altogether the wheelbarrow of Northern China is not to be recommended.

The man-power vehicle, par excellence, is the jinrikisha of Japan. It replaces the *norimon* and *cango*, peculiar forms of the sedan-chair, and has only been in use since 1870. It is said to have been invented by an American, and the first jinrikishas that were used were imported from San Francisco. Probably not less than a hundred thousand of them are now in use throughout Japan, and they are said to have penetrated to the remotest districts.

The jinrikisha is a carriage like a small chaise of the New England pattern; it is on two wheels, and has shafts like a handcart, and there is a hood over the top that can be opened or closed at pleasure. The coolie that draws it places the shafts on the ground to permit you to enter, and, until he picks them up, you are sitting with your head bent forward. The cross-piece of the shafts held against his breast brings the carriage to a level, and then you are ready for a start. The jinrikisha is intended for one person, but occasionally you see two Japanese or Chinese of medium size occupying a single vehicle.

For a short ride in a Japanese city one man to pull your carriage is sufficient, but for a journey into the country, or of several miles, you need two men, or perhaps three. Where you have but one man you should not expect to go as rapidly as with two or three, and you must dismount in sandy places, or when a hill is to be ascended. The speed and endurance of these men is something wonderful. It is nothing unusual for three of them to pull a jinrikisha fifty miles in twelve hours, with only three halts of a quarter of an hour each, and they have been known to make sixty-five miles between sunrise and sunset of a long day.

The writer, with three men to his carriage, traveled from Osaka to Nara, a distance of thirty miles, between 10 A. M. and 5 P. M., with a halt of an hour for dinner. The next day he continued his journey to Kioto, thirty miles more, in a pouring rain, with the same men in the same time. The coolies were as fresh on the second day as on the first, and as cheerful as one could wish, although their passenger was not a light weight, and was suffering from a lameness that prevented his walking up any of the hills.

Riding with a jinrikisha is cheap enough for the most contracted purse. The tariff in the large cities of Japan is ten cents an hour, or fifty cents for a day of twelve hours, and if the traveler wishes to keep his carriage waiting for him, and subject to his call, he can readily make a bargain for not over three dollars a week. Most of the foreigners in Japan keep their own carriages by buying a jinrikisha, and hiring a couple of men for six or seven dollars each per month. They perform the work of general servants about the house and grounds, and whenever the master wishes to ride out he orders the jinrikisha and its accompanying coolies. A carriage of ordinary workmanship costs about twenty-five dollars, and a "swell" one can be had for fifty or something less. Its name is compounded of three Japanese words—jin, man, riki, power, and sha, carriage—jin-riki-sha, man-power-carriage.

The stranger in Japan, China, or India, finds it disagreeable to ride on men's shoulders, or to be drawn by them in a vehicle. Especially is this the case in Japan, where you have the struggling and perspiring man directly before you, and witness the effort he is making to propel you over the ground. Everybody experiences this feeling, and his first ride in a man-power carriage is rarely agreeable. But when you remember that the coolie considers it a favor to be employed, and that nothing would displease him more than to have the offer of his services refused, you will change your mind, and take your ease in a jinrikisha. Regard him as you would the man whom you employ to saw wood or dig potatoes; he is thankful for the opportunity of working, and so is the Japanese coolie who exerts his strength to pull you about. And when you have done with him give a few cents extra, and he will thank you with an expression so heartfelt that you cannot fail to be touched by it.

Many of the Japanese still prefer the *cango* to the jinrikisha, but it is rapidly going out of use in all the localities where the miniature chaise can run. The *cango* is a sort of open-sided basket slung on a pole, and carried by two men in the same way that a sedan-chair is carried. The occupant must double his legs beneath him, and sit perfectly still; this is easy enough for a Japanese, but is torture to a European. No man from Europe or America will ever find the *cango* enjoyable until a system is invented whereby he can unscrew his legs before starting, and screw them on again when his journey is completed.

CHAPTER XX.

PEDESTRIAN TRAVELING.—MOUNTAIN CLIMBING.

The earliest form of traveling was on foot; it was in universal use before the horse and other beasts of burden were subdued to the will of man, and before the railway and steamship were invented. In spite of the lapse of ages, and the many improvements in locomotive means, it continues to be practiced by a great many persons, and will doubtless so continue as long as men have feet to walk with. The large majority of pedestrians are such from necessity, but the class that prefers to walk when it can afford to ride is by no means small.

The railway has been the great destroyer of pedestrian travel, and, at the present time, very few people, except those absolutely without money, take to the high-road where there is an iron way to carry them to their destination. Unless there is some reason for the foot journey beyond the desire to reach a certain place, the railway affords the greatest economy of money and time, as the merest glance at the figures will show. Suppose a man wishes to go from New York to Philadelphia, a distance of ninety miles; at thirty miles a day he will be three days on the road if he uses his feet, and three hours if he takes the railway. The fare by railway will be two dollars, and his loss of time half a day; reckoning his meals and lodging along the high-road at one dollar a day his expenses in footing it would be three dollars, without counting the loss of time, which most Americans consider equivalent to money. Far greater is the contrast in a long journey across the Continent, or over a considerable portion of it, so that the most miserly of men is not likely to put his own feet in competition with the wheels of the locomotive.

Pedestrian journeys in America are mainly confined to young men in search of health, who throng the routes of New England and northern New York in the summer months. In Europe the principal resorts of the pedestrian are the mountain regions of Switzerland, Italy, and Germany, and there is a fair amount of the same kind of travel in Norway, Sweden, and the lake and mountain districts of Scotland. Workmen going from one town to another in search of employment are often encountered, and in some countries of the Continent such journeys are obligatory upon apprentices before they can be allowed to practice the trades they have learned.

Fifty years or more ago there was a half-pedestrian system in vogue in the United States, especially on the great roads leading to the west. It was known by the name of "ride and tie," and many an emigrant of those days found his way west by this process. It was about as follows:

Two men, whom we will call Smith and Jones, unite their funds and buy a horse and saddle. Their baggage is stowed in the saddle-bags, so that neither of them has anything to carry beyond his strong walking-stick. On the morning fixed for their departure Smith mounts the horse and starts at an easy pace along the road, while Jones follows on foot. It has been arranged that the first "tie" shall be at a village twenty miles away.

In four hours Smith and the horse have made the twenty miles, and the horse is put up at a tavern and fed, while Smith proceeds on foot. When Jones arrives the horse has had a rest of three hours or more, and is ready for another twenty miles which Jones proceeds to give him. He passes Smith on the way, and arrives at the next village, where he orders supper and awaits the arrival of his comrade. They spend the night in company, and the next morning the journey is continued in the same way; generally the scheme is reversed on successive mornings, the one who was first to ride one day being the last to do so on the next. In this way they make forty miles a day, and each of them has only a comfortable walk while the horse is kept in good condition.

For a pedestrian tour among the mountains, either of Europe or America, the principal requisites are a reasonably strong constitution, good feet, and good shoes to wear on them. Shoes are preferable to boots, as the latter are apt to weaken the ankles, especially if made with elastic at the sides. Besides they are heavier than shoes, and where we are taking a walk of many miles every infinitesimal fraction of an ounce added to the weight of our foot-gear counts against us. Of course there are occasions where boots are required for protection against mud, snow, or sand, but where roads are good and smooth shoes should have the preference. They should be easy without being loose, and sufficiently wide to give freedom to the toes. The soles should be broad, and the heels low and wide; all doubts on this score can be settled by ascertaining the kind of shoes worn by the professional pedestrians in the great walking-matches that have recently become fashionable.

The author of Baedeker's guide-books is a good adviser in the matter of pedestrian excursions, as he has tramped over the most of Switzerland and Germany, and believes that the best way of "doing" them is on foot. He says as follows:—

"A light 'gibeciere,' or game-bag, such as may be procured in every town, amply suffices to contain all that is necessary for a fortnight's excursion. Heavy and complicated knapsacks should be avoided; a light pouch, or game-bag, is far less irksome, and its position may be shifted at pleasure. A change of flannel shirts and worsted stockings, a few pocket-handkerchiefs, a pair of slippers, and the articles of the toilet will generally be found sufficient, to which a light mackintosh and a stout umbrella should be added. A piece of green crape or colored glasses, to protect the eyes from the glare of the snow, and a leather drinking-cup will be found useful. The traveler should, of course, have a more extensive reserve of clothing, especially if he expects to visit towns of importance. This can be contained in a valise, which he can easily wield when necessary, and may forward from town to town by post."

"The first golden rule of the pedestrian is to start on his way betimes in the morning. If strength permit, and a good halting-place is to be met with, a two hours' walk may be accomplished before breakfast. At noon a moderate luncheon is preferable to the regular table d'hote dinner. Repose should be taken during the hottest hours, aud the journey then continued till 5 or 6 P. M., when a substantial meal may be eaten. The traveler's own feelings will best dictate the hour for retiring to bed.

"For wounds and bruises a vial of tincture of arnica should be carried, and it has an invigorating effect if rubbed on the limbs after fatigue." The traveler should not fail to be provided with a few of the simple medicines best adapted to his system, as he may often need them when they are quite unattainable. Avoid drinking water too freely, especially where it comes directly from the melting snows of the mountains. There are many persons who rarely drink water, whether on pedestrian excursions or at other times, and to them the preceding advice will be superfluous. Cold tea is regarded as the best beverage by the majority of pedestrians, and its invigorating powers are often remarkable."

When starting on a pedestrian excursion be careful not to overtax your strength. Five or six hours a day are sufficient to begin with, and when no fatigue results from a single day's work that of the next may be increased. By adding half an hour daily to his task, a traveler will soon be able to devote ten or twelve hours out of the twenty-four to the use of his feet. The most experienced pedestrians advise that the limit should be ten hours, except on extraordinary occasions. An even, steady pace should be adopted, and everything like a "spurt" is to be avoided. Many a traveler has broken down in the effort to do more than he ought, either in going too far in a given time, or walking faster than the accustomed pace to see how many miles he could cover in an hour.

For climbing high mountains, special practice in walking is a necessity. There is a great deal of fatigue consequent upon the ascent of Mont Blanc and his snow-covered brethren of the Alps, partly due to the exertion of walking through the snow, and over the rough rocks, and partly to the rarity of the atmosphere in elevated positions. None but good walkers should attempt these journeys, as it is a serious matter to break down at a point far from roads, and where assistance may be a long time coming. The members of the English and other Alpine clubs generally devote at least a month to the ordinary excursions among the mountains before venturing on a "course extraordinaire," like the ascent of Mont Blanc. The ascent of the Matterhorn is far more difficult than that of Mont Blanc, and the preliminary practice proportionally longer.

The equipment for an Alpine ascent above the snowline is quite simple, but should be of the very best quality. The traveler will need an alpenstock, or strong stick, from five to six feet long; it should be of the best seasoned ash, and one end should be pointed with iron to give it a firm hold on the ice. It should be as light as possible, consistent with strength, and the test to be given is to have it sustain the weight of its owner, when supported at the ends. Ice-axes and ropes are also needed for the higher mountains, and sometimes it is necessary to carry a ladder for crossing crevasses. Mountain-climbing in Switzerland has been reduced to a system, and there are associations of guides who make it a business to accompany tourists in ascents more or less difficult. The ascent of Mont Blanc, formerly so difficult, is now quite easy, as there is a hotel at the "Grands Mulets" where the night is passed, and though the accommodations are limited, they are quite sufficient for the robust traveler. Everything that is needed for the journey can be obtained from the guides at fixed rates, and the only care of the stranger is to see that what he orders is of the best quality.

The regulation time at present for the ascent of Mont Blanc from Chamouny and return is two days. The traveler starts at 7 A. M. and arrives at the Grands Mulets about 3 or 4 in the afternoon. At 4 the next morning he is called, and after a light breakfast a start is made for the summit, which should be reached by nine o'clock. The return to Chamouny is usually accomplished by sunset, but many travelers who have plenty of time at their disposal prefer to spend the second night at the Grands Mulets, and return leisurely on the third day to Chamouny. Each tourist requires a guide and a porter to accompany him, and sometimes half a dozen guides to each tourist are taken. Each guide receives one hundred francs (twenty dollars) for his services, and the porter half that amount, so that the cost of an ascent of Mont Blanc is by no means small. The dangers are now much less than formerly, as the crevasses are all well known to the guides, whose directions should be followed implicitly. The principal peril is from sudden storms of snow, in which travelers are overwhelmed as in a sand-storm in the desert. In 1870 a party of eleven persons perished in a snow-storm; they had been to the summit and were nearly half-way back to the Grands Mulets when the snow-cloud burst upon them. The guides can generally foretell the approach of bad weather, and the cautious tourist will not insist upon making the ascent against their advice.

It has been said that tourists need only go part of the way up the mountain to obtain a certificate of having made the entire ascent, provided they pay for the complete course. It is doubtful if this is the case; not that the guides would be unwilling to oblige a patron, but because the summit is in full view of the village of Chamouny, and parties who make the ascent are watched through powerful telescopes by loungers on the verandas of the hotels.

CHAPTER XXI.

TRAVELING WITHOUT MONEY.

Anyone can travel who has time and money at his disposal, but it requires genius, or its first cousin, improvidence, to travel without it. One who is not a genius, but who possesses common-sense and prudent habits may see a great deal of the world for a very little cash. Bayard Taylor made the tour of Europe in his younger days for less than five hundred dollars, and devoted more than a year to the journey; how he did it is told in his volume entitled "Views Afoot." He has had many imitators, and some of them have traveled for less than he did; of this class was Ralph Keeler, who claimed to have seen Europe for less than two hundred dollars, but he went through many hardships that the majority of men would decline to undergo.

In the fall of 1880 an account was published of a printer who made a tour around the world in four years, and had only fifty dollars in his pocket when he started. According to his story, he left San Francisco in 1876 as steward of a sailing-ship, which he quitted at Honolulu for work in a newspaper office there. After setting type for a month he arranged to take care of some horses that were being shipped to Melbourne, and in this way he reached Australia. He remained in that country nearly a year, tramping through it, and occasionally working at his trade. He shipped on a coasting-vessel as a sailor in the fall of 1877, was wrecked on a reef, and picked up by a ship that carried him to Suez. Through Egypt and the Holy Land he went as servant to travelers, and as a vagrant, and in this way managed to get to Constantinople, and thence up the Danube to Vienna. From Vienna he walked northward to the shores of the Baltic, where he again became a sailor during the summer of 1878. In the fall of that year he re-crossed Europe, most of the way on foot, till he reached Rome, and from there he proceeded to Spain, and thence to Paris. He was in the French capital till July, 1879, when he had earned money enough to carry him to London, where he remained some weeks, and then sailed for Charleston, S. C. From Charleston he walked through most of the coast States, and when the account was published he had reached Detroit on his way to San Francisco. When asked if he had experienced any real hard times, he answered :—

"I suppose you would call it hard to go twenty-four hours without food, but I have done that many times and it didn't hurt me, and I have lived for weeks at a time without knowing what a bed was, and without clean clothes, except as I would wash my own shirt and wear my coat buttoned closely while it was drying." He said further that such little conveniences as stockings, collars, cuffs, and handkerchiefs never entered his thoughts.

Not many would care to travel after the manner of this wandering printer, but there is a fair number of Americans who set out to see the world with very little more money than this man had in his pocket at the commencement of his journey. If the annals of the American consulates could be published a great many of us would be surprised to know the number of appeals to the consular pocket for aid. The story usually told at the consulates is that the traveler's remittances have failed to reach him, and he desires a loan for a few days till his letters arrive.

They generally do not come, and when the money that was borrowed is gone another appeal is made and with the same excuse. When the consul's patience is exhausted (and also his purse), the adventurer makes a final petition for sufficient money to carry him to the next city, where the same story is told, and the same process goes on. In this way a tourist may live comfortably for a couple of weeks or so in each of the principal cities of Europe, provided he can find the consuls able and willing to "lend" him what he wants.

The foregoing is intended as a hint to the enterprising American who has neither conscience nor money and is desirous of traveling abroad. The best time for him to begin his travels on this plan is just after a change of the presidential administration has caused a sweeping removal in the consular offces and the appointment of a new set of incumbents. A new consul is anxious to be polite and obliging, and will often prove a rich mine to the adventurer, while the old one has become case-hardened in the service, and is sceptical about the stories that the unfortunates tell him, and you should gauge your appeal according to the time a man has filled a consular office. If he is newly-arrived you can make three or four loans of ten dollars or so while waiting for your remittances, and can then borrow more to move on with. If he has been there a year or two you can hardly expect more than a couple of preliminaries, or perhaps only one, and if he has been there three or four years you cannot expect him to do more than pay your second or third-class passage to the next place.

The adventurer who seeks to travel for nothing sometimes claims to be the correspondent of a newspaper, and not unfrequently he writes letters for a daily or weekly journal. If he cannot obtain the loan he wants he revenges himself by writing an abusive letter about the consul who has refused him, and sometimes he gets the latter into trouble. Nine-tenths of the abusive letters about our consuls abroad come from the fellows who try to borrow money and fail. As a general thing the American consuls in Europe and Asia are capable men who render their country good service for inadequate pay; the government gives them no contingent fund from which to make up their losses from loans to swindlers, and all these sums must come out of their own pockets. The evil is so great that there is not a consul who has been a year in the service who does not tremble when a strange American presents himself at the consulate and wishes to see the representative of his country. The chances are three to one that a "loan" is wanted, and the tale that accompanies the application is so pitiful that it would melt the heart of a bronze dog. Some of the consuls require strangers to state their business to the clerk before they can see the chief, but it needs more courage to demand it than is possessed by the majority of American officials.

Some of our representatives abroad have painful recollections of visits from "inspectors of consulates" appointed by the government to make tours of inspection in various parts of the world. Two at least of this gentry made it a practice to ask a loan of fifty dollars of each consul before inspecting his office; if the money was forthcoming the office was speedily examined and found to be in excellent condition, but if the consul was not in a lending mood he was reported to have his books in bad shape, and to be personally unfit for the position he was filling. It is needless to say that the great majority of the consuls saw the point, and imitated the example of Captain Scott's coon by "coming down" before the fire was opened. And no one of them to this day has been repaid a penny of the borrowed money.

Memorandum : If you can add the title of "Inspector of Consulates " to your other accomplishments you will vastly improve your chances of swindling your way around the world. The most of these officials are men of excellent character, and if you try the rôle you must assume the manners of a gentlemen, however much you may be devoid of his instincts.

There is a fair number of American adventurers in the European cities who live by searching out their countrymen as fast as they arrive and making loans more or less small. These fellows watch the hotel registers and the lists of strangers in the newspapers, and their methods of conducting their operations are numerous and varied. London and Paris contain more of them than any other cities, and perhaps London has a greater number than its French rival. One of the most ingenious devices for fleecing the stranger was adopted by an American who lived some years in Paris ; he had no patent upon it, and as he is dead now anyone who chooses may take it up. It was as follows :—

He operated around the Grand Hotel, and other resorts of Americans, and managed to make himself acquainted with as many new-comers as possible. He was particular in cultivating anyone to give his card and ask that of the stranger, and to ascertain at what hotel the latter was stopping. Immediately they separated he called at the hotel in question and left his card, so that the stranger would be impressed with his new-found friend. Then the next morning about eight o'clock a messenger would come in great haste with a note from the swindler, which ran about like this :—

"DEAR SIR :—I regret to inform you that I have been run over by an omnibus, and while I was insensible my pocket was picked of all the money I had about me. You may not be aware that in this country a man who gets run over is fined for being in the way; I am at the police-station of the 12th arrondisement, and they refuse to let me go till I pay fifty francs. As I cannot draw money at my banker's at this hour of the morning, I venture to ask a favor of you. I beg that you will oblige me by sending fifty francs by the bearer, and as soon as the banks open I will go to my banker's and get the money to return to you immediately. You can expect me a few minutes past ten o'clock, and I shall hope to find you in. In case you are gone out I will leave the money with the concierge."

The appeal was so reasonable that many a stranger was taken in. The swindler endeavored to keep out of the way of his victim, but if met and interrogated he always declared that he left the money with the concierge, and the latter had doubtless pocketed it. He thrived for a while, but at length the gentle but firm hand of the police was laid upon him, and he was forced to emigrate. The Continental police are apt to interfere with schemes of this sort, and an enterprising man has little chance among them.

The only successful traveler without money is of the class usually designated as the "tramp." He has increased in numbers in the last few years till there is altogether too many of him; so much is this the case that several of the state legislatures have been compelled to pass laws for his suppression, and thus his operations have been greatly curtailed. But in the states where no laws have been made against him he flourishes in all his glory; he generally lives well by begging at kitchen doors, or at houses along the country roads, and he is satisfied with lodgings in a barn or under a haystack. In summer he traverses the country, and in winter the cold drives him to the city, where he stays till the trees bud and blossom again, and the robin sings in the orchards. Then he returns again to the country, and so he goes on from year to year, unwilling to accept honest employment, and giving no equivalent for his support. It is his evident impression that the world owes him a living, and the only duty devolving upon him is to collect the debt.

During the World's fair at Paris in 1867, one of the London papers published a scheme whereby a man could spend three days at the Exposition for 50 francs. It was something like the following :—

	fr.	c.
Lodging three nights at 3 francs per night,	9	00
Breakfast three days at a Duval restaurant, at 1 fr. 50 c.,	4	50
Omnibus to Exposition, at 50 c.	1	50
Admission to Exposition, 1 fr. daily,	3	00
Lunch and glass of beer, 2 fr. 50 c. daily,	7	50
Return from Exposition, same as going there,	1	50
Dinner, with wine, at Duval restaurant or Table d' Hote, 4 fr. daily,	12	00
Theatre in the evening (gallery), 3 fr.,	9	00
Extras,	2	00
Total,	50	00

A Paris paper, a few days later, made an improvement on the above, and showed how a man could spend three days at the Exposition for nothing. This is the way it was done :—

Lodging three nights at police stations, 00 per night, 00
Breakfast at hydrant, three times, 00 each time, . 00
Ride to Exposition by hanging on steps of omnibus, 00
Admission, make a bundle of your coat and enter as
    an exhibitor, ... 00

Lunch, similar to breakfast with addition of samples, obtained in the alimentary section of the Exposition, ... ∞
Return same way as going, ... ∞
Dinner at hydrant with remains of lunch, . . ∞
Theatre in evening, beg a check from somebody leaving, ... ∞

Total, ... ∞

It would be difficult to find a cheaper system than this, though it is on record that once during a period of steamship opposition between San Francisco and Oregon, the Pacific Mail Steamship Company advertised a free passage and a chromo to anybody who wished to make the voyage. A hundred or more of the impecunious ones of San Francisco thought it would be a good opportunity to go to Oregon and back for nothing, and have a week's board, and so they took passage. Nothing was said about the return; the opposition company made terms with the Pacific Mail just as the steamer reached Portland, and the old rates of fare were at once established. The majority of the tourists had great difficulty in getting home again, and some of them became permanent residents of the region to which they had unintentionally emigrated.

CHAPTER XXII.

SKELETON TOURS FOR AMERICA AND EUROPE.

It is well to have your route laid out beforehand when you start on a pleasure tour, at least in a general way, so that you can approximate the necessary time and money for the journey. To facilitate the traveler's plans a few skeleton routes will be given, together with an estimate of the time necessary for a rapid journey to cover them. It should not be understood that the routes given embrace a tenth or a twentieth of those that exist; any railway or steamship agent can give you dozens or perhaps hundreds of routes of travel, and after you think the subject is exhausted you can easily find a rival agent who can give you a selection from many more. The lines of travel that are here laid out are intended to embrace the chief cities of Europe and America, together with the principal pleasure-resorts. The traveler will pay his money and take his choice, or rather he will take his choice and then pay his money.

The American tours take New York as a starting and also as a returning point, for the obvious reason that it is the largest city of America. For the European tours London or Liverpool will be taken as the terminal points, since nine-tenths of the Americans who visit Europe land at Liverpool and proceed thence to London with more or less directness.

Any one of the American routes can be covered in from

one to two months, with a sufficient amount of time for seeing enough to satisfy an ordinary tourist. This does not allow for a stay of a week or more at each of two or three points, but only for a visit of sufficient length for doing the necessary sight-seeing, and a very little more. As there are no antiquities in American cities, and comparatively few stock sights, a tour of a given number of miles or places will take less time than a similar tour in Europe. A few hundred years hence we may be able to point to ancient buildings and ruins around which cluster many historical associations, but at present, to use a Hibernianism, all our antiquities are modern.

Without further preliminary the following routes are presented :—

New York, Philadelphia, Baltimore, Washington, Lynchburg, Charlotte, Atlanta, Montgomery, Mobile, New Orleans. The Mississippi River, passing Baton Rouge, Port Hudson, Natchez, Vicksburg, Memphis, and Cairo to St Louis; rail via Springfield to Chicago and back to New York by Detroit and Niagara Falls.

New York, Philadelphia, Baltimore, Washington, Lynchburg, Danville, Charlotte, Atlanta, Montgomery, Mobile, New Orleans. The Mississippi River, passing Natchez, Vicksburg, Memphis, and Cairo; thence on the Ohio River, passing Evansville and Louisville to Cincinnati, and back to New York, by Pittsburg and Altoona.

New York, Philadelphia, Baltimore, Washington, Norfolk, day steamer on the James River to Richmond, Gordonsville, Goshen (for Natural Bridge), White Sulphur Springs, Kanawha Falls, Huntington, steamer on the Ohio River to Cincinnati, St. Louis, Springfield, Chicago, through the Lakes to Buffalo, Niagara Falls, Toronto, the Thousand Islands and Rapids of the St. Lawrence to

HOW TO TRAVEL. 203

Montreal, Lake Champlain, Lake George, Saratoga, Rutland, Boston, Springfield, Hartford, New Haven, and New York.

New York, Philadelphia, Baltimore, Washington, Cincinnati, St. Louis, Springfield, Chicago, rail or steamer through the Lakes to Buffalo, Niagara Falls, Toronto, the Thousand Islands and Rapids of the St. Lawrence to Montreal, rail or boat to Quebec, Gorham, stage to Glen House, Summit of Mount Washington, Crawford House, Fabyan House, Bethlehem, Profile House, rail to Concord, Nashua, and Boston, and Sound steamboat to New York.

None of the routes thus given will carry the traveler farther west than St. Louis. The tourist who wishes to extend his journey to the Rocky Mountains, to Utah, or to the Pacific Coast will be pretty certain to make either St. Louis or Chicago his point of departure, and therefore we will make up our routes from those cities. From St. Louis we can go as follows :—

St. Louis, Kansas City, Denver, Cheyenne, Ogden, Salt Lake City, Virginia City, Sacramento, and San Francisco, where we pause to consider the sights of California. These include the wonderful Yosemite Valley, the North Pacific Coast Railway through the Redwood forests, the Geysers, and the wine-growing regions of Sonoma, and other valleys north of San Francisco Bay.

From San Francisco we can go to Oregon, either overland or by steamship; in either case we arrive at Portland, whence a journey may be made up the Columbia River and back again. As this book goes to press there is no satisfactory route for reaching the East except by returning to San Francisco, but in a few years it will be possible to ride in railway carriages from the head of navigation on the Columbia to St. Paul, in Minnesota, and thence through the states of the Northwest to Chicago.

Suppose we go back from Oregon to San Francisco and are ready to return to the East. We may go as we came as far as Cheyenne, and thence to Omaha, where we have the choice of four routes to Chicago. Or we may turn to the southward, over the Southern Pacific Railway, which will carry us to Los Angeles, and thence to Yuma, by way of the Desert, where at one point we are 266 feet below the level of the sea. From Yuma the route is eastward over the dry plains of Arizona, and among the mountains to the Rio Grande, and thence through New Mexico and along the valley of the Arkansas to Kansas City. From the latter point there is a bewildering choice of railways to St. Louis or Chicago.

The majority of tourists would doubtless prefer going by one route and returning over the other. In case you take the northern route for the westward journey Chicago would be the best point of departure, while if the southern route is chosen the start should be made from St. Louis. In either instance Denver and the mining and grazing regions of Colorado may be visited by a detour— by the northern route from Cheyenne, and by the southern from Pueblo.

Let us turn now to Europe. The voyage over the Atlantic will occupy about ten days each way, and therefore three weeks should be added to all the estimates of time in the following tours. And as before stated the time allowed for the tour itself is only what would give a hurried view of each place, and the objects of interest along the route. If the tourist wishes to go leisurely he should double the figures, and he will not be far out of the way. Or he may add 50 per cent. with the knowledge that he is just avoiding a "rush" through the country.

A tour of twenty days may be made, embracing the following cities :—

Liverpool, Glasgow or London, Antwerp, Rotterdam, The Hague, Amsterdam, Utrecht, Cologne, The Rhine, Wiesbaden, Brussels, Paris, Rouen, Dieppe, Brighton, London, Glasgow, Liverpool or London.

One of forty days will include most of the foregoing, and also Strasburg, Basle, Luzerne, Brunig Pass, Interlaken, Berne, Lausanne, Villeneuve, Martigny, Chamouny, Geneva, Macon, Dijon, Paris, and back to point of departure in England.

One of sixty-five days, embracing England, France, Italy, Austria, Germany, and Belgium, will include Liverpool, Glasgow or London, Dover, Calais, Paris, Macon, Mt. Cenis Tunnel, Turin, Genoa, Leghorn, Rome, Naples, Florence, Venice, Verona, the Austrian Tyrol, Innspruck, Munich, Salzburg, Vienna, Prague, Dresden, Berlin, Hanover, Cologne, Brussels, Antwerp, London or Liverpool.

One of about the same time, and embracing England, Belgium, the Rhine, Germany, Bavaria, Italy, Switzerland, and France, will take the tourist through Antwerp, Brussels, Cologne, the Rhine, Mayence, Heidelberg, Stuttgart, Munich, Lake Constance, Coire, the Splugen Pass, Colico, Lake Como, Bergamo, Verona, Venice, Florence, Rome, Leghorn, Pisa, Genoa, Turin, Milan, Arona, the Simplon Pass, Brieg, Martigny, Chamouny, Geneva, Lausanne, Berne, Thun, Interlaken, the Brunig Pass, Lucerne, Basle, Paris, and thence to Great Britain for the return to America.

One of sixty days will embrace England, France, Italy, and Switzerland, and will include, London, Paris, Dijon, Macon, the Mt. Cenis Tunnel, Turin, Genoa, Pisa, Rome, Naples, Florence, Venice, Verona, Milan, Como, Lugano, St. Gothard Pass, Andermatt, Lucerne, Interlaken, Berne, Neuchatel, Pontarlier, Paris, London or Liverpool.

Leaving out Italy the tour can be made in thirty days, as follows :—London, Paris, Troyes, Mulhausen, Basle, Lucerne, the Bernese Oberland, Interlaken, Berne, Freiburg, Lausanne, Geneva, Macon, Dijon, Paris, London, Glasgow or Liverpool.

The list may be extended indefinitely; enough has been given to show the possibilities of travel, so as to visit the most of the countries of Central and Southern Europe. For the probable cost the reader is referred to preceding pages of this volume, where the expense of travel is set down as nearly as it can be estimated. But, as before stated, no general rule can be made, and the cost of a journey will depend very largely upon the tastes of the traveler, and his financial ability to gratify them.

The American who visits Europe for the first time is apt to be in a hurry, and to endeavor to see too much. He will very likely return with a confused notion of his experiences, and will be obliged to refer to his note-book to know what he has done. Instances have occurred of tourists who could not tell whether St. Paul's Cathedral was in London or Rome, and who had a vague impression that the tomb of Napoleon was beneath the Arc de Triomphe. They told of the wonderful wood-carving to be seen at Venice, and thought that Michael Angelo, John Titian, and Sir Christopher Wren were among the most famous painters Switzerland had ever produced. They ascended the Volcano of Mount Blanc from Vienna, and had a delightful view of the eternal snows of Vesuvius from their hotel windows at Berlin; where they also visited Trajan's column, and the Falls of Schaffhausen. In short they came back with things decidedly mixed, and all from making their journey too quickly.

Moral—Don't be in a hurry.

CHAPTER XXIII.

GENERAL DIRECTIONS, WITH ROUTES, DISTANCES, ETC., FOR A JOURNEY ROUND THE WORLD.

If stout old Sir Francis Drake, the first navigator to sail around the globe, could appear on earth to-day, he would be quite justifiable in standing transfixed with astonishment. The announcement that he could encircle our sphere in less than eighty days would be too much for his equanimity, when he reflected that the voyage in the *Elizabeth*, from Plymouth back to Plymouth again, consumed nearly two years, and compelled him to cross the Equator no less than four times. The performance of the modern steamship would be likely to bewilder him, and he could scarcely comprehend the transit of the American Continent in a single week. From New York to Omaha, without change of cars or clothes, would be beyond his understanding, and from Omaha to San Francisco in a Pullman car would appear to his old-fashioned mind like the work of the magician. There is good reason to believe he would not be thankful that he had been awakened from his sleep of three centuries. To the question, "What would Admiral Drake say if he were alive now?" the historic Irishman might respond, "He would say he's glad he's dead!"

From the two years required for the circumnavigation of the globe in the time of Sir Francis, the progress down to our day was not very rapid. For two hundred years after that eventful voyage of the *Elizabeth*, there was little if any reduction in the time for a similar cruise, though there was a material diminution in the profits to be derived from semi-piratical adventures along the route. The brave old Admiral made his enterprise remunerative in a high degree, both to his government and himself; the courts are said to be troubled at the present day about the rightful ownership of some dozens of millions which belonged originally to the estate of Sir Francis Drake, and have increased through the operations of time and the tables of simple and compound interest.

There was a glorious uncertainty about the voyages of Sir Francis Drake and Captain Cook that exists no longer. It was a problem if ever those navigators should return; and, in the case of Captain Cook, the solution was not to the satisfaction of that enterprising explorer and his friends. But, setting aside the ordinary uncertainty of human affairs, a voyage of circumnavigation to-day is no more problematic than a trip from New York to Chicago. A man may start for a journey around the world, and fix almost to a day the date of his return. On the third day of July, 1877, the writer sailed from San Francisco for Japan, China, India, and other Eastern countries, intending to return by way of Europe. A friend was at the dock to see him off, and, as they shook hands in farewell, the latter said:

"I am going to Paris next spring; when will you meet me there?"

The outward-bound voyager thought a moment, and then said: "I'll meet you in Paris on the 15th of April."

And so they separated, one to go west, and the other, a few months later, to go east.

On the evening of the 14th of April the first-mentioned

tourist landed at Marseilles, and the next day he was at Paris; his friend, who had been notified by telegraph, was at the station to meet him, and the meeting, as we see, was exactly on the day appointed. A traveler can arrange his time with absolute certainty, if he will take the trouble to study the tables of the steamship and railway lines, and determine the period of his detention in each city and country along his route. And this is precisely what was done in the instance above mentioned.

A man in New York thinks nothing of making a business appointment for a week from to-day; he is going to Chicago in the meantime, but will be back on the date he names. It is just as feasible for him to say, "It is now the 13th of June; I must go to Hong Kong for a little business which will keep me a couple of days, and the movements of the steamers are such that I shall lose a day and a half waiting there when my business is ended. If you will call at my office at noon on the 24th of August, we will go to lunch and talk this matter over; I really haven't time to attend to it to-day. I may possibly have to go to Calcutta; if so, I'll telegraph you, and we'll make the appointment hold over till the 18th of September, as I shall arrive by the steamer of the 17th. Good-day; I leave by this evening's train."

Year by year the travel around the world increases, and doubtless it will continue to increase as people become familiar with the requirements of time and money for the journey.

A ticket around the world can be bought at a price varying from one thousand to twelve hundred dollars, according to the line of steamers chosen for certain parts of the route, and whether one passes through India or adheres to the steamer from Singapore to Suez. The time required is from three months upward, according to the

14

abilities of the traveler to spare it, and the amount of money at his disposal. The old adage, that time is money, is nowhere more applicable than on the journey around the world. You can't have a good time unless you have the money to pay for it, and you can't have a good time with your money unless you have time enough to spend it properly.

"How much does it cost to go around the world?" is as difficult to answer as "How much does a horse cost?" One man will get along with a quarter of what another will consider absolutely necessary, and can live luxuriously on what will starve another. Tastes and ways differ in travel as in anything else, and an exact rule cannot be set for everybody. A youth who has not learned by practical experience the value of a dollar, who indulges in ways of living more or less riotous, and, above all, who occasionally whiles the weary hours at the seductive game of poker with chance travelers, will require a liberal allowance to enable him to make the circuit of the world in what he would call "style." This allowance might be anywhere from five or six thousand dollars upward, and would probably leave occasional souvenirs in the shape of unpaid bills, which are altogether too numerons at present for the reputation of our countrymen. But to the man of unwasteful habits, who knows the worth of his money, and quietly makes up his mind to have it, who uses his eyes and his brains, finds what is proper to pay in each instance, and then pays it, the journey can be made in ten months, at an expenditure of about four thousand dollars. Ten months will allow for sufficient stoppages along the route, and the sum mentioned will enable him to travel first-class on all ships, and stop at first-class hotels—if the majority of the caravansaries in the East can be called first-class. Generally the only features about them that warrant that name are their bills. The traveler can also purchase a fair allowance of inexpensive "curios," as souvenirs of his tour, without going beyond the last-named figures.

If ladies are of the party the expenses will be a trifle more than where it consists entirely of the sterner sex. Ladies need have no hesitation in attempting the tour of the world; they might even go unaccompanied by gentlemen, but it is not advisable for them to do so. Hotels are to be found everywhere on the great routes of travel, and even on some of the by-ways there is passable accommodation. In the tropics where the heat is so great as to compel passengers to sleep on deck when going from one port to another, one side of the deck is reserved for ladies and the other is allotted to the men.

It is not advisable for a traveler to buy his ticket at once for the entire journey, but to take it in sections as he goes along. From New York, or any other American city, to Yokohama is enough for the first section; beyond Yokohama the routes divide, and your movements depend upon circumstances which generally are not easy to foresee. Therefore, when you have determined to buy a ticket around the world, buy it as you go along, and not all in a lump.

The best way of going around the world from America is by going westward. The seasons can be taken more easily in their natural course in this way than by going eastward, and each country on the route can be seen in the best time for seeing it. The monsoons can be taken in a favoring direction, and the typhoons, those scourges of the Eastern waters, can be avoided. From May to July is the best time for leaving San Francisco—not earlier than the first of May, and not later than the first week of July. This will give the summer months in Japan, the autumn for China and Siam—if the latter country is included—and the winter for Java, the Straits, Ceylon, and India. By the end of February one should leave India, spend a fortnight or three weeks in Egypt, and then go on to Europe. He can land in Naples late in March or early in April, and then go north with the season till he reaches that Mecca of the wanderer—Paris. Thence, if he does not possess the ingenuity to find his way home, he has traveled to very little purpose; whether he will be anxious to find his way home from Paris at an early date depends largely upon circumstances—and upon Paris.

It is advisable for the intending traveler to have his finances so arranged that he will run no risk of being stranded penniless in some Eastern port, and compelled to wait till a remittance reaches him. A letter of credit for the whole amount needed on the journey is the best thing to have; but if this is not attainable, he should carry a credit for at least half the amount, and arrange for remittances in sterling drafts on London to meet him at points previously designated. These should be forwarded in duplicate in registered letters, and by different mails, so that a loss of one will not be likely to mean the loss of both. And in order to take these registered letters from the post-office, and for other purposes of identification, every traveler should carry a passport.

In taking out a letter of credit, be sure and have it from a house that has correspondents in the principal cities and the open ports of the East. The same precaution should be observed relative to drafts that may be forwarded to meet the traveler at any of the points he is to touch; and he should not conclude that because he is personally cognizant of the high standing of a banking-house, it will be all right wherever he goes. A draft made by a well-known house in New York, on the Barings of London, reached the writer in Singapore; when he proceeded to turn it into cash he was surprised to find that nobody in Singapore had ever heard of the makers of the draft, and if he had been without introductions, and had had no letter of credit in reserve, he would have been in a very awkward predicament. Too much precaution cannot be observed about one's means of obtaining money in the far East; and to be stranded on the other side of the world without cash is very inconvenient.

We will suppose you have equipped yourself with the necessary letter of credit; the next thing is to have a suitable frame of mind for the journey, and the next a light and properly garnished trunk. The frame of mind is an important consideration. If you are a morose, ill-tempered brute, determined to see nothing good in any country but your own, you had better stay at home; and if a friend has arranged to travel with you, it would be an act of kindness to advise him to drop you and go with some one else, or alone.

Arrange your time-table as nearly as possible before starting, and then tell your friends where letters will reach you. Have them sent to the principal post-offices—Yokohama, Hong Kong, Singapore, Calcutta, Bombay, etc.—according to the dates you expect to be in those cities, and when you are about leaving those places you can instruct the post-master as to your subsequent address. If you do so your mail matter will be forwarded, and with proper care you will be pretty certain to get all your letters. Do not have newspapers sent after you, as they are not very likely to turn up on account of the accumulating postage.

As to baggage, you don't want a large amount to start with. A couple of ordinary suits of clothing, and a dress-suit for dinners, will be the basis; remember that the dress-suit is indispensable, as its absence will sometimes deprive you of the pleasure of attending an interesting ceremonial, and that a gentlemen in the East, as well as in Europe, is expected to wear an evening garb when invited to dinner. A light overcoat should be taken, and a heavy one for rough work; the latter should be of coarse but strong material, and will often come handy at sea when storms are blowing, and on land when the owner is compelled to camp out or travel through severe weather. A rug or shawl may be taken, if one has a fancy for it, but it is not at all necessary, as the stout overcoat supplies its place, and serves the additional purposes of an overcoat. Take the same underclothing that you would take for a six weeks' trip anywhere in the States; when your stock is exhausted you can buy a fresh supply in any of the ports or inland cities of the East, particularly the former. Clothing of all kinds is as cheap in Hong Kong, Shanghai, Yokohama, Singapore, Calcutta, Bombay, or the other great ports, as in New York, and in some of the cities I have mentioned it is cheaper. It would be well to have your shirt-maker get you up a dozen shirts of a kind specially adapted to the journey, and if you are inclined to be a "swell," you might take two or three dozen. Have them made of the strongest muslin you can find; pay no attention to fineness, but a great deal to strength. The front, or "bosom," may be as fine as you please, but I wouldn't be too particular about it; as to the rest, the nearer you can come to sailcloth or sheet-iron the better.

The laundress in the far East is invariably a man, and, to judge by the way he knocks your clothing to pieces, he must be the strongest man in the community. He is native and to the manner born, and his manner is not at all pleasing. In Yokohama, and other Japanese cities, he is, of course, a Jap; in China, he is the "wanchee-washee" man, with whom San Francisco and New York are familiar; in Java, he is a Malay, and in India he is a Bengalee. No matter which one you have first, you will think he is worse than any of the others can possibly be, and when you try the others you will find that your first love was the mildest of them all. The Bengalee is the worst of the lot for destructiveness, but he is only an infinitesimal distance ahead of the Chinese.

The Eastern way of washing is to pound the garments with a club, when clubs are handy, but as they are generally out of the way, and firewood is dear, the artist contents himself with laying your shirts and other things on a stone, and pounding them with another stone; and the rougher these two geological products are, the better for his purpose.

Three or four washings will generally make an end of handkerchiefs; shirts and other garments may survive a sixth or eighth journey to the lavatory, but the tenth or twelfth will usually send them to the rag-bag. Therefore I advise that all underlinen should be of the strongest material, and fineness a secondary consideration.

When you reach Yokohama you will probably want to buy some clothing suitable for the warm climate of the East. A *sola topee*, or sun-hat, is the first requisite; it is made of pith, has a white cover which can go to the wash every few days, and an internal arrangement so that the wearer's head is constantly cooled by the air which circulates around it. Then you will want some suits of white linen, about ten of them, which will cost you from five to six dollars a suit; a couple of suits of blue serge, at ten or twelve dollars each. These, with your ordinary clothing, will be sufficient for your wants, if you exercise proper care in keeping close at the heels of the washman; you will generally find that your washing will be promptly done, but it is always best to have an extra provision laid up for a rainy day. In the East everybody carries a goodly amount of baggage, and as there is always a plentiful supply of porters, and the allowance of the steamship companies is liberal, you need not mind the addition of a trunk or two.

Well, we are off from New York; we are not in a frightful hurry, and are determined to see as much as we can for our time and money.

The transcontinental trains between New York and San-Francisco are a daily affair each way, and the regular time of running through is seven days. The price of a ticket varies according to the harmony, or the lack of it, between the Eastern roads; $140 may be taken as a fair average for the through ticket, with an addition of $25 or $30 for sleeping-coaches and meals.

From San Francisco, the departures are semi-monthly for Japan and China; the steamers of the Pacific Mail and Occidental and Oriental Companies perform the service alternately, so that each line sends a ship every month. They were formerly in opposition, but are now working harmoniously; a passage-certificate bought of the one is good on the ships of the other, and there is nothing to choose between them, so far as the comfort of the voyage is concerned. The running time to Yokohama is about twenty days, and no matter what the ship or which the company that the traveler patronizes, he is pretty certain to be pleased with his fare and treatment. A ticket from San Francisco to Yokohama costs $250, and if bought in New York it entitles the passenger to an allowance of two hundred and fifty pounds of baggage overland, instead of the ordinary allowance of one hundred pounds.

After the "globe-trotter," as the tourist is called in the East, has done with Yokohama, Tokio, and the eastern part of the empire, he can take a steamer any Wednesday afternoon for Hiogo, which is the port of Osaka and Kioto. This is a voyage of a day and a half; and when the western part of the empire has been seen, another steamer may be taken to Shanghai, passing through the famous inland Sea of Japan, and halting at Simoneseki and Nagasaki. The line is weekly each way, and is known as the Mitsu Bishi (Three Diamonds); it is a Japanese organization, sustained by a government subsidy in the shape of a mail contract, and its ships are mostly of American build. Old travelers on the line between New York and San Francisco by the Isthmus route will find an acquaintance in the steamer *New York*, transformed to the " *Tokio Maru*," and the *Oregonian* to the "*Nagoya Maru*"; the *Golden Age* is the "*Maru*" something or other, and so are several of the former vessels of the Pacific Mail Company. A ticket from Yokohama to Shanghai costs $45, and it makes no difference whether you buy it through or in sections. There are chance steamers at frequent and irregular intervals, that carry passengers at a reduced rate, but they are less comfortable than the Mitsu Bishi Company's boats, and more uncertain. The crews of the Mitsu Bishi steamers are Japanese, the waiters in the cabin are Chinese, and the captains, officers, engineers, and stewards, are Americans, English, or some other Caucasian nationality. When the equipage of one of these steamers is drawn up for inspection, the affair is emphatically *une revue des deux mondes*.

From Shanghai one can ascend the Yang-Tse as far as Hankow, a distance of a trifle over six hundred miles, and there are boats of the China Merchants' company every three or four days. The price of a ticket varies; it was once $400 each way, but at the time of my visit to Shanghai it had fallen to $18, in consequence of an opposition by an English company. It was the intention, as soon as the opposition ended, to raise it again to $50, where it probably now is. The steamers are large and comfortable, and the table is excellent.

The China Merchants' Company has a weekly line to Tien-Tsin, whence one may go overland to Pekin, a distance of ninety miles. There is said to be a smooth way of the world and a rough one; where the smooth one may be I will not attempt to say, but there is little doubt that the rough one is the stretch of ninety miles between Tien-Tsin and Pekin. About two thousand years ago the road was built, and it has never been repaired since the contractors left it; it was made of large and irregular boulders, badly laid down, with no attempt at evenness, and has been a good deal damaged by old Tempus Edax Rerum in the twenty centuries that he has been gnawing at it.

You can make the journey to Pekin on horseback, by cart, or by a mule-litter, or you can go on foot. For a vigorous man, the saddle is recommended; for a more luxurious one, the mule-litter; for a brave and small one, the cart; and a man who has a touch of the walking mania can try pedestrianism. The mule-litter is a box like a covered chair, slung on a couple of poles; these poles are long enough, and just far enough apart, to serve as shafts for two mules—one in front and the other in the rear—and are suspended over the saddles of the beasts by stout straps. The pace is not unpleasant, and the movement would soon become monotonous were it not that the suspensory apparatus is constantly giving way, and letting the box to the ground with a general shaking up as the result. Occasionally the mules run away, indulge in kicking-matches, or otherwise disport themselves in ways more or less exciting; so that the traveler is in no danger of perishing with *ennui*.

The Chinese cart is a small box on a single pair of wheels; it is not long enough for an average man to lie down in, and too low for him to sit erect. The occupant is doubled up very much as if he were in a wine-cask; the cart has no springs, but the body rests directly on the axle, so that every jolt, however small, is felt by him. When all these facts are considered, in connection with the character of the road, it will be readily seen that a traveler who journeys from Tien-Tsin to Pekin in a Chinese cart, feels, on arrival, very much as though he had been passed through a patent clothes-wringer.

There is another route, via Tung-Chow. A Chinese boat is taken to the latter point, which is twelve miles from the capital; the usual way is to go to Pekin by the road, and return by Tung-Chow and the river. In this way the current favors, and the descent can be made in a couple of days, while the ascent takes four or five. Few travelers to Pekin fail to visit the Great Wall, which is about a hundred miles northwest of the city. Saddle-horses and mule-litters are the modes of conveyance, and the most of the provisions which you expect to consume on the journey must be taken along. The journey from Shanghai to Pekin and back again will require about a month in time, and $400 in money, including the visit to the Great Wall.

Brief allusion has been made to the steam lines in the far East on another page. A more detailed account will be given here.

From Shanghai to Hong Kong there is a weekly service, which is performed alternately by the Peninsular and Oriental Steam Navigation Company (English), and the Compagnie Messageries Maritimes (French). These lines are usually called the "P. and O.," and the "French Mail," and it may be roundly stated that they run from

England and France to China and Japan. One week there comes the P. and O. boat, and the next the French Mail, and so they go on alternately each way weekly, year after year. The fares are about the same, but the French line includes wine in the price of passage, which the English does not. As far as I could observe, the French steamers are the most comfortable, their table is better, and there is more civility on the part of the officers. It is noticeable that the majority of the passengers on the French steamers are English, and I have known Englishmen who were intensely patriotic in other matters to delay their departure a week to go on a French ship instead of an English one.

The itinerary of the P. and O. Line from Shanghai to Southampton touches the following ports:—Hong Kong, Singapore, Penang, Pointe de Galle, Aden, Suez, Port Said, Alexandria, Malta, and Gibraltar. There are branch lines between Hong Kong and Yokohama, Singapore and Batavia, (Java,) Pointe de Galle and Australia, Pointe de Galle and Calcutta, Aden and Bombay, and Alexandria and Brindisi. The French route is from Shanghai to Hong Kong, Saigon, Singapore, Pointe de Galle, Colombo, Aden, Suez, Port Said, Naples, and Marseilles, with branches between Hong Kong and Yokohama, Singapore and Batavia, Pointe de Galle and Calcutta, Aden and the Mauritius. Both lines receive a heavy subsidy from their respective governments in the form of mail contracts, and they do a great deal to maintain English and French prestige throughout the East. For several years the P. and O. had a virtual monopoly of the business, and looked with disdain upon the efforts of the French to enter the field. But not only did the French Line establish itself, but other lines have sprung up, and manage to flourish without the advantage to be gained from a contract for carrying the mails. There is one known as the "Holt Line," which performs a semimonthly service each way between England and China; and there are numerous irregular steamers in addition, so that there is no lack of communication between the Occident and the Orient.

The rates of fare in the East are decidedly high, when we compare them with the price of passage over the Atlantic and on the seaboard lines of the United States. From Yokohama or Shanghai, by the English line, to Southampton, or to Marseilles by the French one, the fare is £105, or $525 in round figures. The local fares are higher than this in proportion. It is $63 from Shanghai to Hong Kong—a run of three days; and $108 from Singapore to Pointe de Galle—a voyage of five days. To Java, by the branch line from Singapore, a voyage of exactly forty-eight hours, requires a disbursement of $46. You will save about 20 per cent. on your fare by purchasing a through ticket; but, as already hinted, the saving is accompanied by a restriction of one's movements that more than balances the advantage in the reduction.

At the agencies in the East they do not assign you to a room on the steamer when you buy your ticket, but tell you that you will get it from the steward when you go on board. They give as a reason for this the impossibility of knowing what rooms are reserved, as the tickets are generally bought before the ship arrives in port, and before there is any communication between the purser and the agent. This excuse will not hold good at the beginning point of the voyage, and so they plumply tell you that it is not their custom to assign the rooms except on board, and they can make no deviation from their rules. Generally the ships are not crowded, and so the custom works well enough; in case of a rush of passengers it also works admirably—for the company. The agent can continue to sell tickets to all applicants and assure them that there is abundance of room, although he knows that he has sold twice or three times the capacity of the steamer. The ship that performs the branch service for the French company between Singapore and Batavia has accommodations in her cabin for sixteen persons—eight rooms, with two berths in each room. The agent at Singapore blandly assured the writer that there were very few passengers engaged, and he would be certain to have a room to himself—when all the time more than forty passengers were booked, and the agent had the list in his possession. It may be impolite to say he lied, but he certainly was not mathematically exact. When the steamer sailed she had fifty-two passengers, and they were packed like negroes on a slave-ship. Of course there was much grumbling, but the officers of the steamer referred the matter to the agent—whose fault it was; and the agent was safe on shore, and out of reach of the angry travelers.

Two things are necessary to one's comfort in traveling on steamers in the tropical East—*pajamas,* and a bamboo chair. A pajama suit consists of a loose sack and drawers of the Chinese pattern, and nearly every foreigner in the East adopts them, in place of the night-shirt of civilization, for sleeping purposes. They may be of muslin, silk, grass-cloth, or anything else that suits the wearer's fancy —some prefer one thing and some another, and there is no way of harmonizing tastes. Any Chinese tailor can make you a pajama suit at a few hours' notice; and if you would be comfortable, you will order half a dozen suits at least.

Around the hotels and on board ship it is perfectly *en*

règle to be in pajamas between the hours of 9 P. M. and 8 A. M.; and on the steamer it is interesting to observe how universally the passengers avail themselves of the permission. Through the tropics, it is generally too hot to sleep below; nearly everybody takes to the deck and makes it his home by day and by night. The reclining chair comes in play here, as it can serve as a bed for most persons, and at any rate it is a capital lounge. It can be bought very cheaply in all the Eastern ports, and no traveler's equipment is complete without it. And the man who neglects to provide himself with pajamas in the first port he reaches will have reason to regret his action. He might even do a more unwise thing than purchase a supply before he leaves San Francisco, provided the Chinese have not all gone thence before he reaches the Pacific coast.

The hours for meals vary somewhat on the different lines, but may be taken as resembling in general the hours on the transatlantic ships, with the exception that they are fewer. As soon as you rise you can have a preliminary coffee or tea, or you may have it before you rise, if it so please you. Then from eight to ten you have breakfast, which consists of omelets, meat of two or three kinds, and curry, the latter being universal and perennial. Somewhere between noon and 1 P. M. there is a cold lunch with fruit, and at 5 P. M. comes dinner. This is not much unlike the steamship dinner of other parts of the world, except that the curry comes up warm and smiling on every occasion, and is eaten by nearly everybody. Few people like it when they first eat it, and few people eat it half a dozen times without acquiring a taste for it that is akin to love. It is conceded that curry is necessary to keep the liver in a proper condition of activity, and the man who does not eat it is very liable to find himself out of order internally in a very short time. It is surprising that such a warm substance as curry should be the proper thing in a hot climate; but the weight of testimony is emphatically in its favor, and we should respect the verdict of time and experience.

There is no pleasanter steamship life anywhere than in the East, so far as the associations are concerned. The brainless idiots that add a pang to existence on the transatlantic voyage are rarely seen so far away from home as the coast of China; the majority of the people you meet there are the possessors of at least a fair amount of intelligence, and know how to use it. Among twenty passengers on a steamer, you will find three or four globe-trotters, like yourself; as many merchants; as many clerks and other employés of Eastern houses; two or three men who have been or still are in the consular or diplomatic service; a banker or two; two or three soldiers of fortune who have been serving one of the Oriental governments in one way or another; and the balance will be made up of nondescripts, who cannot be classed in any regular list. If there are any of the gentler sex, they will be the wives, widows, sisters, or daughters of men who have been making a home in the East; and you will occasionally encounter some of them who have made a dozen voyages back and forth, and know every wave of the sea along the route. The great majority of the passengers are sure to have had sufficient attrition against the world to wear away their rough corners; you will find them social without forwardness, and communicative without being garrulous.

If the traveler is limited in time and money, he will avoid the north of China, and also the western part of Japan; he will proceed direct from Yokohama to Hong Kong, and can take for this purpose a ship of either of the transpacific lines or of the English or French mail companies. The former are preferable, as the fare, when combined with that from San Francisco, is lower, and the steamers are larger and better than the English or French mail-packets. From Hong Kong one can go daily to Canton (ninety miles) in about eight hours; and by no means should a tourist omit seeing this most interesting of the cities of China. From Hong Kong, when Canton has been finished, the regular route leads to Singapore—the English steamers going direct, and the French ones touching at Saigon. Those who wish to leave the regular track may go to Siam by steamers that leave every week or ten days, and, though of English build and ownership, are managed by a Chinese agency, and carry their cargoes on Chinese account. They are nominally freight-steamers, but have accommodations for a few passengers; and the same is the case with the steamers that will take the tourist from Bangkok to Singapore when his visit to Siam is concluded.

From Singapore you may make a detour to Java or Manila, but eventually you will find your way back again, since all the routes of the East lead by this point, as, anciently, all roads led to Rome. If you have a month to spare when south of the equator, you may make a circular trip on a Dutch steamer that goes to all the principal ports of Java and the Spice Islands, and comes around in the end to her starting-point. When back in Singapore, and ready to go on to the westward, you have choice of two, or, rather, of three routes: you can go by mail-steamer to Ceylon, and stop at Galle, whence you proceed by land to Colombo, and Kandy; you can go to Calcutta direct; or you may go to Calcutta by a steamer that halts at Malacca, Penang, and Moulmein a day each, and two days at Rangoon. This indirect voyage consumes seventeen days, but it is full of interest. The direct voyage to Calcutta requires six days.

If you do India by way of Ceylon, you will finish the land of spicy breezes, where only man is vile, and then cross from Colombo to Tuticorin, whence you can go by rail to the uttermost parts of the great Indian peninsula; or you may take, once a week, a ship of the British India Steam Navigation Company, which makes the voyage to Calcutta in fourteen days, touching at Madras and a dozen other ports. As the ship is usually halted in the daytime and moving at night, this mode of traveling is not at all unpleasant. From Calcutta the railway will bear us to the north, and we can see Benares, Agra, Cawnpore, Lucknow, Allahabad, Delhi, Jeypoor, and other cities, arriving eventually at Bombay.

Six weeks will serve for seeing India, or, rather, that part of it in the Bengal and Bombay presidencies, and very few who have done the country will care to return.

The distance from Bombay to Calcutta, by the direct route, is 1,409 miles, and the fare (first-class) about $60. Benares and Allahabad are the only cities of importance that lie on the direct line; the others are reached by branches, and it will require another thousand miles of travel to take them in.

We will suppose we have finished with India, and are ready to leave Bombay for Egypt and Europe. The P. & O. Company sends a weekly steamer, and its departure is fixed for Saturday during the prevalence of the southwest monsoon, and for Monday when the monsoon is not blowing. There is another weekly service, formed by the Hall Line and the Anchor Line, making fortnightly departures alternately. There is an Italian line and an Austrian line, each monthly, and there are numerous irregular steamers, so that four departures a week may be fairly counted upon. The fares vary considerably; the P. & O. charges $250 to carry you to Suez, 3,000 miles: the Italian line will take you there for $160; the Anchor and Hall lines for $155, and the Austrian for $150. Patronage appears to be fairly divided among the lines; those who have plenty of money, together with a great many who have not, go by the P. & O. ships, while others who are more matter-of-fact, and do not care to keep up appearances, select the cheaper lines.

To irascible bachelors, the voyage from Bombay westward has a lively terror. From February to May the steamers are crowded with children and their nurses on their way to England, and, no matter what ship you take, you cannot avoid them. Like the poor, they are always with you, and cannot be shaken off; very often the number of juvenile passengers equals that of the adults, and on occasions painfully frequent it is greater. From rosy morn till dewy eve, and from eve till morn again, they make things the reverse of monotonous, and a passionate lover of infantile ways has all the entertainment he desires. Selfish and irreverent travelers are apt to think affectionately of King Herod, and wonder if his like will ever be seen again.

This migration of children is for the reason that they lose health, and generally their lives, if kept in India beyond the age of four or five years. The spring and early summer are considered the best time for them to arrive in Europe, and consequently the traveler at this season finds the steamers filled with them. They are mostly of the spoiled class, accustomed to have their own way, to receive the attentions of a multitude of servants, and to resent with anger the least attempt to thwart them. The companies would doubtless find it to their profit to send an occasional steamer at higher rates, from which children should be excluded, just as our transatlantic lines advertise ships carrying no steerage passengers, and charge more for places thereon.

In Egypt, one can go directly through the canal, and thence to Europe, or he may land at Suez, go by rail to Cairo (eight hours), and when he has done with Cairo he may go in four hours to Alexandria, where he will find three or four steamers a week for Brindisi, Naples, Marseilles, and England, and steamers at least once a week for Syria, Palestine, Asia Minor, Constantinople, the Black Sea, and also for Greece and the Adriatic. He may take his time in Europe, and get home the best way he can.

Following is a table of distances of a journey around the world, without taking into account the numerous detours, which will vary according to the tastes and means of each traveler, and the time he has allotted to himself for his personal gratification, either in the pursuit of pleasure, science and art, or commerce :—

New York to San Francisco, 3,450 miles; San Francisco to Yokohama, 4,764; Yokohama to Hong Kong, 1,620; Hong Kong to Singapore, 1,150; Singapore to Calcutta, 1,200; *Calcutta to Bombay,* 1,409; Bombay to Aden, 1,664; Aden to Suez, 1,308; *Suez to Alexandria,* 250; Alexandria to Marseilles, 1,300; *Marseilles to Paris,* 536; *Paris to London,* 316; *London to Liverpool,* 205; Liverpool to New York, 3,000. Total, 22,172 miles.

(Distances by rail are in italics; by sea in roman.)

Separating the above distance into land and sea travel, we have 6,166 miles of railway, and a trifle over 16,000 miles of water. Allowing continuous progress at the rate of twenty-five miles an hour on land and twelve miles on the water we could swing around the great circle inside of sixty-seven days. And if we take the quickest journeys that have been made over the different portions of the route—the special trains that have passed across the Continent on two or three occasions, and the extraordinary runs of steamers on the Atlantic, Pacific, and Indian Oceans, and in the China and Mediterranean Seas—add them together, and make no deductions for delays in port, we can have a theoretical journey around the world in less than sixty days. Phileas Fogg is left far in the rear, and Jules Verne must resume his pen and make another trial, if he would really astonish us. Give us the highest recorded speed upon railways and ocean steamers, and apply it to the route in question, and we will put a girdle around the earth in the half of eighty days, with several hours to spare.

CHAPTER XXV.

LEGAL RIGHTS OF TRAVELERS.

For the information contained in this chapter the author is indebted to a well-known lawyer of New York, who has had considerable experience in suits of individuals against railway and steamship companies, and is therefore thoroughly competent to write on the subject.

"In considering the legal rights of travelers it is necessary to remember that they are not the same in all countries, nor even in different states of one country. Legal right in England may not be legal right in France or the United States, and a decision of a court in New York may be quite opposed to one in a case exactly similar in Ohio or California. I will endeavor to give a summary of decisions embodying the most important relations of the traveler to the carrying companies, and where there are two cases of similar character, that have been differently decided, I shall prefer the one from the higher court.

"One of the most frequent causes of dispute in the United States is the time for which a ticket is valid. It has been generally held that a ticket for a single trip over a railway is good for any length of time, with the understanding that when the journey begins it shall be completed in a continuous ride. This applies only to single tickets over the road of one company; when the ticket has one or more coupons attached, and is sold at a lower rate than the single fares would amount to if added together, it is liable to be refused on the ground that it is in the form of a contract that expired a certain number of days after the ticket was issued. There have been many decisions on this subject, the majority of them favoring the claims of the company against the passenger.

"An excursion or round trip ticket, sold at a reduced rate, is held to be a contract, and is worthless if not used in the time specified. It is also non-transferable, if so printed on the face, and the conductor may refuse it when offered, on the return trip, by any person other than the one who used the first half. The theory is that in consideration of the reduced rate the company should have the benefit of any chance that the original purchaser does not return within the specified time. The courts of most of the United States, and also those of England and the Continental countries, are in accord on this subject.

"A ticket marked 'good for this day only,' or 'for this train only,' was formerly held to be good for any day till used, but of late years the majority of decisions are in favor of the printed limitation, on the ground that the companies have a right to regulate their business, and that they must know how many people are to travel by a train in order to make it up properly. But in this case the purchaser of a ticket may have his money returned provided he asks for it before the departure of the train, or can show that it is the fault of the company that he has not used it.

"In regard to the validity of a ticket in the reverse direction from what it reads, there have been several decisions both ways, the passenger claiming that he had paid to be carried a given number of miles over the road and he had a right to travel either way, as he chose. A passenger on the New York and New Haven railway recovered damages for injuries received while being ejected from the cars, but it required a law-suit of five years, and repeated trials, to obtain them. He had offered a ticket from New Haven to New York while riding in the reverse direction, and was put off in consequence. In another instance a passenger from Boston to Portland sued for damages, for ejection from the train when he offered a ticket 'from Portland to Boston,' and lost his case; and the majority of the decisions in England and the United States favor this view of the subject.

"It has been held repeatedly that a passenger is entitled to a seat, and cannot be required to give up his ticket until a seat is provided, though he must show it if asked. A passenger on a New York railway found no seats in the ordinary coaches and went into the drawing-room car that formed part of the train. When called on for the extra charge for the seat he refused it, but announced his readiness to return to the ordinary coaches as soon as a place was provided for him there. Thereupon he was ejected by the porter, and he brought suit against the railway company for damages. The latter claimed it was not responsible, as the drawing-room car was the property of a private individual, and not of the railway, but the courts rejected this claim and gave damages to the passenger. Similar decisions have been made in several cases where railway and sleeping-car companies were concerned, the courts holding that the railways are responsible for the management of the cars that compose their trains, although they may not own them. This principle has been affirmed by the Court of Appeals of New York, and by the Supreme Court of the United States.

"It was formerly held that a conductor must allow a passenger to ride when he had lost his ticket, providing he gave reasonable proof of having purchased one before entering the train, but of late years the courts are inclined to the opinion that it is the passenger's place to take care of his ticket, and it is unfair to ask the conductor to hold a court of inquiry concerning it. Besides, the company has no protection against carrying the person who finds the ticket. In Illinois a passenger in a Pullman car lost his ticket after showing it to the porter; the conductor came around before the train started and demanded the ticket, or its equivalent, and refused to take the porter's word about it, whereupon the passenger went to the ticket-office and procured a certificate to the effect that he had bought a ticket. This the conductor refused, and compelled the passenger to ride in the ordinary coach all night. A jury gave $3,000 damages to the passenger, but a higher court said this amount was excessive, and the man was only entitled to what he had paid for the ticket, and moderate compensation for the inconvenience of being deprived of a place in the sleeping-car.

"There have been frequent lawsuits involving the rights of persons traveling on free passes; the railway pass usually bears on its back a printed notice that 'the person accepting this free pass thereby assumes all risk of accidents,' etc., etc. The courts have generally held that this notice is of no consequence, and the holders of free passes have collected damages for injury to their persons, or loss of property, while using said tickets. The theory is that the pass is granted for some consideration which is the equivalent of the money that would be required to purchase a ticket at the office, and therefore the company is liable, and it has been affirmed by the Supreme Court. Since these decisions, some of the railways print the notice in the form of a contract or agreement, which the passenger signs before delivering the pass to the conductor; no suit under this form of pass has been reported, and the companies think they could not be mulcted under it, as they could show a specific agreement on the part of the passenger not to ask for damages in any event. A tramp, or other person, stealing a ride on a train has no redress for damages, nor any other rights which the company is bound to respect.

"Damages have been recovered in several instances for injuries received in railway stations before the intending passenger had entered the train, or even purchased a ticket, and they have also been recovered for injuries received in the station after the completion of the journey. In all these cases it was shown that the person was in the station either for the intention of traveling, or after the completion of the journey, and in one case where the plaintiff could not establish this fact he lost his case.

"In a case where a passenger in an omnibus was injured by the upsetting of the vehicle, through the driver's carelessness, damages were given by a jury. The omnibus belonged to the railway company, and was run by them between the station and neighboring village. The passenger had no ticket, as tickets were only sold at the station, whither he was going, but it was held that his journey began when he entered the company's omnibus with the intention of traveling by the railway.

"The right of a passenger to protection from drunken and disorderly persons, and from ruffians in general, has been established. The courts have decided that the company through its agents must use 'due diligence' for the protection of peaceable passengers, and unless it does so it is liable. A good illustration is that of a railway in Mississippi where some rowdies beat a passenger severely, and the latter sued the company for negligence. It was shown that the conductor simply asked the rowdies not to get him into trouble, and then left the car; the court held that the company was liable for his failure to use due diligence in protecting the passenger, and gave the latter $6,000 damages, but if the conductor had stopped the train, and called the brakemen and passengers to assist him, the damages would not have been allowed, even if the conductor had failed in his effort at protection.

"Suits have arisen out of the loss of property by passengers in sleeping-cars, and in most instances the company is not held responsible, as it is not a common carrier, and the court rules that it is the passenger's duty to take care of his own personal valuables. The same rulings have been made in several cases where property has been lost in an ordinary passenger-car and suit brought against the company, the courts holding that when a man chooses to take care of his valise or hand-bag it is not in the care of the company. So, also, in instances where passengers have been robbed while on railway trains, the courts have exonerated the companies, except where absolute negligence has been shown. In one case some ruffians entered a car and robbed a passenger of $15,000 in U. S. bonds; the courts held that the company was not responsible, since $15,000 was altogether too large an amount of valuables to be carried about one's person, and before the company was to be held liable it should have been notified, and the property intrusted to its care.

"Responsibility for baggage has given rise to a great many suits on the part of passengers, and the decisions are numerous and varied. In general it is held that a passenger can recover for the loss of personal property such as he wishes to use and actually needs on his journey, 'in reasonable amount.' Most of the railway companies in America stipulate on their tickets that the passenger is limited to one hundred dollars in value and one hundred pounds in weight of baggage, and if he has more than one hundred dollars' worth he must declare it, and pay in addition at the rate of a single fare for every five hundred dollars in value. Extra trunks are usually paid for by the piece, rather than by the weight or value, and checks given accordingly.

"In a suit growing out of the loss of baggage the passenger is required to tell the contents of his trunk, and the jury must decide whether the missing articles belonged properly to the traveler's outfit. In one case a man lost a trunk which contained his 'wardrobe.' When he stated, which he did very reluctantly, that the trunk contained sixteen coats of different sizes, and no other garments, the jury thought it a remarkable wardrobe for a traveler, and he lost his case. Money, watches, and jewelry are admitted to be a part of one's baggage, but they must be carefully packed, and not excessive in amount. Discrimination is made in favor of money, as most civilized nations have recognized this article as a requisite of travel. Surgeons' instruments, law books, and papers for a lawyer going to attend court, dresses of actors and actresses, uniforms of soldiers, and in general anything that may be classed under the head of 'tools of a trade or profession' are legitimate baggage, and form a good basis of a suit for damages in case of loss. A gambler once brought suit for the loss of his trunk, which contained a roulette table and other paraphernalia of his 'profession,' together with two revolvers and a bowie-knife. The court decided against him on the ground that his occupation was *contra bonos mores*, and the railway company could not be held to a responsibility for anything intended to demoralize the community.

"Where there is clear proof of the loss of a trunk a railway company will generally pay without litigation, if the claimant is a person of respectability, and there is reason to believe that the statement of contents is correct, provided also that the amount claimed is not enormous. It is better for the company to pay one or two hundred dollars in a genuine case than to go to the courts, where it would be pretty sure to be defeated, but there are some companies that make it a rule never to pay until sued, on the ground that they frighten away a great many timid persons, as well as others who cannot afford the time for a lawsuit.

"A famous case, involving the question of what is necessary to one's personal comfort on a journey, is that of a Russian countess against the New York Central railway. One of her trunks, containing laces to the value of $200,000, was opened while she was traveling from New York to Niagara Falls, and about 200 yards of lace were stolen. It was antique and costly, and valued at $80,000; the trunk was old and worn, and its exterior gave no indication of the wealth within. The Countess sued for the value of the lace, and the company defended the suit on the ground that the lady had no right to carry such property in a common trunk, and that it was her duty to inform the company, through its agent, the baggage-master, of the value of the trunk, and pay the proper price for its insurance. The court held that she was not bound to volunteer information, but it was her duty to answer all proper questions concerning her baggage, and to pay whatever was demanded as extra freight. But as nobody had questioned her she was not in the wrong; considering her station in life the laces were necessary to her comfort, and she was awarded $30,000 in compensation for her loss.

"Suits for lost baggage are far less common in Europe than in America. They generally result in favor of the companies, especially where two or more are concerned.

between Paris and London losses occur from time to time, and when the passenger seeks redress he is told that he must show whether the loss took place in France, England, or on the channel, so that the responsibility can be fixed. Of course he can rarely do so; all he knows is that his trunk started from one end of the route and failed to arrive at the other; the company that took it swears it delivered it safely to the other, while the latter swears that it never received it. The unlucky passenger gets the worst of it, and the matter is complicated by having different languages, laws, and customs to contend with. The courts generally take the side of the companies by throwing the burden of proof on the loser; a similar juggle is not unknown in America, as the patrons of freight, express, and transportation lines in general can testify. A parcel or a box will be lost between New York and San Francisco; the shipper holds a receipt or a bill of lading from the company to whom he delivered it in New York, and it is clearly evident that he can know nothing about the movements of his property after it left his hands. But when he asks for redress he is told to 'prove where the loss occurred and let us know who is responsible.'

"Most of the Continental lines of railway have a fixed tariff for payment for lost baggage, and on proof of disappearance of a trunk or a satchel they pay with reasonable promptness. Baggage is so well cared for on the Continent that losses are rare, but the complaints are not infrequent of robberies from trunks while in transit. Travelers on their way from Italy to England sometimes find that their baggage, which was booked through, has been opened while on the road, and valuables abstracted; suspicion points directly to the railway servants, but when a sufferer asks the railway companies to pay him he is met with the response that he must prove on what road the theft occurred, and must also name the man or men concerned in it. As he is unable to do this he loses his time as well as his property, and his principal consolation is to write an account of the affair to the *London Times* or some other English newspaper.

"The laws regarding common carriers apply to steamships and steamboats the same as to railways, and the decisions in cases arising from loss of the property of passengers are of the general character already described.

"Many suits have arisen consequent upon the failure of railway companies to run their trains at the advertised time, missing connections, or otherwise causing loss to the passenger. The courts have generally held that the advertised time-table of a company has the validity of a contract with the public, and unless it can show that the failure to keep the agreement was quite beyond its control, the passenger must be paid for any immediate loss resulting therefrom. But the allowances are confined to 'direct' rather than to 'indirect' damages, and include extra expense for hotel bills or for special conveyances, and sometimes compensation for injury to health by exposure. A merchant may be able to show that by missing a connection he lost the opportunity to make a valuable contract; a lawyer may prove that a case went against him because the delay on the railway prevented his reaching court till after the judge had rendered his decision; or an actor may show that he disappointed an audience and lost the profits of a performance for the same reason. In all these instances the courts will not hold the companies responsible, as the loss is constructive and not actual. On the other hand the passenger is held guiltless for a free ventilation of his opinions to the conductor or other representative of the company, and he may even indulge in profane expressions, if he is unrestrained by moral training.

"There is a case on record in which a railway train that was running behind time was struck by a tornado, whereby a passenger was injured. A suit was brought for damages on the ground that if the train had been on time it would not have encountered the storm, but the court held that the delay was not in any way the cause of the tornado, and therefore the company had no responsibility in the matter. Accidents from floods, snow-storms, and similar causes are regarded by the courts as 'the act of God,' and if a company can show that it used all diligence to avert disaster, and made every reasonable effort to get the train through on time, it is exonerated.

"Delays on steamships are regarded in the same light. If a steamer meets with an accident at sea, or is detained by storms, the occurrence is treated as a case of *force majeure*, for which the owners of the ship are not responsible, unless negligence or incapacity of the officers can be clearly shown. If a steamer breaks down after starting on a voyage, and returns to the port of departure, her passengers are entitled to be conveyed on the vessel as soon as the necessary repairs are effected, or on some other vessel of the same company, but the company is not required to return the money paid for the passenger's fare unless it has no vessel to start on the voyage 'within a reasonable time.' It generally does so by courtesy, to avoid making enemies, and not infrequently the company pays the hotel bills of delayed passengers for the same reason. In the Mediterranean and the far East a passenger delayed by the failure of a ship to make a connection, or from any other cause, must pay his own hotel bills, and if he lives on board the ship while waiting in port he must pay for his meals, but not for his lodging.

"When a ship is detained in quarantine the passengers must pay for their meals, at a reasonable price, which is usually fixed beforehand. Several suits, growing out of delays in quarantine, have arisen, and almost invariably the decisions have been in favor of the steamship companies. In one instance a steamer touched at an infected port on her way, and thereby subjected herself to be quarantined on arriving at her destination. It was shown that she was not advertised to touch at the port in question, and her agents, at the point of departure, had distinctly stated she would not stop there; the court compelled the refunding of the money paid for board during the ten days' quarantine, and also other expenses caused by the delay, on the ground that there had been a clear violation of agreement with the public.

"The reader who desires fuller information on this subject will do well to consult 'Judge and Jury,' by Benjamin Vaughan Abbott, and 'The Law of the Road, or Wrongs and Rights of a Traveler,' by R. Vashon Rogers. 'Judge and Jury' endeavors to show the law of the land on topics of general public interest, and about sixty pages of the book are devoted to travel and transportation. 'The Law of the Road' is in the form of a story, introducing all the incidents and accidents of travel, and their legal aspects. In both books the decisions of the courts are cited, so that they can be readily found. 'Lawson on Common Carriers' is also recommended as an excellent authority on matters indicated by its title."

CHAPTER XXVI.

WILDERNESS AND FRONTIER TRAVEL.

The rapid extension of the railway across the American Continent, and the construction of lateral lines, have greatly diminished the volume of travel with wagons, and other primitive modes, but have by no means made an end of them. There is yet a large area without settlements, and unprovided with the iron road, and for many years to come the wagon of the emigrant and explorer will wend its way through the wilderness. For those who contemplate pushing beyond the borders of civilization, the writer presents this chapter.

The means of transportation available in frontier or wilderness regions are wagons and pack-animals; the former are adapted to most open and prairie countries, but in mountain regions it often happens that the wagon cannot be used. The pack-animals in general use are horses and mules; the latter are the surest of foot, especially the Mexican variety, which is smaller than the American mule, and can live where the latter would starve. Where snow is to be encountered horses are to be preferred, as the horse will plod on through the drifts long after the mule has given up in despair. The writer of "How to Travel" has an unhappy recollection of crossing the divide between the Arkansas and Platte rivers in the winter of 1860, when paths had to be trodden in the snow for the mules before they would consent to go ahead.

Our horses kept on through snow that was nearly thirty inches deep, but even when they had made a very good path it was difficult to urge the mules forward.

The best pack-saddles for either horses or mules are of the "Grimsley" pattern; they are open at the top, and covered with rawhide that shrinks while drying, and is thus drawn straight. The Grimsley fits well on the animal's back, and saves it from soreness longer than any other form of saddle in use. The Indians have pack-saddles in the form of "saw-horses," and the Mexicans use a leather sack like a mattress, which is stuffed with hay, and has no projections for fastening the load in place. In putting it on a mule they draw the belt so tight that it seems to threaten to cut the poor brute in two, and certainly must give him great pain. All the forms of pack-saddles, as well as the best riding-saddles for frontier use, have broad girths of braided horse-hair, that are far less likely to slip than any girth of leather.

The proper adjustment of a load on a pack-saddle is a work of art that can only be accomplished after long experience. In the first place, the load must be accurately balanced, so that it will not have a tendency to turn over, and, secondly, it must be lashed to prevent its working 'loose, and scattering' itself along the trail. It is not agreeable to find soon after leaving camp that your lashings have loosened, and the load, which was your pride at starting, is being distributed by the wayside. To add to the perplexity, the mule invariably helps the business along by executing a waltz, and kicking at imaginary dogs above the tree-tops. Men have been known to use profane language on such occasions, but a mule never does.

At night the packs should be placed in a row and covered with the saddles and saddle-blankets, to protect them from possible dew or rain, and have them convenient for loading up in the morning. Great care should be exercised to prevent the backs of the animals from getting sore; the best preventive is a well-fitting saddle, but in any case the backs of the beasts should be closely watched. If a horse or mule is found to be sweating when unsaddled, it is well to allow the saddle-blanket to remain until the skin is dry. Grease can be applied to a spot that shows a tendency to soreness, and a piece of bacon-rind may be tied on and left over night. It is not a good plan to wash an animal's back immediately after unsaddling, and while he is hot and sweating; the back should be allowed to cool completely before water is applied.

A very important member of a pack-train, especially when it is composed of mules, is the *madrina*, or bell-mare. She must be chosen for her dignity and docility, and be ornamented with a bell like the ordinary cow-bell of the eastern States. Its tinkle is a great attraction to the mules, and wherever she goes they are sure to follow. When the train is on the march she should be kept in front, and when rivers are to be crossed she must be sent over first. The affection shown by mules for the bell-mare is often very touching; they will crowd around her and struggle for the privilege of rubbing their noses against her sides, and, if she is accompanied by a colt, they show as much fondness for it as girls do for a baby. Many are the stories told by old plainsmen about the bell-mare, and the devotion of the rest of the animals to her; she saves a vast deal of trouble, both in camp and on the march, as she keeps the herd together when all other means would fail.

For wagon travel on long and rough roads, where grain cannot be obtained, oxen are preferable to mules or horses, as they have more endurance, though they move more slowly. They keep in good condition where horses and mules would give out, and in cases of emergency, where the animals must be slaughtered for food, they make orthodox and more attractive beef. Fifteen to twenty miles is a good day's journey for an ox-team, while horses and mules can make from twenty to thirty, if the roads are fairly good. Oxen are less liable to be stampeded by Indians, and are easier to keep from straying; with a few days' training they can be made to work under the pack-saddle if necessary, and in South Africa pack-oxen are in general use. Anderson, who traveled in South Africa, said he had an ox named 'Spring' that he rode for two thousand miles, and found him an excellent beast under the saddle. It is well for a long journey to have some cows along, as they find their own food, and give milk, and, in emergencies, they may be worked in the teams like oxen.

Wagons should be as light as possible, consistent with strength, and the wood should be perfectly seasoned, in order to resist the effects of the changes of the atmosphere. The wagon-body should be water-tight, so that it will preserve its contents when fording streams, and it can also be used as a boat where a river is too deep to be forded. There should be a joint in the pole where it enters the hounds, and the coupling pole should be movable; the joint will often prevent the breaking of the hounds, and the movable perch enables a part of the wagon to be converted into a cart, when a broken wheel or axle prevents the further use of the entire vehicle. Every wagon should have strong bows and a double cover of thick osnaburg to protect the contents from the rain and dew. The bolts that connect the running-gear should be riveted at the ends to prevent the nuts from falling off, as the loss of a nut in the wilderness often leads to the loss of the entire wagon.

The load of the wagon should be closely and securely packed, and everything arranged to prevent chafing in the many jolts of the road. Provisions for the journey should be in the most compact form, and not a superfluous ounce of stuff should be taken along. Bacon and flour are best carried in strong sacks, and all boxes and barrels must be rejected, except one or two light flour barrels for getting water. Sugar and salt must be in canvas bags with an outer covering of india-rubber or oil-cloth, to prevent the moisture reaching the contents, and tea and coffee require air-tight cans for their preservation. Dessicated and canned vegetables are excellent; the former deserve the preference on account of their more condensed form. Citric acid and the essence of lemons should be taken on long journeys where fresh vegetables cannot be obtained, as they are an efficient anti-scorbutic, and it is well to have a few simple medicines in a small box that ought to be kept in a corner of one of the wagons, where it can be easily reached.

The personal outfit of a campaigner in the wilderness is not very elaborate. White shirts should be discarded, and blue or red flannel worn instead. The coat should be short and of some strong woolen material, and the overcoat heavy without being stiff. The trowsers should be thick and soft, and if the wearer intends to do any saddle-riding he should have his nether garments "half-soled," or reënforced with buckskin where they touch the saddle, and thus preserve them from wear. An outfit for a campaign of a hundred days might be about as follows:—

Overcoat, coat, and soft hat, one each, two flannel overshirts, two woolen undershirts, two pairs thick cotton drawers, four pairs woolen socks, two pairs cotton socks, three pairs shoes, one pair strong and high boots, one India-rubber poncho, and six colored silk handkerchiefs. Then add castile soap for toilet purposes, and three pounds bar soap for clothes, comb and brush, and tooth-brushes, and a quantity of needles, thread, pins, buttons, beeswax, etc., in a small bag of buckskin. By the way, don't forget a good quantity of buckskin and an awl; they come handy in many ways for repairing harness, clothing, saddles, shoes, and the like, and you will greatly miss them if you forget them till too late.

For bed and bedding you want two blankets, a quilt, and a pillow, the whole wrapped in a cover of India-rubber or painted canvas, which can be spread on the ground at night to keep out the moisture. For dining-room and kitchen you want for every six persons a camp-kettle, a coffee-pot, a mess, a frying, and a bake-pan, all of wrought-iron. Have an extra camp-kettle for accidents, and a bucket of galvanized-iron for bringing water; don't trust to wood, as it is liable to many accidents from which iron is secure. Your judgment will tell you about knives, forks, and spoons; cups and plates should be of strong tin, and the handles of the former riveted on, never soldered. Pepper and matches should be in glass bottles, with close corks, and kept in the safest place. Every horse and mule should have at least two lariats, or picket-ropes, and every wagon needs an axe, and a spade, and some S's, and extra chain-links for repairs.

So much for the outfit, to which you will add the firearms that suit your fancy and the requirements of the region you are about to visit. Those that use fixed ammunition are undoubtedly to be preferred, if you can be sure of a sufficient supply of cartridges at all times, but where this is not the case, it is best to adhere to the old-fashioned Colt's revolver, loading with loose powder and ball. A Remington, Winchester, or other cartridge rifle may be carried for rapid work in fighting Indians, or killing large game, and a Colt's revolver, with loose ammunition, will be a convenient thing for every day use and ornament.

Now we are off, and must look out for ourselves. Provisions for our sustenance are in the wagons, and we must think of food and water for our riding and team animals. Make short and easy drives for the first few days, till the teams get accustomed to their work, and then we will increase the distance; we will not make more than half a dozen miles the first day, and even if we only go a mile or two, and camp just outside the town, we shall have gained so much. We will make our marches in the early part of the day, have a long rest at noon, especially if we are using oxen, and then go on again till sunset. We must always camp near grass and water, and it is better to make a very long drive than not to do so; if possible, we should have grass and water at the noon halt, but, in case of necessity, we can do without water, and then lengthen the afternoon march so as to reach it.

An old traveler will find water where the novice declares it does not exist; none of the rules are absolutely infallible, and the shrewdest will sometimes be disappointed. Observe the fresh tracks of animals, and the flight of birds, and they will frequently lead to water, especially the tracks of deer and mustangs. Examine the dry beds of streams, and if they are sandy push a long stick or cane as far into the sand as it will go; if you find it moist when you withdraw it, you can be certain of water. Then dig a hole with your spade, and use an empty flour-barrel for a curb, and if the hole is deep you can place one barrel above another. In a little while the water will enter the barrel, and you may draw from this improvised well all you need for your party and your stock.

In countries where streams and springs are scarce, water may be caught during showers by means of tents, awnings, wagon-covers, and even by rubber overcoats.

Drinking-water may be obtained where there are heavy dews by dragging a blanket over the grass, and then wringing it out; it is hardly necessary to add that the blanket should be a clean one. Water from stagnant pools may be purified by thorough boiling, and then mixing with powdered charcoal; in a muddy pond, it may be partially cleansed by boring small holes in the lower half of a barrel, filling it two-thirds full with layers of moss or grass, with alternate layers of clean sand, if the latter can be had. Then place the barrel in the pond till the top is nearly level with the surface; as the water enters the barrel it will pass through the improvised filter; and be found far purer than in its original state.

Always form your camp by the side of a river or stream of some kind, if it is possible to do so, as you thereby make sure of plenty of water for your stock; if in a hostile country, where attacks from Indians are possible, have an eye to the defences of the position. A peninsula in a river is the best place, as the water forms a natural fortification, and you have only the neck of the peninsula to look after; if you cannot find such a spot, take the place that most nearly resembles it, and if you cannot do better, have the river or stream on one side of you. If you camp away from water, select a spot so as to have the crest of a hill on one side of you, where a lookout can be stationed.

It is the custom for large parties traveling on the western plains of the United States to arrange their wagons in a circle, or an oval, with an opening at each end, at every halt. A yard is thus formed, into which the stock may be driven to be harnessed or yoked. It may be enclosed at night, or when hostile attacks are made, and, finally, the yard, or corral, is an excellent redoubt from which to make a defense against Indians. Many a train has been captured by neglecting this precaution, and many another saved by observing it. No good captain of a train will ever allow it to go into camp even for an hour without forming the wagons into a corral. When the stock is driven in, the openings at the ends of the corral may be closed by the simple operation of stretching a chain across.

Where there is a scarcity of water, you will find you can get along without it for many purposes for which at home it is considered absolutely necessary. All your cooking and dining utensils can be cleansed thoroughly without it; knives and forks by thrusting them several times into the ground till every vestige of their recent use is removed, and plates and pans by means of wisps of grass and dry earth, joined to what is known in the Eastern States as "elbow-grease." Great care should be exercised in regions where water contains alkaline matter, as it induces diseases that require a long time for curing.

Fuel is the great need of a traveler next to water. In a wooded country he has no trouble in finding it, but he should never waste it, no matter how plentiful. Never build a fire in a hollow log, or one that is partially decayed, but clear a space of ground, and roll or carry your fuel to it. When you move on in the morning put out the fire, or encircle it, so that it cannot by any possibility spread and cause damage. The danger of a hollow log is that the fire may smoulder there for days, or even weeks, and then break out; if the season is dry, and the forests extensive, many acres and miles of country may be burned over, and perhaps human lives may fall victims to your carelessness.

In the open and treeless country the wilderness-traveler is often hard pressed for the material for a fire. The most commonly used article is the dry dung of buffaloes, known to the Canadian voyageurs as *bois de vache*. It makes a hot fire, with very little smoke, and as the animals haunt the valleys of the streams in search of the best grass, they leave this material in the region of the camping grounds where it is most needed. It is excellent for tinder, and with a burning-glass and a piece of buffalo-chip you can get a fire in a few moments, provided the sun is shining. In many parts of the world the dried excrement of grass-feeding animals forms the only fuel of the inhabitants or of travelers.

If you sleep near a fire at night, and the weather is so cold as to render the heat desirable, always lie with your feet towards it; as long as the feet are kept warm the rest of the body is likely to be so, and with cold feet no one can be comfortable. Unless the surrounding circumstances compel you to sleep with your boots or shoes on be sure to remove them before you go to bed, as their absence makes your sleep far more refreshing than it is with them.

When you arrive at a stream, on whose banks you intend to camp, but which you must cross before proceeding on your journey, make the crossing before you halt for the night. Streams rise suddenly, and it often happens that what was a tiny rivulet at sunset is a roaring torrent on the following morning, and it may be a day, or several days, before it subsides. The rule here given is followed by all experienced travelers on the plains of the great west.

When you break camp in the morning one of the party should remain behind, after the wagons have moved away, and carefully examine the ground to see that nothing has been forgotten. The members of the party may take turns in this duty, or it may be assigned to one person who should be held responsible for whatever may be lost by forgetfulness. It will often happen that some article of camp equipage has been left behind, and its absence is unknown until camp is formed, at the end of the day's march. A thought B had put it in the wagon, and B was certain that A had attended to it, or at least he should have done so. Many a quarrel has been saved by this simple precaution, and also many a deprivation, as the loss of a camp-kettle or frying-pan, when it cannot be replaced, is a very serious matter. Since the writer gave up the wilderness for civilized travel it has always been his custom, after his trunks have been packed and locked at a hotel, to renew his practice of olden times and go through his room with the utmost care, examining every drawer of bureau or washstand, and looking into every closet. Candor compels him to say that once in a while he finds articles of greater or less value that but for this rule he would have left behind.

One of the perplexities of travel in wild countries is the passage of rivers. Shallow streams can be forded, and if the current is not strong a depth of five feet may be passed without serious difficulty. Many streams are full of quicksand, and in such case the rule is to keep your team in constant motion after it enters the water. As long as a man keeps moving on quicksand there is no danger, but whenever he stops his feet begin to sink, and if he remains stationary he will speedily find himself beyond his depth. The same conditions are true of saddle or draught animals, and of the wheels of wagons. Where there are quicksands horses should be led across, and to insure their going steadily forward they should be allowed to drink all they wish before entering the stream. Horses and oxen are more certain to go ahead without halting than mules; the latter are apt to lie down and refuse to move, exactly as they do in deep snow.

In a difficult ford the teams had better be doubled.

The driver should stand on the front of the wagon with a reliable whip in his hand, and be assisted by one or more mounted men on each side of the team. It is well also to have a mounted man ride ahead with a long lariat on picket rope attached to the forward leaders of the team, so as to direct their course. In a swift current the ford should be made obliquely downwards if possible, so that the current can assist the progress of the wagons.

In crossing a stream too deep for fording, boats or rafts may be improvised from wagon beds, or they may be built on the spot. If the current is swift a ferry must be made, and for this purpose (after the spot for crossing has been selected) an expert swimmer goes over with a fish-line or other slender cord in his mouth. By means of this cord a strong lariat can be drawn over; it should be twice as long as the width of the river, and fastened on each shore to a tree, or a wagon tongue set in the ground if there are no trees. To make a ferry-boat from a wagon-bed put it in the center of a wagon-cover or other strong canvas, and then bring the edges up over the sides to the top; the leakage will then be so slight that a man with a cup can easily keep it free from water. The contents of the wagons can be passed in this boat by means of the ferry rope, the animals can swim over, and the empty wagons may be passed by fastening them down to the axles, and attaching ropes to the tongue and also to the rear. They are then drawn over by the men on the farther bank, and kept from drifting by means of the rear rope.

If you are about to swim a stream with a horse it is not a good plan to remain in the saddle, as your weight presses heavily on the animal and restricts his movements. It is better to dismount, tie a cord eight or ten feet long to his bridle, drive him into the stream, and then grasp his tail and be towed over. If he tries to turn back you can direct him with the cord or by splashing water towards his head. If you do remain in the saddle give him a free rein, and do not pull in the least, except when it is necessary to guide him. Horses and oxen are better swimmers than mules; the latter are easily frightened and may suddenly turn down stream, refusing all attempts to bring them to land. They are also more liable to be drowned, and great care should be taken that they do not get water in their ears; as soon as you see a mule droop his ears you may know that he is in danger, and the water should be removed immediately on reaching land, if you are so fortunate as to get him there. For this reason never splash water towards a mule's head, and do not make him jump into the water if possible to avoid doing so.

An excellent ferry-boat may be made from a green or soaked hide of ox or buffalo, or better still, from two or more hides. You will generally find willows growing on the banks of the streams; gather some of the smaller ones, sharpen the butts and drive them into the ground, so as to form an oval figure of the size of your intended boat. Then bring the tops together, weave slender willow rods among the larger ones till the structure resembles a basket with a round bottom, and have a specially strong willow running around all of them near the ground, and firmly fastened, to make the gunwale of your boat. If your boat is made of one hide stretch it over the basket and sew it to the large rod around the top, and let the whole thing stand a few hours in the sun to get dry; then cut off the rods where they enter the ground and you have a boat that will carry four or five hundred pounds with ease. For a larger boat, with two or more hides, you want a more pretentious frame, a stout pole for a keel, and two smaller poles for gunwales. This water vehicle is known on the plains as a *bull-boat*, and can be easily constructed, provided the traveler has a supply of willows, some green or soaked hides, and a fair amount of common sense. Where a traveler expects to encounter streams that cannot be forded he would do well to carry two or three dried hides, and then he will have the material for covering a bull-boat always at hand.

While we are speaking of hides, another use of them may be mentioned. It often happens that emigrants, or settlers in a new country, wish to salt a quantity of beef or other meat but have no cask or other receptacle in which to place it. In this emergency dig a hole in the ground, of such dimensions that the hide of the slaughtered animal will just line it; then place the hide in the hole, with the flesh side up, fasten the edges to the ground with wooden pegs, and you have a salting cask that you may use, *sans peur et sans reproache*. An animal's hide is also useful to bake him in, and in this way: Skin and dress your game and then sew what you intend to bake into the hide. Build a good fire in a hole in the ground with a sort of rude oven of stones around it, and keep it going till the ground and stones are hot. Now sweep out the ashes, throw in your roasting piece, cover it with dry or green leaves, put back the hot embers as quickly as possible, and then continue the fire long enough to cook the meat beneath it. The writer has practiced this form of cookery on several occasions and found the result very satisfactory.

If your supply of fuel is limited, and you have much cooking to do, dig a narrow trench for the fire and place your kettles and pots above it; make the trench with one end towards the wind, and build a small chimney of stones or earth at the other end. Another way is to dig a round hole a foot deep, and place the kettles in a circle on its border, half of each kettle being on the ground and half over the fire. If you lose all your kettles and frying-pans it is well to know that you can improvise a frying-pan by taking two large flat stones and laying one above another, with a few pebbles between to keep them apart. Build a fire around them, and when they are well heated sweep away all the ashes and put your slices of meat between the stones; you will be well satisfied with the frying process that ensues.

But space is limited and we must pause. The writer could go on for many more pages, giving advice to travelers in the wilderness, of varying degrees of usefulness, and mainly drawn from his own experience as a frontier campaigner years and years ago. But the demands of the printer, and the interests of the non-migrating reader, forbid an extension of the chapter. If more on the same subject is desired it will be found in an eminently practical little volume entitled "The Prairie Traveler," by Captain (since General) R. B. Marcy; the author is thoroughly familiar with the subject, as any old officer of the army can testify.

COLUMBIA BICYCLE.

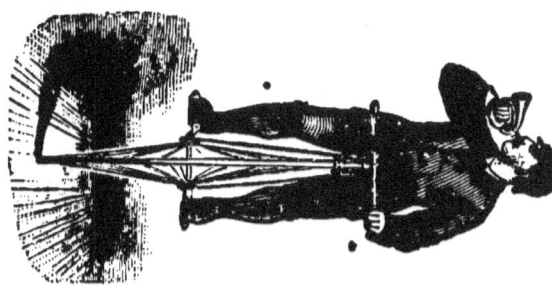

The permanence of the Bicycle as a practical road-vehicle is an established fact, and thousands of riders are daily enjoying the delightful and health-giving exercise. The beautiful model and elegant appearance of the "COLUMBIA" excite universal admiration; it is carefully finished in every particular, and is confidently guaranteed as the best value for the money attained in a Bicycle.

FROM THE PRESIDENT OF THE LOCAL TELEGRAPH CO.,
PHILADELPHIA, PA.

"I am familiar with the various methods adopted by enlightened nations for healthful sports, agreeable pastime, and exercise, and I must say that, in my opinion, a consistent use of the wheel far surpasses them all, both for body and mind. The very marked improvements made by yourselves and our English friends, in Bicycles, within the past year or so, convince me that they will soon be no longer a luxury, but a necessity." (Signed,) HENRY BENTLEY.

Send 3-cent stamp for 24-page catalogue, with price-lists and full information.

THE POPE MFG. CO., 597 Washington St., BOSTON, MASS.

ESTABLISHED 1850.

INMAN LINE
United States & Royal Mail Steamers.

CITY OF ROME, 8,300 Tons.

	Tons.		Tons.
CITY OF BERLIN,	5,491.	CITY OF MONTREAL,	4,490.
CITY OF RICHMOND,	4,607.	CITY OF BRUSSELS,	3,775.
CITY OF CHESTER,	4,566.	CITY OF NEW YORK,	3,500.

NEW YORK TO LIVERPOOL, - THURSDAYS OR SATURDAYS.
LIVERPOOL TO NEW YORK, - TUESDAYS OR THURSDAYS.

RATES OF PASSAGE, $80 and $100, according to accommodation, all having equal saloon privileges. Children between two and twelve years of age, half fare. Servants, $50.

ROUND TRIP TICKETS, $144 and $180.

TICKETS TO LONDON, $7, and to PARIS $15 and $20 additional, according to the route selected.

THE STEAMERS of this Line, built in watertight compartments, are among the strongest, largest, and fastest on the Atlantic.

THE SALOONS are luxuriously furnished, have revolving chairs, are especially well lighted and ventilated, and take up the whole width of the ship.

THE PRINCIPAL STATEROOMS are amidships, forward of the engines, where least noise and motion is felt, and all replete with every comfort, having double berths, electric bells, and all latest improvements.

LADIES' CABINS and bath-rooms, Gentlemen's smoking and bath-rooms, Barbers' shops, pianos, libraries, etc., provided.

MEALS SERVED *a la carte.*

These Steamers do not carry Horses, Cattle, Sheep, or Pigs.

For further particulars apply to
JOHN G. DALE, Agent, 31 and 33 Broadway, New York.
GEO. A. FAULK, " 105 South Fourth St., Philadelphia.
L. H. PALMER, " 3 Old State House, Boston.
F. C. BROWN, " 32 South Clark Street, Chicago.

WM. KNABE & CO.,
112 Fifth Avenue,
NEW YORK.

204 and 206 W. Baltimore Street,
BALTIMORE, MD.

Manufacturers of Pianos.

"GUION LINE."
United States Mail Steamers

SAILING WEEKLY

Between New York and Liverpool.

(CALLING AT QUEENSTOWN.)

THESE STEAMERS are built of Iron, in watertight compartments, and are furnished with every requisite to make the passage across the Atlantic both safe and agreeable, having bath-room, smoking-room, drawing-room, piano, and library; also experienced Surgeon, Stewardess, and Caterer on each Steamer. The staterooms are all upper deck, thus insuring those greatest of all luxuries at sea, perfect ventilation and light.

CABIN PASSAGE, $60, $80, and $100, according to Location, etc.

INTERMEDIATE.—This is a class that affords people of moderate means a respectable way of traveling. Beds, bedding, wash-basins, etc., together with good food, separate dining-room from either cabin or steerage being provided. Passage, $40 single; $80 round trip.

STEERAGE PASSAGE at Low Rates.

DRAFTS payable in Ireland, England, and Scotland at low rates.

APPLY TO

WILLIAMS & GUION,
29 BROADWAY, N. Y.

59 Wall Street, - NEW YORK,
209 Chestnut Street, PHILADELPHIA,
66 State Street, - - BOSTON,
AND
ALEXANDER BROWN & SONS,
COR. BALTIMORE AND CALVERT STREETS,
BALTIMORE.

BUY AND SELL BILLS OF EXCHANGE
ON
GREAT BRITAIN AND IRELAND, FRANCE,
GERMANY, BELGIUM, AND HOLLAND.

ISSUE COMMERCIAL AND TRAVELERS' CREDITS
IN STERLING, available in any part of the world, and
IN FRANCS, for use in MARTINIQUE and GUADALOUPE.

MAKE TELEGRAPHIC TRANSFERS OF MONEY
BETWEEN THIS AND OTHER COUNTRIES,
THROUGH LONDON AND PARIS.

To TRAVELERS.—Travelers Credits issued either against cash deposited or satisfactory guarantee of repayment. In Dollars, for use in the United States and adjacent countries; or in Pounds Sterling, for use in any part of the world. Application for Credits may be addressed to either of the *above houses* direct, or through any first-class Bank or Banker.

HOUSES IN LONDON AND LIVERPOOL.

MESSRS. BROWN, SHIPLEY & CO.

HATCH & FOOTE,

BANKERS,

No. 12 WALL STREET,

NEW YORK.

We buy and sell U. S. Bonds, execute orders in Stocks, Bonds, and Miscellaneous Securities, and transact a general Banking Business. Interest allowed on deposits.

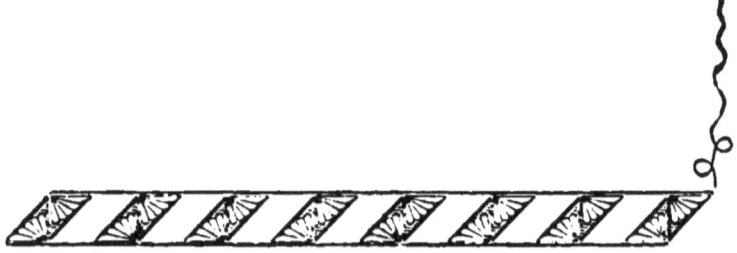

OREGON
Railway and Navigation Co.,
OWNING AND OPERATING THE
WALLA WALLA & COLUMBIA RIVER R. R.

OCEAN DIVISION.
The only direct Mail Line from
San Francisco to Portland, Oregon.
Carrying WELLS, FARGO & CO'S EXPRESS.

"GEORGE W. ELDER."   "OREGON."   "COLUMBIA."

Regular Steamships from Portland to San Francisco and return, every Five Days until further notice.

Connections made at Portland, Oregon, for all points in Oregon, Washington and Idaho Territories, British Columbia, and Alaska.

K. VAN OTERENDORF, Superintendent.

Columbia & Willamette Division.

Connecting with Northern Pacific R. R. at Kalama and Ainsworth; and with Walla Walla and Columbia River R. R. at Wallula.

GEO. J. AINSWORTH, Superintendent.

Walla Walla & Columbia River Railroad.

Connects at Wallula (on Columbia River) with Steamboats of O. R. & N. Co. This Line, being rapidly constructed, is now open to Weston, Oregon.

CONSIGN ALL FREIGHT "VIA OREGON RAILWAY & NAVIGATION CO."

H. VILLARD,   T. F. OAKES,
President.   Vice-Pres't and Gen'l Manager.

A. L. STOKES, General Eastern Passenger Agent,
52 Clark Street, CHICAGO.

To Travellers Visiting New York.
The International Exchange
AND READING ROOMS,
Madison Square, New York.

(Entrances 953 Broadway, and 185 Fifth Avenue, corner of 23d Street.)

C. A. O'ROURKE & CO., Proprietors.

Strangers to the United States, or to New York, can find at this institution the information and facilities most useful to them. Among the features of the establishment are:

1. The leading newspapers of the principal cities of the world are kept on file. The latest issues of these journals are received by every mail.
2. Information for travellers as to the places of interest in the city, and how to visit them. Also in regard to travel, routes, cost, etc., to all points of the United States, Canada, Mexico, the West Indies, and South America. Accommodations secured in advance at leading hotels in all cities. Interpreters and guides furnished.
3. Theatre, Railroad, and Steamship Tickets can be purchased at regular rates. Diagrams of the seats, and Telephonic communications with leading Theatres.
4. Foreign Money Exchanged.
5. Direct Telegraphic communication at regular rates with all parts of the world.
6. The important news of the world, especially if of financial or commercial interest, received at the Exchange and Bulletined.
7. Notification of Steamship arrivals, and of arrivals and departures of Mails. Subscribers can receive their Letters at the Exchange.
8. Quotations of Railroad, Mining, Produce, and other Stocks, received at the Exchange by telegraph.

Americans sojourning in New York *en route* to Europe can avail themselves not only of the general advantages of the Exchange, but can obtain information in regard to routes of travel, principal places of resort, cost, etc., on the other side of the Atlantic.

The International Exchange counts among its annual subscribers a very large number of the leading business and public men of New York.

Subscription price $25.00 per year, $10.00 per quarter, $5.00 per month, payable in advance.

The Traveller, published weekly by the International Exchange contains, besides matters of general interest, information in a concise form most useful for travellers.

AMERICAN EXCHANGE IN EUROPE,
(LIMITED.)
HEADQUARTERS FOR AMERICANS IN EUROPE,
AND
Post-Office Address for Travelers' Correspondence,
449 STRAND, LONDON, ENGLAND.

PRESIDENT,	GEN'L MANAGER,
JOSEPH R. HAWLEY.	HENRY F. GILLIG.

The following Particular Advantages for Travelers:

1st.—The largest number of American newspapers on file in Europe.
2d.—The only place in Europe where the directories of American cities and towns can be found.
3d.—The only place where arrivals are published weekly, and circulated throughout the world.
4th.—The only place where TRAVELERS CAN OBTAIN THEIR LETTERS EVERY DAY in the year, and offering facilities to travelers for correspondence with their friends.
5th.—The only place where the arrival of Steamers on both sides of the Atlantic is made known by telegraph immediately on being signalled.
6th.—The only channel for economical telegraphic communication between America and Europe by a code containing innumerable phrases specially compiled for travelers, and relating to domestic as well as business matters.
7th.—The only place in Europe where all the leading American newspapers are kept on sale.
8th.—The only place where there is a separate reading and writing room for ladies.
9th.—The only place where all the lines of Steamers and Routes of European travel are *impartially* represented; where *impartial* information and advice on all subjects relating to travel can be obtained; and where every requirement of the traveler is supplied.
10th.—The only place of the kind in Europe managed exclusively by Americans.

Over six hundred Newspapers, two hundred city and state Directories, three hundred official State and Municipal Reports regularly filed in the Reading Rooms of the Exchange.

Travelers' Branch open daily from 9 A. M. to midnight.

Passage Tickets issued available by any line of Steamers.

Freight and Parcels booked at through rates to all parts of the world.

BAGGAGE AND GOODS STORED.

N. B.—Printed Addressed Envelopes can be obtained Free of Cost at the Branch Office, 102 Broadway, New York, and at Hotels, Railroad and Steamship Ticket Offices throughout the United States, Canada, and Europe.

HENRY F. GILLIG, *General Manager.*

E. REMINGTON & SONS,

MANUFACTURERS OF THEIR CELEBRATED

MILITARY BREECH-LOADING RIFLES,

CARBINES AND PISTOLS,

of which more than 1,500,000 have been sold to nearly every Government in the World.

ALSO,

Long, Mid, Short-Range and Sporting
BREECH-LOADING RIFLES,

Which have won for themselves world-renowned reputation for accurate shooting at Creedmoor, New York; Dollymount, Ireland; Wimbledon, England; Ontario, Canada, and many other ranges throughout the civilized world.

LIKEWISE

Double and Single-Barreled Shot Guns

Equaled by few and inferior to none extant.

Revolving, Repeating and Single Shot Pistols;
ARMY, NAVY, POLICE, HOUSE AND POCKET SIZES,

ONE TO SIX SHOTS.

CARTRIDGES, LOADING IMPLEMENTS, SHOOTING CANES, BULLETS, PRIMERS, SHELLS, ETC., ETC.

MANUFACTORY:
ILION, HERKIMER COUNTY, N. Y., U. S. A.

SALESROOMS:
283 Broadway, New York,
71 State Street, Chicago, Ill.,
21 So. Howard Street, Baltimore, Md.

LIGHTEN YOUR LABOR
BY USING
THE PERFECTED TYPE-WRITER.
SEE WHAT IT WILL DO.

FROM THE AUTHOR OF "HOW TO TRAVEL."

NEW YORK, MARCH 4, 1881.

E. REMINGTON & SONS:—Gentlemen:

In reply to your inquiry of yesterday I beg to say that I consider the Type-Writer invaluable to any one who has a large amount of writing to do. For clearing off an accumulation of correspondence on returning from a journey it is admirable, and for preparing printer's "copy" it is unrivaled. If I could not get another Type-Writer I would not willingly take ten thousand dollars for the one I now have. It is little more than two years since I bought it, and in all that time its repairs have cost exactly fifty cents. Besides all my private correspondence, magazine articles, and newspaper matter, I have written four books with this machine and shall complete a fifth in a few days. The saving of time to me is not far from 25 per cent., and in this one item the Type-Writer has paid for itself several times over.

Very truly yours,
THOS. W. KNOX.

MANUFACTURED AND SOLD ONLY BY

E. REMINGTON & SONS,

PRINCIPAL OFFICES:
281 and 283 Broadway, New York.

BRANCH OFFICES:
38 Madison St., Chicago.   124 So. 7th St., Philadelphia.

LINDO BROS.

DIAMONDS, FINE WATCHES, RICH JEWELRY, SILVERWARE, ETC.

| PURCHASES AT HIGHEST PRICES. | 1205 BROADWAY, OPPOSITE GILSEY HOUSE. | Dessins et évaluations faite pour la monture de Diamants. |

M. Crane,

53, 55, and 57 Park Place,

New York.

Electrotyping

and

Stereotyping

In all its Branches.

Fine Electrotypes from Engravings a Specialty.

Specimens of work sent on application, and
Satisfaction Guaranteed.

THE PERMANENT CURE OF CATARRH.
Rev. T. P. Childs' Treatment the Only Effectual Way.
CHILDS' CATARRH SPECIFIC
Is no new untried cure, but a Positive and Certain Remedy.
WE, ABOVE ALL THINGS, DESIRE TO ESTABLISH CONFIDENCE IN OUR TREATMENT, SO THAT EVERY SUFFERER FROM CATARRH AND BRONCHITIS MAY FEEL CERTAIN OF SUCCESS IN ITS USE.

193 E. Fayette St., Baltimore, Md., Dec. 20, 1879.
REV. T. P. CHILDS.—I have the pleasure of informing you that after a faithful use of your remedy for eight weeks ending March 28, 1879, I am completely rid of a stubborn case of catarrh of three years' standing—breathing tubes clear as a whistle, appetite good, and digestion good.
Yours, THOMAS B. HAND.

REV. T. P. CHILDS: Dear Sir—I think you have the true theory and practice for cure of nasal catarrh, and also for the treatment of respiratory organs. My throat is now so well restored that I can lecture daily without any difficulty, and find no difficulty whatever in preaching. You are at full liberty to use my name for the benefit of others.
Yours very truly, E. B. FAIRCHILD, D.D., LL.D., Chancellor of the University of Nebraska, Lincoln, Neb.

WHAT THE EDITORS SAY.
"While not supposing that all cases of catarrh will be cured by the prescription advertised, the publishers of the Illustrated Christian Weekly, after diligent inquiry, have reason to believe that it has in many cases proved effectual."—*Illustrated Christian Weekly*, New York.

"The publishers of the Congregationalist, with multitudes of other people, are somewhat suspicious of patent medicines as a rule, and when we received the advertisement of Mr. Childs we at first declined its insertion; but, on making inquiry, we received such satisfactory replies, and one especially from a well-known Congregational pastor not far from Rev. Mr. Childs, the proprietor of the medicine, that we withdrew our objections."—*Congregationalist*, Boston.

CHILDS' CATARRH SPECIFIC will effectually and permanently cure any case of catarrh, no matter how desperate. It can only be obtained at Troy, Ohio. The treatment is local as well as constitutional, and cannot be obtained at the drug stores. We especially desire to treat those who have tried other remedies without success.

Child's Treatment of Catarrh, and for diseases of the Bronchial Tubes, can be taken at home, with perfect ease and safety, by the patient. No expense need be entailed beyond the cost of the medicine.

REV. T. P. CHILDS, TROY, OHIO.

THE POLAND SPRING WATER

Has cured numerous cases of BRIGHT'S DISEASE OF THE KIDNEYS, as well as other forms of disease resulting from BLOOD POISON, such as MALARIAL FEVER, RHEUMATIC FEVER, DYSPEPSIA, CONSTIPATION, GRAVEL, DIABETES, SCROFULA, DROPSY, ETC.

Although an exceedingly pleasant water to drink, it possesses those peculiar properties that restore to action the Kidneys, Liver, and other Internal Organs that may have become sluggish in their movements. Thus by cleansing the blood the body is restored to its original vigor, and the complexion to its original freshness and beauty. Were it more generally used there would be far less demand for drugs and cosmetics.

The following gentlemen of this city will cheerfully bear testimony to its remarkable curative qualities:

J. W. Pottle; S. Jacoby, 103 Broad Street; J. M. Schuyler, 114 Wall Street; C. E. Blumenthal, M.D., 54 West 45th Street; W. G. Tuller and Ira Thorn, Fifth Avenue Hotel; J. Munroe Taylor, 113 Water Street; C. Y. Wemple, Vice-Pres't Manhattan Life Insurance Company; Root & Childs, 87 Worth Street; J. B. Libby, of H. J. Libby & Co., White Street; Deering & Milliken, 79 and 81 Leonard Street; G. N. Dickinson, of Lee, Tweedy & Co.; A. A. Vantine, 827, 829, and 831 Broadway; Edward Carroll, of Falconer, Carroll & Co.; C. P. Tooker, of Kiggins, Tooker & Co., 125 William Street; John R. Ames, Board of Education; George A. Dresser and Wm. Silver, Queens Insurance Company; W. H. Scott, M.D., 8 East 41st Street; Henry C. Houghton, M.D., 44 West 35th Street; H. K. White, 548 Broadway; Wm. H. Lindsley, 279 Broadway; M. M. Stanfield, Victoria Hotel; Wm. B. Bogle, of Bogle & Lyles; I. F. Slader, Brandreth House; F. J. Allen, Astor House; J. H. Small, 111 Front Street.

The undersigned have within their personal knowledge cases in which POLAND SPRING WATER has proved highly beneficial.   H. L. BRIDGMAN.   THOS. W. KNOX

☞ For sale in large or small quantities by

O. HUTCHINSON, the Authorized Agent,
145 NASSAU ST., NEW YORK

150 Bowery, New York,

Duplicate Wedding Presents,

SURPLUS SILVERWARE, DIAMONDS, WATCHES, JEWELRY, BRONZES, AND PAINTINGS.

Inscriptions erased and Silverware refinished and sold

50 PER CENT. BELOW MANUFACTURERS' COST.

Constant Bargains in New and Second-hand

WATCHES.

FINE DIAMONDS BELOW PARIS PRICES.

ESTABLISHED OVER 30 YEARS,

Dealing only in Fine Goods. A visit to 150 Bowery will well repay the curious, or those who want the best Goods at surprisingly low prices.

TOURJEE'S TOURS,
FOURTH SEASON,

The most enjoyable, economical and successful excursion tours ever planned to the

OLD WORLD.
ALL TRAVEL AND HOTELS FIRST-CLASS.
COMPANY SELECT.

Important additions to our former tours. Extra inducements without extra charge. Early registration important. Parties contemplating a visit to Europe should send for circular giving full particulars.

E. TOURJEE,
Music Hall, Boston.

The following is from the Physicians' Pocket Manual and Year Book.

"Three years ago, he planned a new way of seeing the wonders of the Old World, and what have now become famous as the Tourjee Excursions are such as every intelligent person will heartily endorse.

The cost to each excursionist varies from $175 to $700, and these figures include first-class transportation, hotel accommodations, carriage drives, lunches and all incidentals. From the time he embarks to the day he returns to New York, the tourist is not obliged to take out an additional cent from his purse. We heartily endorse these pleasant trips, and believe that they merit the appreciation of the medical profession. In the previous excursions, quite a number of eastern medical men participated, and several will have gone over the ground again the present year. The advantages which they offer for recuperation, both to physicians and patients, are unsurpassed, and we hope that many a year will have passed before they shall be discontinued. The old way of seeing the Old World has always had many drawbacks; the new way affords thrice the benefit for less than one-half the expenditure."

FRANK LESLIE'S ILLUSTRATED PUBLICATIONS.
RATES OF SUBSCRIPTION, POSTAGE PAID.
WEEKLIES.

FRANK LESLIE'S ILLUSTRATED NEWSPAPER—The only pictorial record of current events, devoted to news, literature, art, and science, . . . $4.00

FRANK LESLIE'S CHIMNEY CORNER—The best American family journal, story paper, and home friend, 4.00

FRANK LESLIE'S LADY'S JOURNAL—The highest exponent of fashion and taste, ... 4.00

FRANK LESLIE'S ILLUSTRIRTE ZEITUNG—In the German language. A weekly compendium of news and literature, ... 4.00

FRANK LESLIE'S BOYS' AND GIRLS' WEEKLY—An illustrated journal of amusement, adventure, and instruction, ... 2.50

MONTHLIES.

FRANK LESLIE'S POPULAR MONTHLY—The cheapest and most attractive monthly magazine, . . 3.00

FRANK LESLIE'S SUNDAY MAGAZINE—The best pictorial religious periodical, ... 3.00

FRANK LESLIE'S LADY'S MAGAZINE—Regarded universally as a fashion standard, ... 3.50

FRANK LESLIE'S PLEASANT HOURS—Cheap and entertaining. Devoted to fiction. Every article complete, 1.50

FRANK LESLIE'S BUDGET OF WIT—Filled with intelligent humor, ... 1.50

ANNUALS.

FRANK LESLIE'S ILLUSTRATED ALMANAC FOR 1881— A charming annual, with colored Plates, . . .25

FRANK LESLIE'S COMIC ALMANAC—A racy annual compendium of fun, humor, and information, . .10

The various publications of this house embrace a wide range of popular reading. The illustrations are of the highest order, by the most skilful artists. The literary matter is contributed by authors and writers of great reputation and acknowledged popularity. Most liberal outlays are made to secure the best talent in the market, both instructive and amusing.

No "traveling agent" is authorized to collect money for our publications. Remit by money-order, draft on New York, or registered letter, at our risk. Address

FRANK LESLIE'S PUBLISHING HOUSE,
53, 55, and 57 PARK PLACE, NEW YORK.

THE ASSOCIATED LINES
OF
Southern Railway Travel,
COMPRISING

PIEDMONT AIR LINE,   CENTRAL SHORT LINE,
ATLANTIC COAST LINE,   THE BAY LINE.

Concentration of control under ONE MANAGEMENT.
Special U. S. FAST MAIL, and Double Daily PASSENGER ROUTE.
SHORTEST LINES BETWEEN NORTH AND SOUTH.
Extended Pullman Sleeping-Car Service.
First-class equipment and all standard appliances.

New York, Philadelphia, Baltimore, and Washington
TO
New Orleans, Mobile, Montgomery, Atlanta,
AND INTERMEDIATE POINTS; ALSO,
Charleston, Macon, Savannah, all points in Southwest Georgia, and Florida.

IMMIGRATION.

Arrangements have been perfected by which a complete system of settlers' and immigrants' fares from leading Eastern cities exist to each station upon the lines of railways of this organization, and the attention of immigrants and all persons seeking investments in the Southern States is invited to exhibits soon to be published concerning unimproved lands, improved farms, sites for manufacturing purposes, supplies and location of growing hard woods, deposits of minerals, metals, and building materials, together with facts of physical attractions, accessibility to railway or water transportation, or desirable markets.

Full information concerning the Lines, points reached, matters of tickets, schedules, sleeping car reservations, etc., etc., to be had on application to

306 Washington St., Boston.   *838 Chestnut St., Philadelphia.*
229 Broadway, New York.   *511 Pennsylvania Ave., Washington.*

AND ALL LEADING TICKET OFFICES EAST.

A. POPE, General Passenger and Ticket Agent.

Piano-Fortes

Possess all the delicate tone and action qualities claimed by the leading makers. An inspection will surely prove the fact. The new

TREBLE REFLECTOR

(Wing & Son's invention,) gives a remarkable bird-like quality to the HIGH TREBLE NOTES.

As to Prices.

This establishment can furnish a remarkable instrument in its musical qualities and encased after a new and unconventional design for the sum of **$400**.

Send for the reports of HOFFMAN and other celebrated Pianists to the office of

Wing & Son,

1298 and 1300 BROADWAY, N. Y.

FOR MAGAZINES AND NEWSPAPERS,
AMERICAN AND FOREIGN.

SEND FOR OUR CATALOGUE,

NOW READY FOR DISTRIBUTION.

It gives CLUB RATES *for all the prominent Publications, American and English.*

☞ We make the import of Foreign Periodicals, by mail or otherwise, a specialty. The following are samples of our prices per year, post-paid:

ENGLISH.		AMERICAN.	
Academy,	$4.15	Harper's Magazine,	$3.45
Athenæum,	4.30	" Bazar,	3.45
Agricultural Gazette,	5.50	" Weekly,	3.45
Architect,	6.00	" Young People,	1.35
Boy's Own Paper,	2.00	American Architect,	5.50
Building News,	6.50	American Journal of	
British Architect,	5.75	Science and Art,	5.00
Chamber's Journal,	2.50	Blackwood,	3.45
Chemical News,	4.75	Contemporary Review	
Engineering,	8.80	(*reprint*),	2.15
English Mechanic,	3.25	Literary World,	1.80
Graphic,	8.75	Lippincott's Magazine,	2.65
Illustrated News,	8.75	Popular Science Monthly,	4.35
London Times (Weekly),	3.25	Appleton's Journal,	2.65
Pall Mall Budget,	7.40	Sunday Magazine,	2.65
Punch,	3.75	American Law Review,	3.45
Queen,	9.25	New Englander,	3.87
Saturday Review,	7.40	Atlantic Monthly,	3.45
Spectator,	7.40	Scribner's Monthly,	3.45
Art Journal,	8.50	St. Nicholas,	2.65
Cornhill,	3.60		
Fraser,	8.00		
Hamerton's Portfolio,	8.50		
London Society,	3.60		
Contemporary Review,	7.25		
Nineteenth Century,	7.25		
Fortnightly,	6.50		
Revue des Deux Mondes,	14.25		

☞ LIBRARIANS and MANAGERS OF BOOK CLUBS and READING ASSOCIATIONS are especially requested to notice this. TIME, LABOR, and MONEY are saved by ordering through our agency.

☞ Send for our Catalogue, giving prices of nearly Two Thousand Periodicals, AMERICAN, ENGLISH, FRENCH, and GERMAN, at club-rates. Free to any address upon request.

ALBERT H. ROFFE & CO., 11 BROMFIELD STREET, BOSTON, MASS.

DAILY OCEAN EXCURSIONS TO
ROCKAWAY BEACH,
BY THE ENTIRELY NEW PALATIAL STEAMERS,
GRAND REPUBLIC AND COLUMBIA.

Universally conceded to be the largest, finest, and best adapted Excursion Steamers in the world, combining everything that contributes to the safety, comfort, and luxury of pleasure seekers.

THE GRAND REPUBLIC,
LEAVES: With Band and the Columbia Glee Club,

22d Street, North River, - - -	at	10.00 A. M.
Pier 6, " " - - -	"	10.20 "
Jewell's Wharf, Brooklyn, - - -	"	10.40 "

LEAVING ROCKAWAY, Upper Landings, at 4.00 P. M.
Lower Landings, " 4.30 "

THE COLUMBIA,
With Deverell's 13th Reg't Band and Concordia Glee Club, Cornet Soloist,
LEAVES: Xylophone, etc.,

West 22d Street, -. -	at 9.00 A. M.	and	2.00 P. M.
Pier 6, North River, -	" 9.15 "	"	2.15 "
Jewell's Wharf, Brooklyn,	" 9.30 "	"	2.30 "

DIRECT FOR ROCKAWAY BEACH.
LEAVING ROCKAWAY, Upper Landings, at 5.30 P. M.
Lower Landings, " 6.00 "

The best order and discipline maintained. Ladies with Children are perfectly safe in traveling under the care of the Captains, aided by efficient Officers and a platoon of Police.

Passage Cards, 35 cents. Excursion Tickets, 50 cents.
Children from 5 to 12 years, Half-price; Under 5, Free.

THE MUTUAL LIFE INSURANCE COMPANY,

OF NEW YORK.

Nos. 144 AND 146 BROADWAY.

F. S. WINSTON, PRESIDENT.

R. A. McCURDY, VICE-PRESIDENT.

Assets, January 1, 1881,

OVER

NINETY-ONE MILLIONS

OF DOLLARS.

THE BOY TRAVELERS IN THE FAR EAST. PART I.

Adventures of Two Youths in a Journey to Japan and China. By THOMAS W. KNOX. Illustrated. 8vo, Illuminated Cloth, $3.00.

THE BOY TRAVELERS IN THE FAR EAST. PART II.

Adventures of Two Youths in a Journey to Siam and Java. With descriptions of Cochin-China, Cambodia, Sumatra, and the Malay Archipelago. By THOMAS W. KNOX. Illustrated. 8vo, Illuminated Cloth, $3.00.

These volumes will serve an admirable purpose in the education of our young people.—N. Y. HERALD.

That which Mayne Reid did for a past generation Col. Knox is doing for readers of to-day. He is producing books of travel fascinating alike for old and young.—N. Y. JOURNAL OF COMMERCE.

Great favorites with youthful readers.—CHRISTIAN-AT-WORK, N. Y.

The best, most instructive, and pleasing books for boys ever issued.—BOSTON POST.

PUBLISHED BY HARPER & BROTHERS,

FRANKLIN SQUARE, NEW YORK.

☞ HARPER & BROTHERS will send any of the above works by mail, postage prepaid, to any part of the United States, on receipt of price.

"Whoever would derive the most information, enjoyment, and satisfaction from travel, should always use the best Guide=Books."

OSGOOD'S AMERICAN GUIDE-BOOKS.

"These books contain everything which the traveler wants to know, in precisely the shape he wants to have it." —BOSTON JOURNAL.

Arranged on the celebrated Baedeker plan, indorsed by all European travelers.

The history, poetry, and legends of each locality, tersely and clearly given.

Scores of maps, city plans, and panoramas.

Giving prices and locations of all hotels and boarding-houses, summer resorts, and routes.

There are FOUR VOLUMES, bound in flexible cloth, and each of about 500 pages, with many maps and plans.

NEW ENGLAND,   THE MARITIME PROVINCES,
THE MIDDLE STATES,   THE WHITE MOUNTAINS.

"They are simply indispensable to tourists in the regions named; and those who have sallied forth without them have omitted the really most important part of their equipment."—LITERARY WORLD.

"As for accuracy, the amount of work done by the editor has been enormous. To say that the books are better than any American books of the sort that have hitherto appeared would be superfluous; there is no comparison to be made between them and their predecessors."—THE INDEPENDENT.

REVISED ANNUALLY. PRICE $1.50 EACH.

∗ For sale by all Booksellers, or sent postpaid on receipt of price, by the Publishers,

JAMES R. OSGOOD & CO., BOSTON.

ESTABLISHED 1801.

The Evening Post.

BROADWAY AND FULTON ST., NEW YORK.

NEVER was this paper more able, bright, and newsy than at present.—*St. Paul Press.*

YOUNGER, fresher, and altogether a better newspaper than ever.—*Trenton Gazette.*

EXCEEDINGLY welcome visitor to the evening companionship of reading people.—*Philadelphia Ledger.*

VERY few American journals equal the EVENING POST for reputation and influence among thinking people.—*Newspaper Directory.*

EVEN its advertising columns are jealously guarded against questionable or objectionable advertisements.—*Newspaper Guide.*

NOW the ablest evening paper in the world. Faithful and accurate as a newspaper.—*Mohawk Valley Democrat.*

ITS readers include a large proportion, if not a majority, of the literary and business world.—*N. Y. Daily Bulletin.*

NOTHING is to be found in its columns which would exclude it from the most refined family circle.—*Pittsburgh Post..*

GENERALLY acknowledged to be the door by which access is to be gained to the New York homes.—*Rowell's Newspaper Guide.*

POLITICALLY it is the ablest and most independent journal of republican proclivities in New York.—*Philadelphia Times.*

OUR contemporary's prosperity speaks well for its management, and for the moral tone of its readers.—*Newburgh Journal.*

SUITED for the family circle as well as for the office of the man interested in politics and news.—*Pittsburgh Post.*

THE EVENING POST has a very large circulation among the respectable reading public of this city.—*New York World.*

DAILY, $9; SEMI-WEEKLY, $3; WEEKLY, $1.50.
Favorable Terms to Clubs.   *Specimen Copy Free.*

THE W. C. BRYANT CO., PUBLISHERS,
BROADWAY AND FULTON ST., NEW YORK.

THE NEW YORK TRIBUNE.

THE TRIBUNE is now spending more labor and money than ever before to maintain the distinction it has long enjoyed of having the largest circulation among the best people. It secured, and means to retain it, by becoming the medium of the best thought and the voice of the best conscience of the time, by keeping abreast of the highest progress, favoring the freest discussion, hearing all sides, appealing always to the best intelligence and the purest morality, and refusing to cater to the tastes of the vile or the prejudices of the ignorant.

THE LIBRARY OF UNIVERSAL KNOWLEDGE, embracing Chambers' Encyclopædia complete, omitting only some of the cuts, with extensive additions by an able corps of American editors, treating about 15,000 additional topics, thoroughly Americanizing the entire work, adding to it over 25 per cent. of the latest, freshest, and most valuable matter, the whole making 15 handsome Octavo Volumes of 6 by 9¼ inches in size, printed in large type on good strong calendered paper, and neatly and substantially bound in cloth.

We can offer this valuable work in connection with THE TRIBUNE as follows:

FOR $15. { THE LIBRARY OF UNIVERSAL KNOWLEDGE complete in 15 octavo volumes, substantially bound in cloth as above described, and THE WEEKLY TRIBUNE 5 years to one subscriber.

FOR $20. { THE LIBRARY OF UNIVERSAL KNOWLEDGE as above described, and THE SEMI-WEEKLY TRIBUNE 5 years to one subscriber.

FOR $19. { THE LIBRARY OF UNIVERSAL KNOWLEDGE as above described, and ten copies of THE WEEKLY TRIBUNE one year.

FOR $28. { THE LIBRARY OF UNIVERSAL KNOWLEDGE as above described, and twenty copies of THE WEEKLY TRIBUNE one year.

For further particulars concerning this and other valuable premiums, address

THE TRIBUNE, NEW YORK.

The Hartford (CONN.) Courant.

THE OLDEST NEWSPAPER IN AMERICA.

A REPRESENTATIVE JOURNAL OF NEW ENGLAND.

Established: Weekly, 1764; Daily, 1836.

Hawley, Goodrich & Co.,
Publishers.
{ Joseph R. Hawley,
Wm. H. Goodrich,
Chas. Dudley Warner,
Stephen A. Hubbard. }

New Courant Building, State St.

THE COURANT is the Oldest Newspaper in the United States, and, with less than half a dozen exceptions, the oldest print in the English language. It was founded in October, 1764, and has been published uninterruptedly, under the same title, ever since.

Terms: Weekly, $1.50 a Year; Daily, $8.00.

THE BEST ADVERTISING MEDIUM
IN THE STATE.

☞ Send for sample copies, which will be sent FREE.

IN AN

OLD AND STRONG COMPANY.

THE ÆTNA LIFE

OF HARTFORD, CONN.,

Issues Policies upon all Desirable Plans at Rates Lower than those of most Companies.

THE ÆTNA LIFE INSURANCE COMPANY.—In mentioning this Company we must reiterate the well-known fact that it stands at the very head of the list of life insurance companies. For thirty years it has stood the storms of financial fluctuation, and now remains the strongest life insurance company in the country. Its management is in the hands of experienced and trustworthy men, as is shown by referring to the condition of the Company shown by their statement of affairs.—HARTFORD JOURNAL.

STATUARY
IN
GRANITE,
MARBLE, AND
BRONZE,
Artistic Memorials,
AND
BUILDING WORK
IN ALL KINDS OF GRANITE.

Original Designs and Estimates furnished Free on application.

WORK DELIVERED IN ALL PARTS OF THE COUNTRY.

ADDRESS

THE NEW ENGLAND GRANITE WORKS,
HARTFORD, CONN.

QUARRIES AT WESTERLY, R. I.

BUY THE
"HARTFORD"
WOVEN WIRE MATTRESS

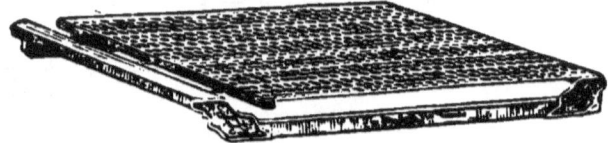

FOR DURABILITY, COMFORT, AND ECONOMY.

WARRANTED NEVER TO SAG.
    NEVER TO LOSE ITS SHAPE.
        NEVER TO MAKE A NOISE.
            NEVER TO NEED A REPAIR.

The "*HARTFORD*" Mattress is *durable*. It will last a *life-time*. One-third of every person's life ought to be spent in sleep, hence the necessity for a *perfect sleeping arrangement*. The "*HARTFORD*" Mattress affords the greatest comfort; *conforming to the body*, it makes a *most delightful bed*. The "*HARTFORD*" Mattress will never wear out or need a repair. Requiring over the Mattress only a *blanket* or a *very light mattress*, much is saved in the way of expense in not being obliged to purchase heavy hair mattresses or other over-bedding. The "*HARTFORD*" Woven Wire Mattress is free from the disagreeable noises so annoying in the upright spiral spring. The "*HARTFORD*" Mattress always keeps its shape, being as elastic and flexible after fifteen years use as when first manufactured. Investigate its merits. Buy only the genuine "*HARTFORD.*" Take no other. Beware of imitations and infringements. Every Mattress marked "*HARTFORD.*" For prices, catalogues, or any desired information,

ADDRESS

Hartford Woven Wire Mattress Co.,
Box 148, Hartford, Conn., U. S. A.

HENRY ROBERTS, Secretary.

"THE HARTFORD" SEWING MACHINE.

THE LATEST PRODUCTION,

Combining all the BEST POINTS of former models of Machines with new excellencies of its own.

The lightest running Machine ever made.
SIMPLE, STRONG, DURABLE.
The only High-Arm Machine making the "Pearl Stitch."
All Bearings of Steel or Forgings.
Self-Adjusting Tensions.
The Original and Simplest Cylinder Shuttle.
Elegant Ornamentation.

"THE GENERAL FAVORITE,"

FOR SHOEMAKERS, SADDLERS, TAILORS, ETC.,

IS THE

STANDARD AMONG AMERICAN MANUFACTURERS.

Weed Sewing Machine Company,

HARTFORD, CONN., U. S. A.

ESTERBROOK'S
Steel Pens.

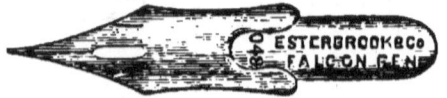

The Most Popular Pens in Use.

For sale by all Stationers.

Leading Nos. 048, 14, 130, 333, 161.

Samples and Catalogue on Application.

THE ESTERBROOK STEEL PEN CO.,
Works, Camden, N. J.   26 John St., New York.

N. P. FLETCHER & CO.,
Hartford, Conn.,

PUBLISHERS, AND MANUFACTURERS OF THE CELEBRATED

Fletcher Ink Extracts.

These preparations are soluble concentrated compounds, containing the coloring matters and mordants used in the best Inks. By the addition of water only, an Ink of beautiful color and fine quality is at once produced. *Invaluable for Travelers*, as the dry and powdered Extracts can be carried in small space and used at convenience. Used for the last six years in the best Banks, Insurance Offices, and Counting Rooms of the United States.

COLORS: Rose-Scarlet, Brilliant Green, Blue, Violet, and Black.

Full descriptive circulars mailed on application.

FAIRBANKS' SCALES.
THE WORLDS' STANDARD.
HIGHEST AWARDS, WORLD'S FAIRS.

LONDON, 1851.	PHILADELPHIA, 1876.
NEW YORK, 1853.	SYDNEY, AUSTRALIA, 1877.
PARIS, 1867.	PARIS, 1878.
VIENNA, 1873.	SYDNEY, AUSTRALIA, 1880.
SANTIAGO, CHILI, 1875.	MELBOURNE, " 1881.

At the World's Fair in Paris, in 1878, Fairbanks & Co. received seven medals, more than were awarded any other American exhibitors; at the Sydney, Australia, World's Fair, in 1881, in competition with manufacturers from the United States, Great Britain, and France, they received a special award above all others; and at Melbourne, Australia, World's Fair, in 1881, also in competition with American, English, and French manufacturers, Fairbanks' scales received the four highest awards.

THE CHEAPEST SCALE MANUFACTURED!
QUALITY CONSIDERED.

Correspondence solicited.   Price list furnished upon application.

OVER ONE MILLION OF THESE SCALES IN USE.

PRINCIPAL WAREHOUSE, **FAIRBANKS & CO., NEW YORK.**

FAIRBANKS & CO., BALTIMORE, MD.
  FAIRBANKS & CO., NEW ORLEANS.
    FAIRBANKS & CO., BUFFALO, N. Y.
      FAIRBANKS & CO., ALBANY, N. Y.
        FAIRBANKS & CO., MONTREAL.
FAIRBANKS & CO., LONDON, ENG.
  FAIRBANKS, BROWN & CO., BOSTON, MASS.
    FAIRBANKS & CO., PHILADELPHIA, PA.
      FAIRBANKS, MORSE & CO., CHICAGO.
        FAIRBANKS, MORSE & CO., CINCINNATI, O.
FAIRBANKS, MORSE & CO., CLEVELAND, O.
  FAIRBANKS, MORSE & CO., PITTSBURG, PA.
    FAIRBANKS, MORSE & CO., LOUISVILLE, KY.
      FAIRBANKS & CO., ST. LOUIS.
        FAIRBANKS & HUTCHINSON, SAN FRANCISCO.

Agent for Fairbanks' Scales in the RUSSIAN EMPIRE, **J. BLOCK,** { MOSCOW AND ST. PETERSBURG

LIBERAL AND IMPORTANT CONCESSIONS
IN LIFE INSURANCE CONTRACTS.

Examine the New Form of Policy
ISSUED BY

The United States Life Insurance Company,

Before Insuring Elsewhere.

NOTE THE LIBERALITY OF ITS TERMS.

After the premiums for three or more years have been paid, upon receiving the required notice from the assured, the Company will continue the Policy in force without further payments, for its FULL FACE, for such a period as the ENTIRE RESERVE will carry it.

Should the death of the insured take place during the continued term of insurance as provided for above, the full face of the Policy will be paid—no deduction being made for forborne or unpaid premiums, excepting in the event of the death occurring within three years after the default.

The new form of ENDOWMENT Policy provides: That if the ENTIRE RESERVE is a greater sum than the single premium required to carry the full amount of insurance to the end of the Endowment term, the EXCESS shall be issued as a single premium to purchase a pure Endowment, payable at the end of the term, thus guaranteeing to the Policy-holder in every event the full value of his RESERVE.

NO SURRENDER of the Policy is required—only a notice from the Policy-holder, on blanks furnished by the Company.

AFTER THREE YEARS, ALL RESTRICTIONS and CONDITIONS in regard to travel, residence, occupation, and cause of death are removed, thus making the Policies after three years INCONTESTABLE FOR ANY CAUSE EXCEPTING FRAUD.

All Forms of Life and Endowment Policies Issued.

THE UNITED STATES
Life Insurance Company in the City of New York,
261 BROADWAY.

OFFICERS.

T. H. BROSNAN, PRESIDENT.
C. P. FRALEIGH, SECRETARY.
A. WHEELWRIGHT, ASSISTANT SECRETARY.
CHAS. H. MILLER, CASHIER.
GEO. H. BURFORD, ACTUARY.
A. H. BUCK, MEDICAL DIRECTOR.
JOHN P. MUNN, MEDICAL EXAMINER.
HEGEMAN & BUEL, COUNSEL.

BOARD OF DIRECTORS.

CHARLES E. BILL, Banker, 13 Broad Street.
ISAAC N. PHELPS, Banker, 45 Wall Street.
CLINTON GILBERT, Treasurer Greenwich Savings Bank.
WM. H. BOLLES, Retired Merchant, Garden City, L. I.
HENRY W. FORD, Pres. Bank of the Republic.
EDGAR S. VAN WINKLE, Counsellor, 48 Wall Street.
W A. OGDEN HEGEMAN, Counsellor, 261 Broadway.
THOMAS GARDINER, Retired, 13 East 62d Street.
N. F. GRAVES, Pres. N. Y. State Bkg. Co., Syracuse, N. Y.
D. KELLOGG BAKER, Provisions, 335 Greenwich Street.
JAMES BUELL, Banker.
H. K. THURBER, Wholesale Grocer, 116 Reade Street.
P. VAN VOLKENBURGH, Dry Goods, 62 Worth Street.
EDWARD H. AMMIDOWN, Dry Goods, 87 Leonard Street.
JULIUS CATLIN, JR., Dry Goods, 132 Church Street.
JNO. A. LIVINGSTON, Sugar Refiner, 91 Wall Street.
HENRY C. HULBERT, Paper, 13 Beekman Street.
JAMES R. PLUM, Leather, 42 Spruce Street.
GEORGE G. WILLIAMS, Pres. Chemical National Bank.
ANTONY WALLACH, Mfg. Jeweler, 11 Maiden Lane.
OLIVER P. BUEL, Counsellor, 261 Broadway.
GEO. W. PERKINS, President Mercantile National Bank.
TIMOTHY H. BROSNAN, President.
HENRY L. CLAPP, Scales, 311 Broadway.
RAPHAEL BUCHMAN, Clothing, 465 Broome Street.
EDWARD VAN VOLKENBURGH, Dry Goods, 62 Worth St.
CHARLES P. FRALEIGH, Secretary, 261 Broadway.
JOHN P. MUNN, M.D., 50 East 31st Street.

UNITED STATES MUTUAL ACCIDENT ASSOCIATION.

Office, 409 Broadway, - New York.

INCORPORATED OCT. 11, 1877.

$3.00 will procure a certificate of membership entitling the member to $5,000.00 in the event of death by accident, and $25.00 weekly indemnity for totally disabling injury. Over 4,000 Business Men now members.

CHARLES B. PEET, PRESIDENT.
JAMES R. PITCHER, SECRETARY.

BOARD OF DIRECTORS.

CHAS. B. PEET, of Rogers, Peet & Co.
WM. BRINCKERHOFF, of Wm. Brinckerhoff & Co.
E. E. PERRY, with Wheeler & Wilson Manufacturing Co.
WILLIAM E. TEFFT, of Tefft, Weller & Co.
FERDINAND P. EARLE, of Earle's Hotel.
DECATUR M. SAWYER, of Gowing, Grew & Co.
WM. BRO. SMITH, 229 Broadway, New York.
W. S. GILMORE, Crouch & Fitzgerald.
WM. GIBSON, with Morrison, Herriman & Co.
LEOPOLD WORMSER, with L. Levenson & Co.
JAMES S. LEEDS, of Wm. T. Lloyd & Co.
GEORGE C. CLARKE, of Tefft, Weller & Co.

PORTABILITY COMBINED WITH GREAT POWER

FIELD, MARINE, TOURIST, OPERA, IN **AND GENERAL OUT-DOOR DAY AND NIGHT DOUBLE PERSPECTIVE**

GLASSES

Will show Objects Distinctly Two to Six Miles.

SPECTACLES AND EYE-GLASSES,

TO STRENGTHEN AND IMPROVE THE SIGHT,

ADJUSTED TO ALL DEFECTS OF VISION.

Catalogues sent by enclosing stamp.

SEMMONS, OCULIST AND OPTICIAN, 687 Broadway, New York.

MUTUAL BENEFIT LIFE CO.

118 Asylum Street,

HARTFORD, CONN.

Accident Protection at Actual Cost!

ADMISSION:

$3 for any Amount up to $5000.

Future Expenses 25 cents per month as long as continued, and assessments to cover losses only, at table rates.

ANY MAN HIS OWN AGENT.

Send for Application, which anyone may fill out, and return to Company with fee.

WEEKLY INDEMNITY, $5 to $25.

☞AGENTS WANTED EVERYWHERE.

THE TRAVELERS
Life and Accident Insurance Co.,
HARTFORD, CONN.

OLDEST AND LARGEST IN AMERICA.

JAS. G. BATTERSON, PRESIDENT.

RODNEY DENNIS, SECRETARY.

CASH ASSETS, $5,519,000
SURPLUS, 1,467,000
BENEFITS PAID, 5,650,000

GENERAL ACCIDENT POLICIES, by the year or month, written by Agents.

REGISTERED ACCIDENT TICKETS, one to thirty days, at Agencies and Railroad Stations.

PERMIT FOR FOREIGN VOYAGE at slight addition to cost of ordinary Policy.

Accident Policies Written, ... 650,000
Accident Claims Paid, ... 55,000
Amount Paid for Accidents, . . . $4,000,000

REGULAR LIFE INSURANCE, all best forms, with ample security, at Low Cash Rates.

www.ingramcontent.com/pod-product-compliance
Lightning Source LLC
Chambersburg PA
CBHW031902220426
43663CB00006B/728